HERITAGE OF CONQUEST

HERITAGE OF CONQUEST

the

ethnology

of

middle

america

BY SOL TAX
AND MEMBERS OF THE VIKING FUND SEMINAR
ON MIDDLE AMERICAN ETHNOLOGY

cooper square

publishers, inc.

new york

1968

Published by Cooper Square Publishers, Inc.
59 Fourth Avenue, New York, N. Y. 10003
Library of Congress Catalog Card No. 68-9464

Printed in the United States of America

CONTENTS

PART III. CONCLUSIONS: THE OLD AND THE NEW

PREFACE

THIS book is about the peoples of Mexico and Central America; mostly it is about that region where the Toltecs and Aztecs and Mayas once built their temples and spread their power. But this book is not about these ancient glories, but about the people today, mostly the uneducated rural people. Whether these are mainly Indians; whether they can be called descendents of the Aztecs and Mayas; what has happened to the area since Cortes and Alvarado brought horses, steel, and saints—these are questions for the book to answer. It tries to answer them professionally, for it is written by most of the specialists in the field of Middle American Ethnology.

This book also records how a group of scholars seek to develop and unify their understanding through discussion and mutual criticism. Scholars hampered by their traditional isolation show here how truth is approached through the conflict and congruence of minds. It thus reports an event in the immense intellectual adventure.

Anthropologists are people who go to live in tribes or villages with alien cultures, to get insight into different ways of life. They have a lot in common because they have read the same books and share a common scientific tradition. But they differ in their interests and personalities and since scholars are supposed to cultivate the fringes of what is known, they develop different theories. So when they also go to different places one expects them to collect quite different impressions. Characteristically the ethnologist spends years working over the data he has collected in his "community," wondering all the time what his colleagues are getting in other places. Of course he reads all that they publish; but publication is usually years behind, and always seems to miss the question he is interested in. Nor is it idle curiosity, for each new observation leads to more significant questions. As the years go by and the reports come in, we begin to see a pattern, vague and partial, that ties what each has discovered to what all have found. "I begin to suspect that . . ."

becomes a well-known phrase. But it takes years for the returns to come that may verify the suspicions.

In the past fifteen or twenty years the amount of anthropological field work in Middle America has probably increased more rapidly than that in any comparable area. North American, Mexican and Guatemalan institutions have trained increasingly more anthropologists to spend longer field seasons in rural and Indian communities. Communication among scholars lagged far behind. In an attempt to close the gap, field notes were microfilmed and passed around. But we needed to exchange impressions in the flesh. The Wenner-Gren Foundation for Anthropological Research made this possible. Not only did the (then) Viking Fund support the enterprise financially, from beginning to end, but the Seminar partook of its gracious hospitality in New York.

In preparation for a week-long meeting, a dozen of us divided the labor of treating the major topics on which we wanted to compare notes. We wrote papers and passed them around for comment. By the time we met in New York we were ready for intimate discussion. An unusual feature of the Seminar was that during the week together not a moment was spent "reading papers."

Scholars try also to be gentlemen; and common courtesy in discussion is good and necessary. But false politeness that inhibits frank criticism is fatal. So we began our meeting over dinner with the following statement:

"We have all seen different parts of the elephant—different parts of Middle America or different kinds of people; and, though we reinforce our senses with the tools of our discipline, we use different tools and so see different things. In short, we are what good scientists must first be—specialists.

"That all of us together may reveal the elephant that none of us has seen, to put our special information into the perspective of the whole—that is the idea of the Seminar. A few of us have forsaken our modesty to commit to paper our ideas about the whole of Middle America, in the certainty that we must be wrong in much of what we think, but with the hope that if others with different experience will correct us where they can, we shall become much less wrong about much more of what we think.

"Our only fear is that somebody will be afraid to correct us—that somebody who could help us with his knowledge keeps his peace for fear of offending—that somebody will forget that the only authority which science and scholarship can respect is the authority of knowledge.

To discourage misplaced courtesy and false modesty that could spell failure for this enterprise—that is the purpose of these remarks."

It worked. The members of the Seminar respected each other sufficiently to be able to be disrespectful. Punches were never pulled; when a statement made was not disputed we could therefore assume it was genuinely accepted. Only so could our conference reach agreement (often to our surprise) on some major propositions about Middle America.

The first paper in this volume was prepared years before the Seminar, but it served, like the others, as a basis for discussion. Kirchhoff's term "Mesoamerica" became our common currency, and is now firmly a part of the scientific vocabulary. The boundaries of Mesoamerica (a smaller part of Middle America) are shown on our map. The second paper was likewise prepared for another purpose, and "adopted" by the Seminar. It served both as a sample for the topical papers that we prepared and as a basis for criticism and discussion. Each of the following seven papers became the subject of a separate half-day session at the Seminar. The last two papers were prepared for the discussions on acculturation and social change. The parts of the discussion that qualify the papers are included in this book. The reader may assume that where a statement is not qualified or contradicted the participants in the discussion found no serious fault with it. The last two sessions left the particular topics for more general considerations of the relations of pre-Columbian and modern cultures, and of the course of cultural history since the Conquest. The conclusions to which the Seminar came finally were summarized publicly at a session of the Twenty-Ninth International Congress of Americanists, for discussion by scholars who had not directly participated in the Seminar.

At the Seminar, we were in the peculiar position, for scholars, of having to form judgments without benefit of even our notes. This had the great advantage that we *did* form them, and could compare what were, for us, broad and daring conclusions. We determined, however, not to put them on record until we had checked them in privacy with books and papers at hand. We spent almost eighteen months after the Seminar doing just this. It is remarkable that in fact we had few second thoughts. Although several of the papers have been rewritten, chiefly for stylistic reasons, careful consideration has not shaken any of our major conclusions. They stand now—and here—as a level of understanding on which we may stand firmly while reaching for more knowledge.

The authors of the papers and participants in the discussions will become familiar in the pages that follow. A person essential to the conference, both in its preliminary phases and during the Seminar itself, was Dr. Betty Starr, who recorded and transcribed the discussions. Immediately following the Seminar she left to study a village in Veracruz, but returned to continue work in preparation of this volume. For a very large part of the work after the conference, most of the editorial tasks, and the maps included in the volume, I am indebted to Stuart A. Johnston.

Sol Tax.

The University of Chicago
April 25, 1951

PARTICIPANTS IN THE VIKING FUND SEMINAR*

contributors

RALPH BEALS. University of California. Field work: Yaqui-Mayo of Sonora; Mixe of Oaxaca; Mountain Tarascan of Michoacán.

FERNANDO CAMARA BARBACHANO. University of Puerto Rico. Field work: Tzeltal and Tzotzil groups of Chiapas; Chacaltianguis and Tuxtilla, Veracruz; Andean communities in Peru.

JULIO DE LA FUENTE. Museo Nacional de Mexico. Field work: Extended research among the mountain and valley Zapotec of Oaxaca; the Otomí of Hidalgo; the Huastec of Veracruz; the Quechua of Peru.

JOHN P. GILLIN. University of North Carolina. Field work: San Luis Jilotepeque (Pokomán) in Eastern Guatemala; Carib of British Guiana; Indian and non-Indian communities in the Andes.

CALIXTA GUITERAS HOLMES. Museo Nacional de Mexico. Field work: Tzeltal and Tzotzil groups in Chiapas; Huastec and Nahua of Northern Veracruz.

PAUL KIRCHHOFF. University of Washington. Field of interest: Ancient Middle America.

GERTRUDE PROKOSCH KURATH. Michigan Folklore Society. Field work: Mexico.

BENJAMIN D. AND LOIS PAUL. Harvard University. Field work: San Pedro la Laguna, Guatemala.

ROBERT REDFIELD. University of Chicago. Field work: Tepoztlan, Morelos; Maya of Yucatan; Midwest Highlands of Guatemala.

* Sponsored by the Wenner-Gren Foundation for Anthropological Research, Inc., and held in New York City, August 28 through September 3, 1949.

SOL TAX. University of Chicago. Field work: Chichicastenango and Panajachel, Midwest Highlands of Guatemala; Zinacantan, Chiapas.

CHARLES WISDOM. University of Connecticut. Field work: Chorti of Eastern Guatemala.

participants in the discussions

GEORGE M. FOSTER. Smithsonian Institution. Field work: Sierra Popoluca of Veracruz; Tzintzuntzan (Tarascan-Mestizo) of Michoacán; Spain.

ANTONIO GOUBAUD CARRERA. Guatemalan Ambassador to the United States; formerly Director of the National Indian Institute of Guatemala. Deceased, March, 1951. Field work: Kekchi of San Juan Chamelco, Alta Verapaz, and other Guatemalan communities.

WIGBERTO JIMENEZ MORENO. Museo Nacional de Mexico. Field work: Mexico.

BERNICE KAPLAN. Detroit, Michigan. Field work: Paracho, Michoacán, Mexico.

ISABEL KELLY. Smithsonian Institution. Field work: Lowland Totonac of the Papantla area of Veracruz, Mexico.

ARDEN R. KING. Middle American Research Institute. Field work: Alta Verapaz, Guatemala.

DOROTHY LOUISE KYTE. Columbia University. Field work: Los Morros, Guerrero, and general reconnaissance of Guerrero, Mexico.

GABRIEL LASKER. Wayne University. Field work: Physical anthropology in Mexico.

JUNE HELM MACNEISH. University of Chicago. Field work: Los Angeles, a Mestizo community in Tamaulipas.

DONALD MARSHALL. Peabody Museum.

J. ALDEN MASON. University of Pennsylvania. Field work: Tepecano and Tepehuan of the Sierra Madre Occidental.

DANIEL F. RUBIN DE LA BORBOLLA. Director, Museo Nacional de Mexico. Field work: Mexico.

DORIS Z. STONE. Costa Rica. Field work: Northern Guaymi of Panama; Talamancan tribes, Boruca, Guatuso, and Chorotega of Costa Rica; the Lenca, Payo and Suma of Honduras, and the Matagalpa of Nicaragua.

FRANZ TERMER. Museum für Völkerkunde, Hamburg. Field work: Guatemala, Mexico, Honduras and Salvador.

FRANCES TOOR. Mexico. Field work: Mexico and Peru.

MELVIN M. TUMIN. Princeton University. Field work: Pokoman of San Luis Jilotepeque, Eastern Guatemala.

ALFONSO VILLA ROJAS. Papaloapan Commission. Field work: Quintana Roo; Yucatan, Tzeltal of Chiapas.

CHARLES WAGLEY. Columbia University. Field work; Northwestern Guatemala (Santiago Chimaltenango), and Brazil.

MARK HANNA WATKINS. Howard University. Field work: Cakchiquel of Guatemala.

NATHAN L. WHETTEN. University of Connecticut. Field work: Rural Mexico and Guatemala.

PART I. GENERAL INFORMATION

MESOAMERICA: Its Geographic Limits, Ethnic Composition and Cultural Characteristics*

by Paul Kirchhoff

IN THE geographic classifications of the native cultures of America which take in the whole Continent or which at least deal with a particular region from a continental point of view, one may easily distinguish two types.

In the first of these, one accepts one or the other of the usual divisions of the American Continent, based on political geography or biogeography. Most Americanists either divide the Continent simply into North and South America, or interpose between the two parts a third, whether it be "Mexico and Central America" or, as some American (U.S.) anthropologists call it, "Middle America." In the first case, as a general rule, one accepts as the boundary between North and South America, the biogeographical dividing line which follows the course of the San Juan River, between Nicaragua and Costa Rica. In the second case, one includes in

* Translated by Dr. Norman McQuown from *Acta Americana*, Vol. I, No. 1, 1943.

"Mexico and Central America" all the territory between the northern frontier of the Mexican Republic and the eastern border of Panama; in "Middle America" the same region, excluding at times the north of Mexico, including at times the Antilles.

Both divisions and their variants which we have noted here have serious drawbacks when they are used for anything more than a mere geographic localization of cultural phenomena of the native world, or in order to set the geographic limits for programs of investigation or publication. The biogeographic boundary between North and South America, although it coincides with a local boundary between regions with clearly marked cultural characteristics, nevertheless does not constitute a cultural boundary between North and South America, inasmuch as to the north of it, the culture of the Sumo and the Misquito and even that of the Paya and Jicaque, is just as "South American" as that of the Chibcha of Central America. In reality, this term lacks any precise meaning, since in South America, whatever the extension we wish to give to the term may be, there are cultures as different one from another, as those of the Fuegians, the Caribs and the Inca. On the other hand, the remaining cultures of Central America and Mexico do not give evidence of any "North American" characteristics, but, on the contrary, perhaps have more in common with certain cultures of South America than with any of North America. Actually, their similarities to certain North American cultural areas, such as those of the Southeast and in part of the Southwest of the United States, are evidenced in large measure in traits which both have in common with certain cultural areas of South America.

The drawbacks of the triple division mentioned are perhaps even greater. Neither the aggregate of the republics of Mexico and Central America, nor "Middle America" in any of the senses just mentioned, constitutes for the anthropologist a region which stands out from the other cultures of the Continent, and which therefore merits especial study. In fact, those who accept one or the other of these triple divisions, far from considering "Mexico and Central America" or "Middle America" as a cultural unit—opposed as such to North or to South America—, continue to recognize as basic the division between North and South America, assigning certain cultures of this region to North America and others to South America.

The second type of geographic classification groups the native American cultures in five large areas:

1. The food-gatherers, hunters and fishers of North America.
2. The interior cultivators of North America.
3. The superior cultivators ("High Cultures").
4. The inferior cultivators of South America.
5. The food-gatherers and hunters of South America.

The anthropologists who accept this type of division, which, like the previous one, has many variants which we do not mention, recognize either explicitly or implicitly that within the areas of the so-called superior cultivators are included, by way of exception, individual tribes or even whole cultural areas which cannot be considered superior cultivators, neither with respect to their general cultural level, nor with respect to plants and techniques of cultivation. In the same way, at times food-gatherers and hunters are included in the areas of the inferior cultivators.

Their inclusion within the areas of superior culture is justified by the fact that notwithstanding their lower cultural level, they share with the other tribes of the area in which they are included a considerable number of cultural traits; whether this be due to the fact that these tribes have been left behind by the more advanced tribes, thus preserving a part of the old common culture, or to recent cultural diffusion. This point of view leaves their individuality to the cultural areas (in the sense of a group of tribes with cultures which are not merely superficially similar, but are fundamentally alike) and allows one at the same time to group them in "superareas" and subdivides them into "subareas." Within the area of the inferior cultivators of North America, the "Southeast" and the "Southwest" (in the sense of "The Greater Southwest" or "Arid North America") constitute such superareas; and within the area of the superior cultivators one can mark out a superarea "Mesoamerica" whose geographic limits, ethnic composition and cultural characteristics at the time of the Conquest, we propose to study in this article.

The present work is based on a series of studies of distribution initiated by the International Committee for the Study of Cultural Distribution in America, created by the XXVIIth International Congress of Americanists. Although these studies are still far from being complete, it is already possible to present certain general outlines for the purpose of posing new problems. This aim of our article has made unnecessary the inclusion of notes or bibliography.

On the basis of the studies mentioned above, one may postulate that at the time of the Conquest, there were present in Mesoamerica a series of tribes which we may group in the following five divisions:

1. Tribes which speak languages not yet classified, such as the *Tarascan,* the *Cuitlatec,* the *Lenca,* etc.

2. All the tribes of the *Maya, Zoque,* and *Totonac* linguistic families. According to certain investigators, the languages of these three families, to which one should probably add the *Huave,* form a group which we might call *Zoque-Maya* or *Macro-Mayan.*

3. All the tribes—except two—of the *Otomi, Chocho-Popoloca* and *Mixtec* families, which seem to form, together with the *Chorotega-Mangue* family, a group called *Otomangue;* and all the tribes of the *Trique, Zapotec* and *Chinantec* families, which some investigators consider related to the previous group, forming a great group called *Macro-Otomangue.*

4. All the tribes of the *Nahua* family and a series of other tribes of *Uto-Aztecan* affiliation, among them the *Cora* and the *Huichol,* whose grouping in families is still not definitive.

5. All the tribes of *Tlappanec-Subtiaba* and *Tequistlatec* families which belong to Sapir's *Hokan* group.

An analysis of the ethnic composition of Mesoamerica, at the time of the Conquest, shows the following:

a. Of all the linguistic families which form part of Mesoamerica, only one, the *Otomi,* has some members (the *Pame* and the *Jonaz* which are perhaps only subdivisions of a single tribe), which do not belong to the Mesoamerican cultural unit.

b. Two linguistic groups, formed by some of these families, the *Zoque-Maya* and the *Macro-Otomangue,* should their reality be demonstrated, would be found to be entirely within Mesoamerica.

c. Tribes of these two groups, and also of the *Nahua* reach, probably as a result of migrations, to the farthest geographic limits of Mesoamerica, both in the North (of the *Zoque-Maya* group, the *Huastec;* of the *Macro-Otomangue,* the *Otomi;* and of the *Nahua* family, the *Cazcan* and the *Mexicans*) and in the South (of the *Zoque-Maya* group, the *Chol-Chorti,* of the *Macro-Otomangue,* the *Chorotega,* and of the *Nahua* family, the *Nicarao*).

All of this shows the reality of Mesoamerica as a region whose inhabitants, both the very old immigrants and the relatively recent ones, were united by a common history which set them apart as a unit from other tribes of the Continent, their migratory movements being confined as a general rule, once they had entered the area of Mesoamerica, within its geographic limits. In some cases tribes of different families or linguistic groups took part in these migrations together.

In spite of the fact that it had linked its fate firmly to that of Mesoamerica, the *Nahua* family, both because it had many linguistic relatives, more or less close, outside of Mesoamerica, and in view of its traditions concerning one or a number of migrations from the North, shows itself to have played, within our area, a cultural role very different from that of the linguistic families listed under "2." These, like the tribes not yet linguistically classified, seem to lack linguistic relatives within any reasonable distance of Mesoamerica, which leads us to believe that they both, i.e., the *Maya, Zoque, Totonac, Tarascan, Cuitlatec,* etc., not only have lived for a long time within the territory occupied by the cultural aggregate of Mesoamerica, but that they have perhaps played an important part in the very process of its formation.

The *Macro-Otomangue* group, or at least its *Otomangue* subgroup composed of the *Otomi, Chocho-Popoloca, Chorotega* and perhaps the *Mixtec* families, in spite of its dissemination within the territory of Mesoamerica, does not give us the impression that it is equally deep-rooted or that it has played as important a role in the formation of Mesoamerica as the *Zoque-Maya* group, but it seems more probable that it entered the Mesoamerican orbit when the area already existed as a cultural unit. Tribes of these families not only appear curiously associated in their geographic distribution with *Nahua* tribes (almost as in South America, and the Antilles, the Arawak with the Caribs), but in several cases we also have historical traditions concerning common migrations of the Toltecs of *Nahua* speech with *Otomi* peoples (according to Sahagún), or with *Mazatec, Popoluca* and *Otomi* (according to the *Historia Tolteca-chichimeca*), and of the *Nicarao* with the *Chorotega* (according to Torquemada). Furthermore we have on the one hand traditions about a migration of the Otomies from the northwest (according to Ixtlilxochitl) and on the other the fact that the *Pame* and the *Jonaz* live to this day outside the Mesoamerican territory, immediately to the north of it.

The numerical and geographical isolation which we find in the *Tlappanec-Subtiaba* and *Tequistlatec* families at the time of the Conquest, suggests that the role that they played in the history of Mesoamerica either was never very important, or goes back to a very distant past; unless one must consider them as relatively recent immigrants to a Mesoamerica already formed.

The proper estimation of the role of each linguistic family or group in the history of Mesoamerica, together with the solution of the problem of determining since when a cultural superarea has existed and what has been its geographic extension, and what its cultural foci have been in different periods, presupposes, in addition to the completion of the already begun studies of cultural distributions at the time of the Conquest, the carrying out of similar studies for different pre-Columbian periods; the utilization of both of these types of studies for the division of Mesoamerica into subareas which will be different in number and extension for different periods; and more excavations in regions which at the time of the Conquest were outside of Mesoamerica, but which in previous times formed part of it, such as have been carried out in a broad zone in the north of Mexico, occupied at the time of the Conquest by tribes of inferior culture.

What we can already assert at this time is that the northern frontier of Mesoamerica was distinguished from the southern boundary by a much greater degree of mobility and insecurity, with alternating periods along it of expansion northward and retraction toward the south. The periods of retraction are due in part to invasions of groups of lower culture situated to the north of Mesoamerica.

This difference between the frontiers to the north and the south, as well as the differences existing between various sections of each of the boundaries, are due, at least in part, to the fact that Mesoamerica is the last link to the north in the chain of superior cultivators. Actually, only in a short section of the southern frontier did Mesoamerica, at the time of the Conquest, border on another area of superior cultivators (the *Chibcha*), while along the rest of this frontier its neighbors were inferior cultivators (the *Jicaque* and *Paya* and the *Sumo* and *Misquito*). In the northern frontier the situation was even more unfavorable, since with the exception of two quite short sections, one in Sinaloa and another insignificant one on the coast of the Gulf, where its neighbors were inferior cultivators, Mesoamerica bordered directly on food-gatherers and hunters.

At the time of the Conquest, the last tribes of Mesoamerican culture on the southern boundary (which runs, more or less, from the mouth of the Motagua River to the Gulf of Nicoya, passing through Lake Nicaragua) were the *Chol-Chorti,* the *Lenca* (and perhaps the *Matagalpa*), the *Subtiaba,* the *Nicarao* and the *Chorotega-Mangue;* on the northern boundary (which runs more or less from the Rio Panuco to the Sinaloa, passing along the Lerma), the *Huastec,* the *Mexicans* of Meztitlan, the *Otomi* and *Mazahua,* the *Tarascan,* the *Coca,* the *Tecuexe,* the *Cazcan,* part of the *Zacatec* (there were *Zacatec* who were food-gatherers and hunters), the *Tepehuan,* the *Acaxé* and the *Mocorito.* Although the southernmost tribes, the *Subtiaba, Nicarao* and *Chorotega-Mangue* are so unmistakably Mesoamerican in their culture that there can be no doubt as to their inclusion in this superarea, such doubts can arise with respect to the *Lenca* on the one hand and with respect to many tribes situated along Lake Chapala and the Rio Sinaloa on the other, since in both cases we find a cultural level quite inferior to that characteristic of tribes most representative of Mesoamerica. Notwithstanding this lower cultural level (which is also found among some tribes and even in some cultural areas in the interior of the territory of Mesoamerica), we include these tribes in Mesoamerica, because of the very considerable number of markedly Mesoamerican cultural traits, which in most cases go precisely to the frontiers which we have indicated. Thus for example, up to the northwestern boundary we find such cultural elements as the cultivation of chile, sweet potato, and fruit trees, the domestication of ducks and "voiceless dogs," metallurgy, the game played with rubber balls, etc. (see below), i.e., elements which Mesoamerica has in common with more southern cultures and which here reach their northern limit.

Culture Traits

In the distribution studies undertaken by the International Committee for the Study of Cultural Distributions in America to clarify the problem of Mesoamerica, studies which in turn profit from all the investigations carried out previously by other scholars, we have found three large distribution groups:

I. Traits exclusively or at least typically Mesoamerican.

II. Traits common to Mesoamerica and to other American cultural superareas.

III. Traits significant for their absence in Mesoamerica.

I

For the purpose of this first exposition of the problems in Mesoamerica, we prefer to combine in a single list, both those traits which are found exclusively in Mesoamerica, and also those, which, although they are sometimes found outside, seem, nevertheless, to be characteristically Mesoamerican. With respect to the latter, we do not refer only to cases in which Mesoamerican traits are found in some tribes outside of Mesoamerica but bordering on it (such as the game with rubber balls among some food-gatherers and hunters of the north of Mexico), where the diffusion is undeniable, but also to cases such as that of the Pawnee of North America or that of the coast of Ecuador or northern Peru, where there is a grouping of traits so typically Mesoamerican that it allows of no other interpretation but that of cultural diffusion.

On the other hand, we include in this list, only a few of the traits exclusively Mesoamerican but rare there, since most of these suppose for their existence that of others more widely found.

We consider as Mesoamerican traits the following:

A certain type of digging-stick (*coa*); the construction of gardens by reclaiming land from lakes (*chinampas*); the cultivation of lime-leaved sage (*chía*) and its use for a beverage and for oil to give luster to paints; the cultivation of the century plant (*maguey*) for its juice (*aguamiel*), fiber for clothing and paper, and maguey beer (*pulque*); the cultivation of cacao; the grinding of corn softened with ashes or lime.

Clay bullets for blow-guns; lip-plugs and other trinkets of clay; the polishing of obsidian; pyrite mirrors; copper tubes to drill stones; the use of rabbit hair to adorn textiles; wooden swords with flint or obsidian chips along their edges (*macuahuitl*); corselets padded with cotton (*ichcahuipilli*); shields with two hand-grips.

Turbans; sandals with heels; one-piece suits for warriors.

Step pyramids; stucco floors; ball courts with rings.

Hieroglyphic writing; signs for numerals and relative value of these according to position; books folded screen-style; historical annals and maps.

Year of 18 months of 20 days, plus 5 additional days; combination of 20 signs and 13 numerals to form a period of 260 days; combination of the two previous periods to form a cycle of 52 years; festivals at the end of certain periods; good and bad omen days; persons named according to the day of their birth.

Ritual use of paper and rubber; sacrifice of quail; certain forms of human sacrifice (burning people alive, dancing dressed in the skin of the victim); certain forms of self-sacrifice (extraction of one's blood from the tongue, ears, legs, sexual organs); the flying game or ritual (*juego del volador*); 13 as a ritual number; a series of divinities. Tlaloc, for example; concept of several other worlds and of a difficult journey to them; drinking the water in which the deceased relative has been bathed.

Specialized markets or markets subdivided according to specialities; merchants who are at the same time spies; military orders (eagle knights and tiger knights); wars for the purpose of securing sacrificial victims.

II

The group of traits common to Mesoamerica and to other American cultural superareas* is divided into various sub-groups for which we give representative examples, with the caution that mentioning a trait for a particular superarea does not imply that it is found in all the component areas:

a. Southeast, Southwest, *Mesoamerica, Chibcha, Andes,* Amazonia: cultivation, ceramics.

b. Southeast, Southwest, *Mesoamerica, Chibcha, Andes,* Northwest Amazonia: cultivation of corn, beans, and squash.

* For this first orientation we recognize, in an entirely provisional form, the following superareas (the names of the superareas of superior cultivators are italicized):

Southwest (of North America, in the sense of "The Greater Southwest" or "Arid North America," i.e., including both inferior cultivators and food-gatherers and hunters).

Southeast (of North America).

Chibcha (excluding those who have cultural affinities with the Andes, such as, for example, the *Muisca*).

Andes (including the arid coast of South America).

Amazonia (including all the tropical forest of South America and the Antilles, but excluding the *Chibcha* of the tropical forest).

c. Southeast, *Mesoamerica, Chibcha, Andes:* human sacrifice.

d. Southeast, *Mesoamerica, Chibcha, Andes,* Northwest Amazonia: cultivation of the sweet potato; blowguns, head trophies.

e. Southeast, *Mesoamerica, Chibcha,* Amazonia: cannibalism.

f. Southeast, *Mesoamerica, Andes,* Northwest Amazon: confession.

g. Southwest, Mesoamerica, Chibcha, Andes: cultivation in the hands of the men; constructions of stone or mud; sandals.

h. Southwest, *Mesoamerica, Chibcha, Andes,* Northwest Amazonia: cultivation of cotton.

i. *Mesoamerica, Chibcha, Andes:* terracing for cultivation; hanging bridges; gourd rafts. Some of the traits of this group, perhaps the majority of them, are known within Mesoamerica only in the southern part.

j. *Mesoamerica, Chibcha, Andes,* Northwest Amazonia: cultivation of sweet cassava, chile (*ají*), pineapple, avocado, papaya, zapote, various kinds of "plums" or spondias (*jobos*); fattened voiceless dog; duck; woven shields, lances; metallurgy; roads paved with stones; markets.

These traits, contrasting with the preceding group, with the exception of woven shields and lances, go as far as the northern boundary of Mesoamerica.

k. *Mesoamerica, Andes:* clans of the *calpulli-ayllu* type; taking out the heart of living human beings; sprinkling sanctuaries with the blood of sacrificial victims.

In addition, there is a considerable group of traits common to the superior cultivators of Mesoamerica and the inferior cultivators of Amazonia:

l. *Mesoamerica,* Amazonia: basket-work blowing fan; flat clay plates on which to cook bread (*comal*); game with rubber balls which cannot be touched with the hands; wooden drum with languettes.

It is worthy of note that the traits of this group which reach the northern and southern boundaries of Mesoamerica are not known among the Jicaque, Paya, Sumo and Misquito tribes which border directly on Mesoamerica and are inferior cultivators like the Amazonian tribes.

Finally, an even more striking group of traits which Mesoamerica has in common with people who are not even cultivators:

m. *Mesoamerica,* food-gatherers and hunters: underground ovens; steam bath.

The traits which Mesoamerica, superarea of superior cultivators, has in common with other areas of superior cultivators or of inferior cultivators, or with both of these at the same time, pose a series of very important problems concerning both the formation of Mesoamerican culture within the aggregate of American cultures based on cultivation, and the relations existing between the superior and inferior cultivators. The division which we have made of these traits into various groups is designed to pose most effectively these problems. It does not seem possible to arrive at definitive conclusions before the distribution studies initiated by the aforementioned Committee have been completed.

One is struck by the fact that Mesoamerica, an area of superior cultivators within which no non-cultivating tribe survives, shares certain traits, lacking among the superior and inferior cultivators of South America, *with the American food-gatherers and hunters,* on whose North American area it borders directly along a part of its northern boundary, whereas it finds itself separated from the South American food-gatherers and hunters by other cultivators both superior and inferior. The fact that these traits go as far as the southern boundary of Mesoamerica, and no farther, tends to separate Mesoamerica from the other great areas of superior cultivators, as well as from the areas of inferior cultivators of South America (with which, on the other hand, it shares such significant traits). But one must remember that these traits characteristic of hunters and food-gatherers are not and cannot be basic to or constitutory of Mesoamerican culture, although undoubtedly they lend it a "flavor" distinct from that of the other areas of superior cultivators, especially those traits which like the steam bath have come to be linked so intimately with Mesoamerican culture. But even though it is true that these traits come to the end of their North American distributional area at the southern boundary of Mesoamerica, they can't be called "North American" because they are also found among the food-gatherers and hunters of South America, unless we want to call these latter likewise "North American."

In order to have been able to reach the extreme south of South America, through all the region recently occupied by superior and inferior cultivators, these traits must have spread before the formation not only of Mesoamerica and the other areas of superior cultivators, but before the beginning of cultivation itself, disappearing later in certain regions.* Their presence in Mesoamerica and absence in the other areas of cultivators in South America, allows of one of two explanations: either they disappeared only in the areas of (superior and inferior) cultivators situated to the south of Mesoamerica, but not in the latter, or they first disappeared in both regions, to be later reintroduced into Mesoamerica from the north by new invasions of food-gatherers and hunters. In any case, the extension of these elements up to the southern boundary of Mesoamerica, even though it does not give to Mesoamerica a "North American" character and does not allow us to draw an ethnographic boundary between North and South America which would coincide with our southern boundary of Mesoamerica, does demonstrate what we have asserted in previous paragraphs and with different arguments: the fact that Mesoamerica is undoubtedly a cultural unit which has had its own history for a long time, common to all its inhabitants, even with respect to those traits which are *not* basic to it.

III

The traits of the third group whose distribution is related to the problem of Mesoamerica are those whose absence in Mesoamerica is characteristic. This group is divided into various sub-groups:

a. Southeast, *Chibcha:* adornment of the edge of the ear.

b. Southeast, Southwest, *Chibcha,* Northwest Amazonia: matrilineal clans.

c. Southeast, Southwest (food-gatherers and hunters of Nuevo Leon), *Chibcha,* Northwest Amazonia: drinking the ground-up bones of deceased relatives.

d. Southwest (Sinaloa-Sonora), *Chibcha,* Amazonia: poisoned arms.

These types of distribution, to which one should probably add others, lead one to suspect that we are dealing with elements once present in Mesoamerica, either merely in the *territory* later to become Mesoamerican or within the Mesoamerican cultural aggregate

* We know only one case of the use of the steam bath among the food-gatherers and hunters of South America. The second South American case, not cited up till now in the comparative literature and one which must be the result of a different and much later diffusion from a Mesoamerica already existing as a cultural unit, is found among the superior cultivators of the coast of Ecuador. Unfortunately there are no details of the steam bath found there, so that we do not know whether it had the structural details which distinguished the Mesoamerican steam bath from that of more northerly tribes.

itself. Especially suggestive is the case of the custom of drinkin ground-up bones of one's deceased relatives, corresponding to w within Mesoamerica we find a custom which may perhaps be in preted as a more evolved phase which has taken its place, the cust of drinking the water in which the deceased relative has been bathed.

With the preceding we might contrast certain cultural traits of the cultivators of South America which go as far as the southern frontier of Mesoamerica, but do not pass it:

e. *Chibcha, Andes:* cultivation of coca.

f. *Chibcha, Andes,* Amazonia: cultivation of palm trees.

The distribution of these two groups of traits leads us to believe that they never were a part of Mesoamerican culture.

Notwithstanding its entirely provisional character, we felt that it was time to present to the readers of this new journal the preliminary results of the investigations of Mesoamerica initiated by the International Committee for the Study of Cultural Distributions in America, not only in order to report on the present state of these investigations, but also in order to stimulate a thorough critical discussion of the method followed and the results obtained to date. The author of the present article, in his capacity as secretary of the Committee, would like very much to receive suggestions as to the best way to continue this work, together with data on other investigations which bear directly or indirectly on the problem of the cultural individuality and the history of Mesoamerica, whether from investigations already completed or from those in process of being carried out.

TRAITS COMMON TO MESOAMERICA AND TO OTHER CULTURAL SUPERAREAS OF AMERICA: AND TRAITS SIGNIFICANT FOR THEIR ABSENCE IN MESOAMERICA

Presence of traits—X *Absence of traits—O*	*South-east*	*South-west*	*Meso-america*	*Chibcha*	*Andes*	*Ama-zonia*
Cultivation	X	X	X	X	X	X
Ceramics	X	X	X	X	X	X
Corn	X	X	X	X	X	X*
Beans	X	X	X	X	X	X*
Squash	X	X	X	X	X	X*
Human sacrifice	X	O	X	X	X	O
Potato	X	O	X	X	X	X*
Blowgun	X	O	X	X	X	X*
Head trophies	X	O	X	X	X	X*

* In the Northwest.

Presence of traits—X *Absence of traits—O*	*South-east*	*South-west*	*Meso-america*	*Chibcha*	*Andes*	*Ama-zonia*
Cannibalism	X	O	X	X	O	X
Confession	X	O	X	O	X	X*
Cultivation done by men	O	X	X	X	X	O
Construction of stone or clay	O	X	X	X	X	O
Sandals	O	X	X	X	X	O
Cotton	O	X	X	X	X	X*
Terracing for cultivation	O	O	X	X	X	O
Hanging bridges	O	O	X	X	X	O
Gourd rafts	O	O	X	X	X	O
Sweet Cassava	O	O	X	X	X	X*
Chile (ají)	O	O	X	X	X	X*
Pineapple	O	O	X	X	X	X*
Avocado	O	O	X	X	X	X*
Papaya	O	O	X	X	X	X*
Zapote	O	O	X	X	X	X*
Spondia	O	O	X	X	X	X*
Fattened voiceless dog	O	O	X	X	X	X*
Duck	O	O	X	X	X	X*
Woven shields	O	O	X	X	X	X*
Lances	O	O	X	X	X	X*
Metallurgy	O	O	X	X	X	X*
Roads paved with stone	O	O	X	X	X	X*
Markets	O	O	X	X	X	X*
Clans of the *calpulli-ayllu* type	O	O	X	O	X	O
Removing heart from living persons	O	O	X	O	X	O
Sprinkling sanctuaries with blood	O	O	X	O	X	O
Basketwork blowing fan	O	O	X	O	O	X
Plates for cooking bread	O	O	X	O	O	X
Game with rubber ball	O	O	X	O	O	X
Wooden drum with languettes	O	O	X	O	O	X
Adornment of edge of ear	X	O	O	X	O	O
Matrilineal clans	X	X	O	X	O	X*
Drinking ground-up bones of deceased relatives	X	X	O	X	O	X*
Poisoned weapons	O	X	O	X	O	X
Coca	O	O	O	X	X	O
Palm trees	O	O	O	X	X	X

* In the Northwest.

chapter 2

GENERAL CHARACTERISTICS OF PRESENT-DAY MESOAMERICAN INDIAN SOCIETY

by Robert Redfield and Sol Tax

THE community consists of a village, a group of hamlets or a rural region, but in any case its residents look toward a common civic and religious center and feel themselves members of the community that has this center, where is housed the image of a saint that is patron to them all. The community tends to be endogamous, and its members are recognizable in terms of some peculiarities of dialect, costume or custom. This sense of solidarity is typically centered in the local group and its way of life, but in some regions it is qualified by some sense of participation in regional or ethnic groups. The controls which shape conduct characteristically include, however, regulations which are imposed upon people from outside the local community; these originate in natural law. Everywhere there is a wider integration than the tribe; the truly isolated community is exceptional. There is a hierarchy of market, political and religious centers extending over large areas.

The community lives primarily by the production and consumption of maize; this crop has central place in the economic and ritual activities of the people. The maize is grown with the aid of the digging stick, machete and hoe; little use is made of animal labour. The diet is predominantly maize, and the *tortilla* is the principal food, but maize is also commonly eaten in the form of gruel, or of boiled dumplings—*tamales*. In preparation for cooking, maize hulls are softened in lime or lye, and the boiled grains are ground on a *metate,* if a modern iron mill has not superseded it. Chile pepper accompanies the maize, and beans play an important, if not secondary, part in the diet. Tomatoes and greens of various kinds are common foods throughout the area. Salt is omnipresent. Coffee, sweetened with crude cane sugar, is widely consumed. Meat (chicken, turkey, beef and pork) is a luxury or festal food. Bread, usually sweet rolls, chocolate and honey are widespread festal foods; bread is often eaten for breakfast.

Whatever the form or material of the house, it is so constructed as to provide separate structure or structures for each family, whether that family consists of one couple and their children or be a compound family. Besides the dwelling some or all of the following structures may occur: a separate kitchen, a granary, fowl pen, pigpen and sweat-house. House-yards are fenced or walled. The household furnishings include pots, gourd or calabash vessels, baskets, wooden chests, wooden stools or benches, straw mats, and a griddle on which to toast tortillas. There is an open fireplace of three stones on which to rest cooking vessels, and it has no chimney. Metal knives and other simple tools of metal are used. Candles or kerosene flares provide light. To this list should be added the metate, some tinware, a few enamelware dishes, some china dishes, and metal spoons and forks. Matches are universal. Pitch pine, where available, is used both for kindling fires and furnishing light. Rope is the common binding material, with many uses. The use of soap is general.

Women wear a skirt and a blouse or cape, wear their hair long, tied or braided, rarely wear footgear or hats, unless travelling, and commonly wear or carry a shawl (*rebozo*). Earrings and rings are worn. Either or both sexes may wear belt or sash. Men wear trousers, commonly short, a shirt, commonly a robe or blanket but in some cases a jacket, and wear sandals frequently. They wear hats with brims and crowns, but in some cases wear head-cloths, wear their hair short and rarely wear jewelry or personal ornaments. Men commonly carry a netted or woven bag and when away from home often carry a calabash water vessel. Heavy loads are carried with a tump-line. Women carry articles on head or hip; men rarely do. If animals are used for transport, the use is secondary.

The work of the cornfield is the affair of the men, and the participation of women involves only lighter labour or is regarded as exceptional. Aside from some festal cookery, the domestic work is the task of the women. Women, as well as men, buy and sell in the market place. In ceremonial activity of native origin the leadership, and often the exclusive participation, comes from the men, while women take a much larger part in ceremonies of European origin. The chief roles and offices in public life are taken by men only, but the wives usually participate with their husbands in some manner; an office, especially one of religious or ceremonial significance, is frequently conceived of as being held by a married couple. In general, women have considerable share in family councils. Occupational and professional specialization is marked in proportion to the size of the group and the technical opportunities. There is also notable regional division of labour, and tradition limits competition in this regard so that local or familial specialization in production tends to continue. The exchange of goods through market competition is familiar, and money, supplemented, occasionally, by maize or other uniform common commodity, is a general measure of value. Economic activity is little limited by "taboos" or religious influences. On the other hand, business never gets "big"; credit institutions are not developed; there is little economic "organization," no "capitalism"; instead, there are small, independent competitors.

While the local group, as expressed in the village or rural cluster under the protection of a common saint, is a principal social unit, the family group is universal, and (with few exceptions) articulates directly with the local community without the intermediacy of clans. Especially in larger, local communities, however, there is generally an organization of territorial subdivisions standing between the family and the whole community. The family is one in which a hierarchical responsibility and power is recognized, older brothers having dominance over younger as fathers are dominant over sons. While relatives in both lines are of consequence to the individual, there is a stress on the patrilineal line and family names are transmitted in the male line. Marriage is negotiated by representatives of the two young people, the boy's people taking the initiative and giving the feast incident to marriage or engagement or paying most of the costs of a marriage provision. The negotiations for the marriage are commonly conducted with appearance of secrecy and take the form of conventionally repeated visits of the petitioners who bring gifts. While rules of residence after marriage are not rigid, there is a tendency for the new couple to establish a home near the boy's parents rather than those of the girl; on the other hand, an obligation of the boy to his wife's parents is in many cases recognized by gifts or service made to them or even temporary residence with them. There is a tendency, in not a few cases, for multiple-family households to form in which related married couples of two generations live together. Marriage is monogamous, and brittle in the early years; after there are children, marriage is typically lasting. Occasional concubinage is accepted in custom, although not formally.

The political organization is physically represented in a building for civil government in the center of the community, and personally by a hierarchy of officials some of which, at or near the top, are recognized by the formal government of the national state within which the local community exists. It is common for this civil hierarchy to be closely interwoven with a similar hierarchy serving the interests of the local church and related festal activities. The local government is featured by distinct division of labour and clear subordination and superordination among its members, and by a change of personnel at annual intervals at fixed dates. This organization, in connection with some merely ritual activities, exercises the police power and organizes and enforces coöperative labour on public works. Formally recognized social classes are not present among those participating in the Indian culture, but differences in prestige due to wealth, power or personal achievement are considerable. The age-hierarchy, especially among males, is notable, and in many cases is measured by the occupation of community offices related to age.

The life cycle is marked soon after birth (which is attended by a midwife) by baptism, a rite regarded as of great importance in the welfare of the child, and one which establishes important new links or ritual kinship between two adult groups. Nursing continues for three or four years. Childhood is a period of little discipline and little organized play; participation in adult activities begins early, except as formal schooling might interfere. There are no puberty rites; it is marriage which signalizes the important transition to mature life, unless entrance into the service of the community by means of an office be considered an earlier transition. Death is marked by the form of the Catholic wake, including vigil, recitation of prayers and the burning of candles. There are, commonly but not universally, repetitions of ritual at periodic intervals after death, especially at the anniversary, and the spirit of these activities expresses the averting of the ghost from the living as much as the commemoration of the dead or concern for the welfare of the soul. In many cases a distinction in death ritual is made between child and adult; the rituals for the child having a formally cheerful character consistent with the idea of baptized infant blessedness. There is no particular fear of corpses. Death is taken in a matter of fact way. Burial is usually in a cemetery within a day of death, and the grave is marked with a cross.

The concepts of disease, lacking systematic identification with symptom syndromes, tend to support, contradict or interact with one another in the explanations given for sickness. Among these conceptions, that of attack or invasion of the body by wind or air, often thought of as with personal characteristics, is common, as is also the identification of illness with disturbed emotional states, such as fright or anger. There is emphasis on the relation of weakened condition to susceptibility to attack from these causes of illness: infancy, pregnancy, over-exertion and exhaustion are such conditions of delicacy. There is also a recognition of contaminating influence (ritual uncleanness) in which illness is brought upon others by those who are in usual states such as pregnancy or menstruation; there is belief that certain persons or even animals may be born with this dangerous influence, located or expressed in the eye. An important conception divides plants, foods, and even persons into two categories, one strong or hot, the other weak or cold, and the ideas as to health and treatment of disease in part follow from a logic of supposed compensation of the one class of phenomena by the other, or from the supposed dangers of too sharp a conflict between the two. Certain persons are thought to perform black magic, and sickness or death is often attributed to the sorcery of an enemy, performed either directly by him or through the intermediacy of a specialist in the black art. An association of the sorcerer with an animal, perhaps an immaterial animal, is common, and the idea is held that certain persons, especially those of evil intent, may transform themselves into such animals or be represented by their forms. The treatment of many ailments is entrusted to specialized or semi-specialist practitioners, whose curing arts include charms, cupping, bleeding, poultices and infusions involving much herbal medicine; such curers are not infrequently thought of as sources of noxious magic too. Among curing devices must be counted ritual and prayer, and the simple lighting of candles at sacred places. Divination, confession, and—less commonly—flagellation, are all elements in the cure of sickness.

The *sacra* include a large number of supernatural beings and also sacred places and objects. The supernatural beings are conceived as in a vague hierarchy with God, of Christian name, as its apex. With God is associated, and in some cases completely identified, Christ. The other members of the hierarchy include the Virgin, various saints and beings of pagan name and attribute; commonly some of the supernaturals combine elements of both Christian and pagan origin. The significance of God lies largely in his vague preeminence; special functions are attached to other beings. Among the supernaturals of pagan origin, partial or complete, are some associated with wind, rain, sky, or mountains, and these are in many cases thought of in connection with the four or five directions. Lightning is connected with some of these beings, and ancient clay or stone artifacts may be associated with the lightning, or with other supernaturals. Some supernatural and personal qualities are attached to sun and moon; eclipses are connected with the actions of these supernaturals and are times of danger, especially for pregnant women. Of natural features, caves, springs and hills or mountain tops tend to be sacred, and the objects or places of religious or magical activity. The saints, as patrons and protectors, are associated with the local community and with the family; they are, at once or in distinct personages, community patrons and domestic or familial patrons. With saints, or somewhat apart from them, crosses of varying degrees of sacred importance are important elements of the sacred. The form or motion of the cross is a powerful protective symbol. The effigies of saints, each ordinarily thought of as unique (although the name of the saint be the same as that of some other effigy) are housed, with the material crosses, on table altars in houses or in temples, or set at sacred spots out of doors; much ritual activity, including praying and the burning of candles and incense, is directed toward them. To the list of *sacra* should be added intoxicating liquors which are widely important, especially in ritual or festal contexts (changes of office, religious ceremonies, weddings, funerals, etc.). Liquor is ritually sprinkled on objects. Tobacco is relatively unimportant ritually, but is occasionally used.

Although there exists a calendar of pagan origin, which includes either an artificial period of two hundred and sixty propitious or unpropitious days and a year of eighteen twenty-day periods with one period of five days to complete the three hundred and sixty-five day year, the calendar that measures much of the activities of the people is that of European origin and form. This calendar fixes the secular activities of the people, such as the changes in governmental offices, the agricultural year (except as that may be a part of the pagan calendar) and the annual cycle of communal ritual. This annual cycle is marked by a temporal alternation of preparation for festival and celebration of festival, and important points in its course are the day of the patron saint of the community, Easter, with importance less universally or emphatically given to Christmas, the Day of the Cross (May third), All Souls and All Saints Day, and the days of other saints. These strictly calendric festivals, in which the day and the saint are the occasions for celebration, are supplemented by or interrelated with agricultural rituals connected with sowing, the first rainfall, the need for rain during the growing season, and the harvest.

The celebration of the day of the saint involves special homage to the effigy of the saint including offering, prayer, and the burning of special candles, possessions, the discharge of rockets and perhaps fireworks, the celebration of festal sports, especially bullfights, and in some cases the performance of ritual dances. The Easter celebrations may be preceded, before the advent of Lent, by a Carnival; general is the celebration of Easter week by ritual enactment of parts of the Passion of Christ. This ritual includes some representation of the Crucifixion, the blessing of water and the kindling of new fire, and the inclusion of some symbol of evil, temporarily dominant but then overcome, in the form of Judas or the Devil. The rituals of All Saints and All Souls center around the conception of the return of spirits of the dead and include offerings of flowers or food to them.

In connection with the calendrical ceremonies, there is an organization of offices and functions which maintain the cult, especially that associated with the cross or saint honored on its day in the calendar. The collective obligation to repeat each year the celebration of the patron, a sacred charge on the whole community, is distributed among its members through this organization. Leadership in the discharge of this responsibility is assumed by one or a few of its adult male members, with their wives, and subordinate shares in the obligation are assumed by others, who also make their pledges or contributions to this end. These are made in anticipation of the fiesta, commonly as a part of the fiesta of the current year; the transfer of obligation from the leaders in the current year to those who will lead in the planning and performance of the fiesta in the following year is expressed, during the fiesta, in the actual transfer of ritual objects—ritual foodstuffs, candle ends, the effigy of the saint itself, or other objects. The group of votaries who have in charge this obligation, and who will pass it to their successors at the festival itself, constitute a perpetual institution, an assigned or dedicated company; as has been noted already, its members may be thought of as a part of the larger institutional hierarchy of governors of the community, sacred and secular together.

The people of this community view the universe as peopled by spiritual beings; many of the features of nature around them are spiritual and personal. Omens are seen in unusual natural events, in the actions of certain animals, especially owls and snakes, and in dreams. Certain days in the Christian calendar, especially Friday, are unlucky and one may wear talismans to safeguard one's fortune. A way of predicting the weather for the year from the weather on the first day of the year is known. Proverbs and riddles are known but not important, and among tales told are some that deal with experiences had by men with supernaturals, some that tell of the beginning of things, others that are concerned with the experiences of Christ when he was persecuted, still others that have to do with the patron saint, and yet other tales in which are recounted the droll doings of tricksters, animal or human.

In this community physical contacts, such as caresses or friendly blows, are disfavored. When intoxicated these inhibitions may be removed. In general there is great modesty about matters of sex and personal hygiene. There is little love-making. The people are disinclined to open conflict, conceal their suspicions and angers, and avoid ridicule or public discussion of themselves by evasiveness or polite fictions when questioned. Personal quarrels are hidden behind appearances of public unity, but quarrels come into the open in the courthouse. Conspicuous ambition is condemned. There is disinclination to assume responsibility if that responsibility is not attached to an office or a well-known role. Industry is highly praised. Ritual conformity is more important than inner piety. Slander and gossip are highly condemned and there is considerable slander and gossip.

Although most Indians are illiterate, writing is highly respected and part of the culture in many ways: there are sacred books, and ordinary documents are almost sacred. A literate person is useful and highly respected and has a special function in the community. There is great respect for and dependence upon law. Personal qualities of leadership are less important than the formal organization. The office makes the man. Diffuse sanctions are important in smaller communities, but even here there is important dependence on formal procedures of social control.

There are no important food "taboos"; no puberty rites, or separation at menses; no fasting, visions, ways of getting "power"; no fear of corpses; no strong kinship patterns such as clans, preferential marriage customs, avoidance and joking relationships and no elaborate systems of mythology.

PART II. ASPECTS OF CULTURE

chapter 3

ECONOMY AND TECHNOLOGY

by Sol Tax

I

IN MIDDLE AMERICA as a whole[1]* are represented three "layers" of technology: a thin top veneer of industrial art, a substantial middle layer of European pre-Industrial technology, and a bottom layer of pre-Columbian Indian technology. These three technologies are not found anywhere in "pure" form—e.g., the workers in an electric power plant lunch on *tortillas* made by pre-Columbian methods—but they *tend* to be associated with different places and kinds of people. In general, the top layer is most heavily represented in the mines and oil fields and factories of more northerly Mexico, and the bottom layer is most fully formed beyond the Isthmus of Tehuantepec.[2] Likewise, wherever there are cities and city people one finds

* Extracts from the discussions in this and the following papers are treated as numbered footnotes, placed where most relevant, and appended to the papers to which they have reference. The discussions serve to amplify, to limit, and to correct the propositions made in the papers, and to indicate areas of general agreement among the members of the Seminar.

at least the products of the modern technology, while the more rural and "Indian" the place is, the more likely it is to be dominantly primitive in technology. Rural non-Indians (Ladinos or Mestizos or whatever they are called) tend to have more traits of the middle layer—the plows and livestock, the blacksmiths, the water-wheels, millstones, pulleys, and so on. On the one hand there is an assumption that with continuing acculturation, the entire area will become "modern" in production methods and in products used; on the other hand there is the fact that 400 years of contact with the iron-age technology of Europe has left the Indians of a large part of this region largely untouched.

At the same time there is in Middle America a significant difference in economic organization ranging from the extreme of self-sufficiency[3] wherein the community (and each family in it) produces virtually all that it consumes, all the way to the extreme of local specialization in which even rural communities (and hence the families within them) produce chiefly for market and buy most of what they consume. Accompanying differences in the importance of trade, markets, and money are obvious; probably there are related differences also in ethical systems and perhaps in personality types. These differences are doubtless connected in part with geography. In homogeneous lowland regions each family and community tends to produce what it consumes, and the same thing; whereas in areas of variegated topography and altitude, there tend to be local differences in resources, hence production. Such considerations may generally explain differences between rural Indian economic life in Yucatan and in highland Guatemala. But within one or another region it would be erroneous to attribute varying patterns of specialization directly to environmental differences; for once a general pattern of trade (for example) is established, factors such as inventive business enterprise and the limitations of customary preference and "know-how" become important.

One might suppose that where the market economy flourishes, there technological acculturation has gone farthest, and the contrary. Not quite so. Self-sufficient areas are often primitive enough in technology, but the market-areas are frequently just as primitive, or more so. It is probable that the market type of economy developed independently of European technology, even to some degree independent of any outside influence. Yet the introduction of new items of material culture, and of new wants, and of different peoples with whom to trade, continually increase the tendency toward specialization and a market type of economy.

II

The extremes of self-sufficiency are reached among isolated tribe-like groups such as the Lacandon and the Indians of Quintana Roo. It is a function of their being tribe-like and isolated, and as such not very interesting. The opposite extreme of mutual interdependence is reached in highland areas of Guatemala, Chiapas, Oaxaca, central Mexico and Michoacán. Perhaps Midwestern Guatemala is the extreme case where there are communities as dependent upon trade for basic needs as are cities. The communities between these extremes partake of the characteristic economies of each. In most places in Middle America the question is the degree to which the local communities enter into a regional market economy. I shall discuss the factors governing this difference in terms of data largely from Midwestern Guatemala.

1. Community specialization is based on geography in three ways:

(a) Varying altitudes limit the agricultural uniformity: coffee can be grown below a certain line, wheat only in higher altitudes; there are tropical fruits and temperate fruits; sheep cannot live on the coast; etc., etc. Differences of altitude divide the country into broad agricultural areas.

(b) Differing natural resources in local areas differentiate their production possibilities: opportunity for irrigation is necessary for the profitable growing of vegetables, grazing land for sheep and cattle; certain reeds are needed for mats and baskets, proper clay for pottery, a lumber supply for advantageous wood-products, the proper stone for *metates,* and so on.

(c) Differences in quantity of land, especially arable land, and other natural resources (in relation to population, of course) strongly influence economic specialties: Neither Panajachel nor Momostenango nor Chichicastenango could grow enough *milpa,* for scarcity of land, to feed its population. In a negative sense this is why Panajachel has gone into intensive vegetable culture, Momostenango into blanket manufacture, and Chichicastenango into distribution and laboring.[4]

But geography cannot account for most of the specialization characteristic of Highland *municipios,*[5] since

(d) Neighboring communities with almost identical topographies and climatic conditions very often have different specialties: Contiguous Chichicastenango and Totonicapán both have pine forests; the Maxeños cut their pine for timber, while the Totonicapeños do not only that, but fashion the lumber into furniture. Likewise, clay is not lacking in either of the two communities; but Totonicapeños are leading potters, while I have never heard of a pot being made by a Chichicastenango Indian. Neighboring Panajachel, Santa Catarina, and San Antonio are all on the shore of the same lake; the Catarinecos make most of their living from fishing and crab-fishing with bought canoes, while the other towns do it practically not at all and the Antoñeros don't have canoes even for transportation. Meanwhile, Catarinecos make mats of the reeds of the lake shore which are found more off the shores of the other towns than of their own; and the other towns don't make mats. Examples of this kind could be multiplied almost indefinitely.

A full explanation of community specialization must take account, therefore, of many factors besides the geography. These will include such facts as that

(e) Specialization tends to be by communities and the production individuality of the communities must be considered as part of their general cultural individuality. Thus fishing is not the only thing that distinguishes Catarinecos as a whole from Antoñeros as a whole, or carpentry and pottery-making Totonicapeños from Maxeños.

(f) Handicraft arts are passed from parents to children, so that continuance is assured in each community while the endogamous tendencies of each tend to keep them exclusively in communities where they have started. This statement may be emphasized by pointing out that, in contrast, agricultural techniques, which can be learned by paid laborers from other communities, more often extend across municipio lines.

(g) A new means of making a living—a new crop, a new industry, or a new "business"—spreads first to relatives and neighbors, thus eventually becomes widespread in one community before it diffuses to a second; this is because social relations are much more intimate within the community than between individuals of two communities.

(h) A new means of making a living, or one known to be common in a neighboring community, is not adopted unless necessary or obviously profitable; the new is in competition with the old, so that differences of communities tend to perpetuate themselves. Thus, the people of Panajachel grow onions while those of San Antonio grow anise; the Antoñeros have learned to grow onions, but will not do so unless anise fails them. A few have tried onions, and they have been very successful; anise meanwhile hasn't been so profitable; if anise continues to "go down" and onions to be profitable, more and more of San Antonio time will be put to onions. But profits being equal, anise will surely win out—and the traditional specialty will remain. Maize is a more general example; it may be stated as a rule that only if necessary will time be diverted from growing *milpa* to some specialty.

2. Economic specialization, where it occurs, is not limited simply to specialization in the kinds of commodities produced. Differences occur more broadly in the way families or communities earn their living. All communities grow milpa, and all have additional productive specialties. Some communities may be said to be specialized in growing milpa when they grow enough for their needs and enough more to provide means of buying other necessities; such communities may have no other source of income. Other communities specialize in

(a) Special crops. Thus Totonicapán grows potatoes and wheat; Sololá and Panajachel grow vegetables; San Lucas grows tomatoes; San Pedro and San Pablo grow maguey; Santa Cruz la Laguna grows fruit; San Antonio grows anise. Also, Chichicastenango raises sheep, Santa Catarina and Atitlán catch fish and crabs; and so on.

(b) Industries. Thus Totonicapán makes furniture and pottery; San Pedro Jocopilas and Santa Apolonia make pottery and the latter also mines lime; Santa Clara makes baskets; Santa Catarina, San Lucas, and Atitlán make mats; San Pablo makes rope and rope-products; Momostenango and San Francisco make certain kinds of blankets, and Chichicastenango another; Nahualá and Santa Catarina Ixtahuacán make metates; and so on.

(c) Trades. Houses for the most part are built in local style by local Indians, so that there are Indian masons, carpenters, *adobe*-makers, tile-makers, and such in the communities where Indians need them for their houses. But only Ladinos use plasterers, and they need *adobe,* tiles, and masons in towns where the Indians don't. The Totonicapeños furnish the masons and carpenters in the midwestern highlands, so may be said to specialize in building trades.

(d) Merchandising. Indians of all communities normally carry their produce or manufactures to market to sell; but some communities specialize in buying produce of other communities in wholesale quantities to take to other markets to sell. Totonicapán, Chichicastenango, and Atitlán are (in this region) the chief specialists in distribution. Further, some communities (like San Pedro Jocopilas and Santa Clara and Panajachel) tend only to produce their goods and take them to only the nearest markets, while others (like Sololá, Totonicapán, and Sacapulas) not only produce, but widely distribute their goods.

(e) Labor. The Indians of all communities work in their own fields; lacking other means of making a living, however, those of some communities hire themselves out in other communities and especially on the coffee plantations of the Coast. Communities that may be said thus to specialize in common labor are, for example, Chichicastenango, Atitlán, Santa Catarina and San Juan on the lake.

Two special points may be mentioned:

(f) There is an order of preference of means of making a living: Indians will not do day-labor if they have another means of making a living; they will not be travelling merchants if they can make a living at home; they will not be artisans or grow special crops at the expense of their milpas. *But,* there are slack seasons in milpa that allow time for other occupations, and, furthermore, if a trade or business is profitable, labor can be hired for milpa; and it must be pointed out that industries such as pottery and basketry and hat-making are largely women's work and do not compete with milpa, which is men's work.

(g) Some communities are specialized in one or two things, others are much more diversified. Thus Panajachel (aside from a little milpa) grows vegetables and picks fruit and that's about all, and San Pablo makes ropes and similar products and (aside from a little milpa) that is all—the Pableñas not even weaving to amount to anything; while Chichicastenango (besides milpa) grows vegetables, makes blankets and hats, distributes many products, and sends droves of laborers to the *fincas,* and Totonicapán grows wheat and potatoes, tans and works leather, makes pottery and furniture and little boxes, distributes products, and sends artisans to work in many towns. The difference can be correlated fairly well with the populated area of the communities and with the number of inhabitants. Thus Panajachel and San Pablo both have small populations concentrated in small towns, while Chichicastenango and Totonicapán are large in numbers and the people are spread over a large area. The point is that with many people, competition and natural individual variations tend towards specializations; and where the people live over a large area, they live in a variety of geographical conditions. Density of population is also probably important, relative of course to the richness of utilized natural resources; a community with more than enough milpa land for all the needs of all the people is likely to have no specialty at all; a poor community (the Indians of which have to "look for ways and means") is likely to have many.[6]

[Totonicapán in this connection raises a special question, and probably illustrates a special process—economic ladinoization. Unlike Indians, the Ladinos regardless of municipio (and except for agriculture which is largely determined by geography) have at a given economic level about the same ways of making a living. In any Ladino community there are apt to be farmers (of milpa and any special crop) and all kinds of artisans—sandal-makers, shoemakers, tailors, masons, carpenters, butchers, bakers, etc. There may be storekeepers, capitalists, dairymen. There may be weavers or potters, and in the larger communities there are. There may also be travelling merchants, or peddlers. All the Ladinos may be considered one culture and one kind of community; the Ladinos as a rule go into any business that promises a profit. Some occupations they stay out of: they aren't normally day-laborers on the fincas, nor do they usually carry their goods to sell in the market. The Indian community of Totonicapán tends towards this pattern; of course, they do not have all the occupations that Ladinos all over the country do, but the Totonicapeños tend (a) to have many businesses and trades, (b) to have many that are more typically Ladino than Indian—cabinet-making, for example, and (c) not to become day-laborers on fincas, and (d) to use tools and techniques of Ladinos. Since at the same time they dress more like Ladinos than do most Indians, and speak much more Spanish and have more education than most Indians, and finally have the mobility (i.e., become residents in towns other than their own) of Ladinos, they may be said to be generally ladinoized. It is probable that their economic ladinoization came first in time, that mobility and education followed as a consequence. It is possible that the process going on among the Totonicapeños is the process that has cost the Eastern Highlands of Guatemala their typical Indian population.

It must be stated that Totonicapán women have lagged behind the men in economic ladinoization; and what is said about techniques does not apply, since they make pottery by non-Ladino methods (whereas many Totonicapán men make pottery on the wheel). It may also be mentioned that there are probably other towns (San Cristóbal, for example) that are like the Totonicapeños, and that many towns are tending in the same direction, although they have not gone as far; one such is Panajachel.]

3. The regional and community specialization gives rise to trade and markets.[7] No community is self-sufficient, and so all are economically interdependent. The following may be said about differences in self-sufficiency:

(a) A community or a family will be more self-sufficient the smaller the variety of consumption goods required, the more that can be gotten out of the soil, or the less money it is necessary to spend. Thus if the community subsists largely on maize-foods, it is apt to be more self-sufficient (other things being equal) than one that requires bread, coffee, meat, chocolate, etc. Thus if practically no furniture is used, and if houses are made of adobe or of cornstalks or of rocks, with a minimum of lime (as most Indian houses are), the community will be more self-sufficient than if tables and chairs and whitewashed or plastered walls are required (as among most Ladinos). Thus, if clothing is made from homespun and woven raw cotton, self-sufficiency will be greater than if it is woven from threads and yarns, still greater than if it is sewed from factory-cloth, and still greater than if it is bought ready-made. On the basis of this criterion, the Indians of Chichicastenango are more self-sufficient than those of Totonicapán (on the basis of clothing, especially) and of Atitlán (on the basis of food). All Indian communities are more self-sufficient than Ladino communities.

(b) Other things being equal, communities that grow enough maize for their own consumption, or specialize in maize, are more self-sufficient than those who do not, or specialize in something else. (A community specializing in maize has to buy all of its pottery, while one specializing in pottery has to buy all of its maize; maize is a far greater part of the family budget than pottery; therefore the industrial community must bring in more from outside.)

(c) This is doubtless the chief explanation of why some regions in Middle America (e.g., Yucatan, etc.) have non-market economies. There are resources permitting the production of enough maize not only for consumption but for the purchase of the few needs that cannot be locally produced.

(d) Since milpa grows at nearly all altitudes, and is about the only thing that does, communities at medium altitudes should be expected to be more self-sufficient than those at extremes. Thus the most favorable altitude for Indians would seem to be about 5000 feet, more or less, where coffee, sugar, some tropical and some temperate fruits, a large variety of herbs, chile, and even cotton can be grown. It is significant, however, that communities at those altitudes do not all seem to take advantage of their position: for example, the Indians around Lake Atitlán do not grow sugar much (and when they do they do not, of course, refine the cane, but sell it); they are as apt to sell their coffee as to use it, and then buy coffee from merchants for home use; they don't eat fruits to amount to anything (since Indians in general don't) and sell what they grow; they prefer the dry red chile from the East to what they could grow enough of; and they grow very little cotton. It is significant because it demonstrates that, except for maize, there is no interest in being self-sufficient;[8] Indians generally prefer occupations that will bring the most cash with which to buy what they please. The whole question of reasons-for-specialization may be tied up with this fact: nobody thinks it worthwhile to try to make a mat, basket, pot, or chair for his own use—thinking is done in terms of commerce. That is why no direct comparison can be made between Yucatan and Midwestern Guatemala, for example. The economic system itself conditions reactions that might serve as evidence of how these systems became differentiated.

(e) The less self-sufficient a community is, the more money it uses and the more important trade and markets are. (Communities specializing in commerce of course cut across this rule.) Thus an Indian community that raises its maize doesn't use much money; San Pedro la Laguna is an example of this, and there barter is often resorted to within the community, while purchases of "imports" are made in quantities once or twice a year when part of the harvest is sold. On the other hand, in Panajachel nobody is without money, and purchases for cash are made every day, inside and outside of the community.[9]

(f) Community self-sufficiency should not be understood in terms so much of internal specialization and exchange as of individual-family self-sufficiency. In each community the tendency is for each family to produce the same products. This is nowhere completely true of course (at the least there is professional specialization of such as midwives) nor is it equally true in all communities; but it is the Indian pattern, and it causes the Indians of each community to "look outward" to buy from and to sell to people of other communities. By and large in an Indian community there is no "domestic trade."

III

Trade and exchange, of course, vary in importance with the amount of specialization. In regions like Oaxaca or Guatemala they are vastly more important and complex than in Yucatan. Yet trade goes on everywhere. It follows about the same pattern, partly because so much of the trade is carried on, or conditioned or stimulated by non-Indians of the same general culture. Indeed, the three general ways by which trade is carried on are pretty firmly connected with *kinds of people* (Indian or non-Indian) rather than with region or anything else. The three methods of selling-buying are:

(1) House-to-house peddling. In general this belongs to non-Indian economics, for the peddlers are almost all Ladinos or ladinoized Indians, and the customers are almost invariably Ladinos. This is partly because the Ladinos live in towns and the Indians typically in open country, and peddling is more practicable in towns. The merchandise carried by these peddlers is dry-goods and notions, things of interest more to Ladinos than to Indians. In special circumstances there is peddling among Indians too, where the Indians live in town; for example, in Panajachel Ladinos often offer pork-products and Catarinecos their crabs and occasional passing merchants other wares from Indian house to house. But even this is rare, and of little importance in the total of trade.

(2) Stores. Stores are almost always run by Ladinos, but they are patronized by Ladinos and Indians alike. In the small towns the stores stock some things (like iron tools) not obtainable elsewhere, other things that are in competition with goods sold in the market.

The Ladinos, living in town (and not travelling to out-of-town markets as often as Indians) patronize the stores more than do the Indians. But Indians buy in stores when they need to (and when the prices are not too much higher than in the market) and—in vacant-town municipios—when they are in town. In addition, stores in Guatemala City and other large towns are patronized by Indians buying dry goods in quantity to sell in markets.

(3) Markets. If peddling and storekeeping are characteristically non-Indian, the same cannot be said for markets. Nor, however, are they peculiarly Indian. The market belongs to both groups, but the market in predominantly Indian regions, like Midwestern Guatemala, is typically an Indian market, and that in predominantly non-Indian regions (central Mexico) is a different kind of market.[10] The non-Indian market I shall not try to describe since I know too little about it; my impression is that the greater noise, the "salesmanship" displays, and the greater use of "bargaining" practices are indicative of differences in the cultures of Indians and non-Indians. I shall describe only the market in predominantly Indian country, particularly Midwestern Guatemala:

(a) If the market was not originally an Indian institution, it certainly is today as clearly as the store is a Ladino institution. With very rare exceptions, only Indians sell in the market-place; and it is the hub of their economic and a good part of their social life. The customers are Ladinos and Indians. Although every town has a market-place, not all towns have regular markets. Whether a particular community has or has not a regular market in its town depends not so much on its size but on its location, the kind of buying public, and accident. If a town is small, off the beaten path, and without Ladinos, it is apt to have a market only on special occasions such as fiestas when many outsiders come for other purposes; but even if the out-of-the-way town is larger, it may have no market unless by accident outsiders come in regularly to furnish a large buying public. San Pedro la Laguna has no market although it has over 2000 people; it is not on any "route," has no Ladinos; the *pedranos* themselves are fairly self-sufficient, buy what they need when they go to other markets to sell. Panajachel is half the size, but has not only a fairly active Sunday market but a fair little market almost every day of the week; it is on a main highway (really at cross-roads) and has a substantial Ladino population; besides, Panajachel is very specialized and therefore has much to buy and much to sell (wholesale) to merchants from other towns. A market like that of Chichicastenango would be large in any event because the population (Indian and Ladino both) is very large; but it is larger because the Chichicastenango Indians are merchants, and buy up pottery wholesale to take elsewhere, and also come in especially large numbers to the market because it is their home market. That at Chiché seems to have been organized (recently) by Ladino authorities to relieve the burden on Chichicastenango by taking away most of the livestock market. So each market has its own circumstances to help account for its being.

(b) During a town's large fiestas, the market is considerably larger than usual. This is both because many people come for the fiesta (so that business will be good) and because people await a large market to make their purchases when the assortment and competition are large and keen. The Indians especially buy such things as furniture, pottery, baskets, bags, mats, rope, and other non-perishables at fiesta markets; that is one reason why Indians are not good customers at ordinary markets and thus why markets are large where there are Ladinos. Other reasons are that Ladinos rather than Indians are buyers of fruit, vegetables, spices, etc., that are more a part of their diet.

(c) Although confused in practice by exceptions, marketing—both buying and selling—is basically a woman's occupation, and this holds for Ladino buyers as well as Indian.[11] That this is true is seen most clearly in small markets (such as Atitlán, Panajachel, and San Andrés) where *local* men are never seen buying or selling; but it is no less true in large markets such as Chichicastenango and Sololá. In all markets, male merchants (i.e., specialists who are selling in "stores") are found in the market-place, as are also merchants of bulky or very heavy goods; but these are always from other towns. Chichicastenango is a definite exception, for Maxeño merchants (bringing chile, bananas, brown-sugar, salt, spices, etc., and varieties of drygoods from afar) do sell in the Chichicastenango market; and Chichicastenango men buy in the market too. Here it may be said that men deal in large quantities, women in small; and that holds for all markets, too—insofar as men are involved.

(d) Government coins are the medium of exchange in all markets; cases of barter are very rare, but every evidence is that barter was much more common a generation or two ago.[12] Together with the growth of the use of money has gone a tendency toward more exact measurement—towards weighing things, for example. It seems to me that entrance of Ladinos into the markets—especially urban Ladinos—has had a lot to do with these changes. Indians have a hard time holding up their end of bargaining with superior-acting Ladinos who don't understand their language: the more exact the weights and standards, the easier it becomes for the Indian. Besides, of course, town Ladinos (not being producers) have nothing to barter; they are the ones with money and their presence helps to keep transactions on a cash basis, among other reasons because they furnish the Indians with cash.

(e) There can be no doubt that a large part of the market is a response of the Indians to Ladino customers. The Indians (and Ladinos) regularly buy at most maize, beans, chile, coffee, *panela,* salt, cotton, and a few other staples. These are brought by merchants who usually bring one item only. Now in addition to such merchants there are (1) Indian women selling small products of the farm and barnyard that other Indians don't buy much of because they have the same things at home, (2) many fruits and vegetables from different regions that Indians rarely buy, (3) merchants (usually Maxeños) with rice, drygoods, and many spices and other staples some of which Indians buy, but more of which Ladinos buy, and (4) market "stores" run by Indians and containing drygoods, notions, dress-goods for Ladinos and of recent years textiles for the tourist trade. The "stores" have recently mushroomed in number and in stock; they tend to carry factory goods, and except for the tourist textiles their goods have a non-Indian source as well as, in large part, a non-Indian destination. Meanwhile such items as pottery and rope (except where they are bought for further distribution) are purchased for the most part by Ladinos, except during certain days of the year when the Indians stock up. Thus if one discounts Ladino influence, the market becomes a smaller affair and changes to some extent its character; in the days of barter, barter was no doubt easier than it would be today.

IV

In regions where the market economy predominates, among Ladinos and Indians alike there is an economic individualism and tendency towards opportunism that extends from the (Indian) community down to the members of households. Thus any man can and will do almost any kind of business from which he thinks he can make money; there are few traditional barriers.[13] Thus also members of the household or family are relatively free to make their own bargains, and keep their own profits for personal (if reasonable) uses. These tendencies are probably part of the general anarchic economy, arising perhaps as natural responses to an "economic mentality" and a money-and-trade system; and I think that they are probably universal among the Indians as well as the Ladinos. *But* I think it probable that Ladinos have stronger tendencies in this direction, and that the Indians vary in them according to their closeness of contact with Ladinos. It is not simply that some Indians are more ladinoized and have taken over Ladino ideas; nor simply that social and family structures are weakened by contact with Ladinos and the complexities arising therefrom; but also that opportunities for *entrepreneurs* big and little are increased a hundredfold by the presence of Ladinos.

Thus the Totonicapeños would be making pottery and growing milpa, for the most part, if this were still Indian country; nobody would need expert plasterers and fireplace-builders, and relatively little furniture would be needed. Thus Panajacheleños wouldn't have a chance, nor a motive, to learn how to grow strawberries for the tables of Ladinos. Thus the Pedrana women, or the Maxeño women either, wouldn't have a sudden boom in cash receipts from tourist-bought textiles. Thus boys and girls wouldn't have the chance to pick up pennies running errands or doing jobs. For that matter, without the Ladinos the economy would be on much less a cash basis to start with; there might be yearnings (and all the potentialities) for economic opportunities, but economic opportunity would simply not knock—or to be more exact, would knock less often.

Here again is a reason for some apparently regional differences. Where Indians live in close economic relationship with urbanized people of different culture, they become more commercial.

V

A series of problems revolves about the general question, "What are the general economic effects of the various social and cultural differences among Indian communities?" These differences, some of which have been discussed above, are:

(1) The type of community. Taken alone, the difference between "vacant town" and "town nucleus" communities seems to

have few correlative economic differences. But when there are Ladinos in the town, the difference is important, since then of course there is increased opportunity for business with Ladinos when the Indians all live in town; Ladinos of course do not typically live in the open country. Furthermore, if the town is situated on a highway or for some other reason has a market, it will have a *daily* market apparently only where the Indians live in town, and in vacant-town communities the daily market (if any) will be patronized only by Indian women who live on the outskirts of town. The daily market itself has, of course, important effects on the economic condition of women.

(2) The presence of Ladinos and foreign Indians. The most striking effect of a population of Ladinos on the economy of a community (of whatever type) is that the local market becomes more important, especially to the local Indians who then have an outlet for home produce.[14] But the most important effect is that they open up possibilities for a variety of petty business dealings, reinforce the cash aspects of the economy, give the Indians an opportunity to learn new things (partly by acting as servants in Ladino homes) and thus changing both their means of making a living and their tastes in living. Furthermore, since Ladino residents require special artisans from other towns, a colony of "foreign Indians" usually results; such a colony, forming an intermediate social class between Indians and Ladinos, tends to act as a bridge towards ladinoization (economic as well as other) of at least a margin of the local Indian population.

(3) Location on the highway. It has been mentioned that towns located on highways and trade-routes tend to have important markets, often daily markets. The location also tends to bring Ladino residents, with effects as noted. Besides, when Indians and others are continually passing through, there is the business of supplying their needs of food and shelter; and if there is no market in town, it is possible to buy from passing merchants. Also, if it is a vacant-town community, there is a tendency for some Indians to move to town for business purposes; the "highway" itself achieves value and importance, and the property that borders it usually achieves a cash value that is not ordinarily attached to other than farm lands.

(4) Religious and social customs. The effects of religious customs on the standard of living and the wealth of the community are

worth special study. Some towns have more fiestas than others, and some celebrate their fiestas with more expensive ingredients (such as liquor and fireworks) than others. Thus both the time and money consumed on these non-economic activities varies, sometimes greatly, with different towns. It may be pointed out that the number of *mayordomías* or *cofradías* does not vary directly with the Indian population; small towns have proportionally more of them, and the personnel required in small towns is proportionally greater than in large towns; so that small towns normally devote more time and wealth to religious services.[15] There is reason to believe that (other things being about equal) small towns are proportionally poorer than large towns. Santa Catarina and San Juan are the smallest towns on Lake Atitlán and are undoubtedly the poorest; they are both notorious for their fiestas. San Marcos is also very small, but it is not poor; and my impression is that it celebrates fewer fiestas. Size and number of fiestas are not the only factors in the question of poverty, of course: Chichicastenango is very large and also very poor, yet the proportion of time and money spent on fiestas is probably smaller than most towns.

Some towns may be found to be "more religious" and "less economical" regardless of the number of local saints. Thus the people of Santa Catarina are the first to visit other towns' fiestas, and indeed ordinary markets, for non-economic purposes; it is becoming poorer all the time and has very little land left. Meanwhile, San Juan has practically no lands left either, and the people for the most part earn their living as day-laborers.

A special point may be mentioned on the question of religious services: when times are good the people can perhaps afford the customary expenditures; with the Depression of the thirties (and an increase in the price of liquor) the *servicios* became a much greater hardship. Yet in the Lake region the elders didn't approve of cutting down expenditures, so that at least for awhile the proportion of total income spent for non-economic "religious" purposes jumped considerably. After a period of lag there was some adjustment in many towns (in San Andrés, for example, if second-hand information is good); in Panajachel the adjustment was made by individuals simply refusing to serve.

It might also be worthwhile to investigate community differences in the amount of time and money (especially for liquor) that custom requires at baptism, marriage, and funerals, etc. If it differs considerably, one could study the differing effects on the wealth and poverty of the towns.

More generally the varying proportions of time spent on economic and non-economic activities of different towns might be compared, making a distinction on the basis of sex for the greater significance of the findings. I would expect that the proportion of time spent on economic activity would be directly correlated with the level of living, and that, furthermore, the amount of time spent on "commercial" as opposed to household economic activities would also be so correlated. If it does not turn out so, one would ask what other factors turn the picture askew. Are there important differences in the economic value of different specializations? If so, isn't there a tendency to switch specializations? Or is it rather the relation of population to natural resources? A special study might be made in this connection of varying birth rates among Indians of different communities.

(5) Recent influences from outside. The motor truck and the sale of textiles to tourists are two new elements in Indian economy that affect some towns more than others. The effect of the first is, in general, to release time from distribution for production. Much of the vegetable crop of Sololá and Panajachel is taken to the city; where almost a week was once required for a round trip, now it can be done in two or three days. Practically nobody walks today on this route, not served by trucks until about fifteen years ago. Yet when I was last in Guatemala most other towns (and such products as pottery, furniture, and all coast-Highland trade) still utilized the old method of transportation. The tendency towards the use of trucks will probably become stronger and stronger. What will be the results on local economies; specifically, to what purposes will the time gained be put? Analyzing the change in towns with different specializations and different resources will probably throw much light on the essential facts of Indian economics.

Meanwhile, in the last five to eight years there has been a great boom in the textile business. Whereas formerly women wove *huipiles* for their own use, now they weave them also to sell—for cash. Thousands of dollars a year now come into Chichicastenango and find their way into the pockets of women; a comparable sum comes into San Pedro and certain other towns. In both Chichicastenango and San Pedro, women formerly had little "cash value" —since neither town has an industry (like pottery, or vegetable-growing) at which women could work. Now it may be possible to see just how the difference affects the position of women. Also, of course, how does the new income affect the whole economy? Since capital is important in Guatemalan towns, I suspect that the eventual effect on the level of living will be out of proportion to the actual change in income.

VI

A similar series of problems revolves about the converse question, "What are the social and cultural effects of economic differences among communities?" Obviously such a general difference as in relative wealth and level of living have accompanying differences of importance; there is a difference even in the personal bearing of the men of rich San Pedro and those of poor San Juan, their closest neighbors on the shore of Lake Atitlán. But the economic differences that lead to special questions are more specific. They are:

(1) Communal ownership of land. The question of communal lands is one on which historians have helped us much more in Mexico than in Guatemala. My supposition is that in the nineteenth century Indian community milpa- and firewood- and waste-lands (at least) were generally communal; that families got what firewood they needed, and that milpa lands were allotted by local authorities for the duration of the land (six or seven years); that house-site lands were always privately owned and inherited; that in town-nucleus communities *all* of the land outside of town was communal, but that in vacant-town communities only "open stretches" were communal and each house had a privately owned and inherited lot of considerable size where milpa could be grown. That is as much as can be reasonably "supposed" on evidence only of the present-day. Whether in vacant-town communities there were privately-owned house-sites, I cannot guess; whether in town-nucleus communities fruit-trees and such in town were privately owned, I cannot guess either. Whether in vacant-town communities the communal land in the country was controlled by the authorities of the whole town or of a smaller unit (such as a *paraje* or a *cantón*) I have no way of guessing either, but I lean towards the latter possibility.

Today there doesn't seem to be much communal ownership of land.[16] In Chichicastenango in some *cantones* little pieces of land seem still to be communally used by the cantón; but the one piece I know is not good for agriculture. In Nahualá, which is also a vacant-town community, everybody says that "all the land is communal and allotted by the year" but while I do not doubt that there are communal lands there, I cannot believe that (a) people move out of their houses yearly, or (b) the milpa-growers exchange plots of land yearly. The milpa-system here entails considerable work on "new land" to burn the bush, etc., and less on succeeding years; and in about six years the piece of land must be left to grow to bush again, and another piece started; I can see no practical way of allotting such lands except for periods of about six years, or the "life of the land." This indeed is the system used in Atitlán, San Pedro, and San Marcos where there are communal milpa lands.

In the lake towns all communities have some communal lands—all *monte* lands (with the people living in town); Atitlán seems to have most, but San Marcos probably has the biggest proportion of all lands communal; San Pedro has only the least desirable milpa lands still communal, and much waste land; Panajachel has only one tract of perfectly barren land still communal; Santa Catarina little more. None of the communal lands are in the towns (where the people all live); there the lands, mostly house-sites, are privately owned and inherited. But in San Marcos (where the people live up the two sides of the valley in two groups) the bottom of the valley, rich fruit-growing country, is communally owned but the trees themselves privately owned. In San Marcos the milpa-land—all of it apparently—is communally owned.

But what are the effects of the difference today between the communities that are different in this respect? The most important difference is probably that where land is communally owned it cannot be sold to Ladinos or to Indians of other towns. San Marcos has apparently not lost an inch of its milpa land, and the people are relatively wealthy and grow all the maize they can without worrying about land; on the other hand Santa Catarina has lost a good portion of its land to Ladinos and a little to other Indians; and now the town has to subsist in large part on what it can earn from fishing and from working by the day in other towns. San Juan is probably the worst off of any lake town as far as land is concerned; the Indians of San Pedro own much more San Juan land than do Juaneros, and the San Juan Indians are for the most part laborers. However, simply because the land is privately owned doesn't mean that it will be sold. There are social controls in Chichicastenango, for example, that effectively keep the lands in the hands of the Maxeños.

Another effect attributable in large part to communal ownership of land is that the population of towns that have it tends to be more homogeneous and exclusive. A foreigner can come into such a town, but he can't buy land; naturally, the elders of the town will not be anxious to give him a piece to work, so foreigners don't usually come in. When they do, they are apt to intermarry and to change to the local costume and do local *servicios* and become otherwise absorbed into the local population. That process of course is rewarded by a share of the land, and it is a process very obvious in San Pedro as contrasted with Panajachel where "foreign Indians" remain apart often for generations.

It might be expected that the elders of a town where the land is communally owned will exercise a greater degree of control over the inhabitants than in other towns; in such matters as religious servicios there are apt to be fewer dissenters. I am not actually sure that it works out that way, however: San Pedro is a town in which for a number of years the Protestant mission was rather more successful than in neighboring towns.[17] It would be good to know how it was reconciled to the religious-political system (since Protestants are not supposed to have anything to do with *santos*) and whether the power of the elders or other effects of the communal ownership of land in any way inhibited the growth of the movement.

(2) Different kinds of specialties of communities should be expected to have varying effects on the social structure. Whether they do or not—and if not why not—presents a series of problems that comparative studies of certain aspects of the social life of certain communities should solve.

(a) Milpa growing. Since milpa is the traditional crop, and milpa products the most important of any in the kitchen, towns that grow all they need and even grow it to the exclusion of other specialties should show some special characteristic. For one thing, wealth being equal the people who specialize in maize probably consume a larger proportion, since it is the only thing they do not have to buy; likewise (since maize is always the biggest part of the budget) money should be less important in such a community. Also, since women do not work in the milpa as they do in other specialties, in a community that makes its living from milpa alone the women might be expected to have a lower position, especially since they have nothing to sell and don't take in any money on their own. It also seems probable that other things being equal a community that specializes in maize will pay more attention to the ritual aspects of agriculture—rain, planting, and harvest ceremonies. It might also be expected that the family will be more closely knit in communities growing mainly maize and having no other specialty since in such a place the source of family income is all the same and there are no opportunities for individual *negocios*. It might be worthwhile to study what the people in such a community do with the leisure time that a milpa-specialty enforces; also, if one wished to study the "*mozo* system" (in which farmers hire each other as laborers) the place to do so is in such a community—and I would not be surprised to find that in such towns the mozo-system is based less on cash than in other towns. One final difference may be suggested: that in towns specializing in milpa the Indians will be less travelled than in other towns. Milpa products are grown everywhere, and it doesn't pay to transport them far in normal times; maize is probably carried less far than any other commodity (except something like firewood).

(b) Industrial communities should show special characteristics as contrasted with agricultural communities (growing maize or other crops as specialties). Thus industrialists, travelling farther as a rule than agriculturists, might be more sophisticated and ladinoized. They should be more secular-minded since they are less dependent on the vagaries of nature and more dependent on trade and money. At the same time that an industrial specialty tends to keep the family together at home more of the time than any other, there is apt to be more independence of the members, since they can all work separately. It would appear also that industrial communities would be more dependent on other specialists and on imported goods for their daily needs, for there is no leisure time to do odd jobs with profit. On the other hand, the people are usually more self-sufficient in the labor market; this is because people of other towns are not usually skilled in the particular specialty; and as a result local skilled-labor is always in demand and the people do not usually have to go to work in other towns. This may be said also for communities specializing in some agricultural product that requires special techniques. It is possible, finally, that the politico-religious organization shows differences as between an industrial and an agricultural community; for in an agricultural town a man can spend every other week in the town hall without great hardship while his crops grow by themselves, while an industrialist loses his time completely. (However, in many industries, such as spinning maguey fiber, making hats, etc., the man can do some work while engaged in his duties.)

(c) Specialties which employ women—whether the specialties are agricultural or industrial—may be expected to have effects on the social life of communities that have them. In general the division of labor is strictest in agricultural—especially milpa—merchandising, and laboring specialties; in industrial communities women often work along with men, and in some cases carry the industrial specialty on their shoulders alone. It is likely that where women work their time becomes worth money, and they are apt to drop some domestic duties such as weaving—or at least spinning—and, if opportunity permits, grinding. Furthermore, the wealth of the community might be expected to be greater. The position of women in the family is likely to be higher, although on the other hand they are likely to have less leisure time. The women who produce seem to be more sophisticated economically; whether or not they take their things to market, they may be expected to know values and take interest in business. Whether this makes them less conservative than other women, or leads to secularization, is a question; but at least in Panajachel it is a factor. Another effect of the requirement of special technical knowledge in women is that such specialized communities are less apt than others to bring in wives from outside, since outside women are economically disadvantageous.[18]

(d) Finally, there are probably some significant social differences accompanying the distinction between merchant communities (where the men take their own or others' produce long distances) and others. It appears that typically merchant communities have larger family units (i.e., extended families, etc.) than the others; and this fact may very well be connected with the necessity of leaving one's wife and children in the care of somebody else—perhaps a brother—while being away from home for days or weeks. At the same time, marital relations among merchants are notoriously loose; the men are supposed to have wives along their routes and the women are supposed to be unfaithful. This is probably true, especially in such communities as Chichicastenango and Totonicapán where the people live in the open country.

It might be expected that merchant towns would be somewhat more sophisticated than others, since at least the men travel so much; but sophistication involves so many other factors (town-type, markets, presence of Ladinos, women in industry, etc.) that it is not easy to isolate this one. Totonicapeños, who are often merchants, are indeed sophisticated; but not necessarily because they are merchants. Maxeños and Atitecos are not as sophisticated as most of their non-merchandising neighbors; but in the case of both, milpa is rather important, there are no industries or specialties in which women take part, contacts with Ladinos are not striking, and so on.

VII

The points I have chosen to discuss are only a few of many that one could select. Even these I have put in what others might think a peculiar order. For example, questions of land tenure are discussed as a subhead in another context, and such common topics as inheritance, sexual division of labor, work cooperation,[19] and so on I have hardly mentioned. For such omissions (as well as less obvious ones like the relations of Indian economy to the world economy and to the laws and administrative activities of the various governments; the economy of the colonies of Indians living on plantations, and so on) I can only apologize. What has interested me most has been to define roughly a *kind of economy* which I think is the one most characteristic of Middle America and to raise some questions about it that might have larger implications.

DISCUSSION

(1)

Whetten: Just what is the universe that we are trying to describe here? I assume it is the Indian culture of *Mesoamerica,* but then we see that several problems arise: (1) the geographical delimitation of the area and (2) just what part of the population we are concerned with after we delimit the area. I find it difficult to decide just what the Indian culture is. My interest in Guatemala has been in fitting together the various groups. In parts of it you have a plantation economy in which people live on fincas, each of which has probably 100 inhabitants. I don't know how many workers this includes. Data by coffee-producers in Guatemala give the finca population in 1945-46 of 282,000 people living as permanent residents, and 142,000 living as temporary residents. The question that then comes to my mind is, are we concerned only with the floating population? If they live there permanently they would have a somewhat different culture than you have in the highlands. So it occurs to me that perhaps that particular part of Middle America should be referred to in some way or excluded.

There comes to mind also—since Mr. Tax states that this paper is concerned primarily with Southwest Guatemala—what about Eastern Guatemala, where, according to most of the data, they are more ladinoized and so on. You could also bring in other countries as illustrations.

Tax: I'd like to bring up a methodological point. One of the differences between a rural sociologist and an anthropologist is that the latter tries to find out what is central to the culture. The use of statistics, for example, is usually a little bit less in our realm. Also, we are not interested so much in the notion of how a Guatemalan makes a living. I haven't taken into account such things as the economy of the Indian groups who are colonizing fincas in this area, in what ways living as colonials on fincas changes their basic ways of doing things. There ought to be a major core of interest here: the characteristic way of life in general of the recognizably Indian groups; taking that as a base, go out from there to see what effects different kinds of life have on this basic culture. What I was trying to delimit here was what I thought of as the basic culture of one type of Indian. We would have to add very much to this. I would like to see a map on which are plotted the places or types of people to whom my description of a characteristic kind of economy is applicable. Such a map would include at least the highlands of Guatemala, Chiapas, and Oaxaca. I don't know about Michoacán. I would like to see how far, and with what variations, this pattern goes.

Beals: The question of how far the statements in this paper would apply to Michoacán calls for detailed discussion. I think there are elements here which we can say are general and elements which in specific areas are not.

I think Mr. Whetten has raised a very fundamental problem on which we don't have enough information. The question is: how far the things which we can describe apply or do not apply to certain types of rural or Mestizo cultures. A number of things apply to Mestizo, as well as to Indian.

Tax: Those people here who have been interested in non-Indian communities may be able to help us.

Mason: Very little of this applies to the tribes north of the Mesoamerican boundary. It is not applicable to the Tarahumara, for example.

Foster: We've got to consider rural Mestizos in many parts of the area far more with respect to the subject of economy and technology than with social organization and other aspects of the seminar.

Whetten: How applicable is the description here to the communities you have in mind?

Foster: That would require taking it apart piece by piece. I'm in more or less general agreement with Tax on his three layers of technology. They are not peculiar to Mesoamerica. We're all concerned with the middle layer. As anthropologists we haven't paid much attention to the cities and factories. On the other hand, there are very few Indians in the area that are not characterized by the market economy. We're primarily concerned with this very thick central core.

Toor: The Lacandon don't have markets because there are so few of them.

Foster: The Popoluca don't have markets either, but there are many of them.

Tax: In the area around Chan Kom there are villages where you would expect to find markets, but there are none, possibly due to homogeneity of production in the area.

Villa: That is the situation at the present time. In earlier times we had market places in Quintana Roo, and a certain kind of specialization. In Quintana Roo they specialized in honey and cotton.

Stone: How much can you say is due to Spanish influence and how much to native influence? In Eastern Honduras you don't have markets; you have traders; you only find this where you have had Mexican influence.

Foster: To what extent do you have arts and crafts in that area?

Stone: You had certain groups who were famous for their weaving, others for hammocks, etc., but no market.

Foster: I think Mr. Tax is driving home a point with which I am more or less in agreement. It seems to me that a market is a concomitant of a certain type of society. When you get a population of a certain density and a certain number of villages, an amount of specialization arises. I have the feeling that markets have come into being that way all over the world. I don't believe that the market is a trait which you must follow by distribution.

Stone: But in eastern Central America where the Mexicans went through, it was impossible to have a market in 45 villages which were constantly at war.

Goubaud: If we could all have a larger map of Guatemala we could delimit the area of which Tax is speaking, and the boundary where this seems to stop.

By and large, those communities which are highly Indian in their culture and less ladinoized are the ones who retain this generalized type of economy. You can trace it to the 5000 foot altitude level, north of Guatemala City, and on west to Alta Verapaz, where the Indian communities lead an independent economic life, definitely related to the economic aspects of the country. In the eastern part of the country you have a cultural island, the Pokomán and Chorti, who again represent patterns of market economy, the surrounding Ladino communities seem to have markets only in the large cities. So that there are definitely two patterns with regard to the economic organization of Guatemala. In one survey we found 194 markets going on during the week, of which about 80% of them were in Indian communities.

Tax: Does this lead us to the conclusion that what I've described here as an Indian economy is really a unique economy?

Goubaud: You can actually draw a line. I've drawn the distribution of the foot loom and the tump loom, which shows a beautiful geographic distribution of those areas where Indian culture is still strong.

Then you have the large plantation section in the southwestern part of Guatemala, in which the Indian is in the mesh of a commercial agricultural economy and has a very subordinate type of economic activity.

Whetten: You would rule out the plantation economy from this discussion?

Tax: I don't think there is any great methodological difficulty here because what you're saying is that here is an economy characteristic of a people who still speak the Indian language and carry on their own customs, that when these people no longer have the Indian customs they no longer have the market economy.

The interesting thing to me is that, assuming that you are going to call this a type of Indian economy in Guatemala, we see that in the South there was a different pattern of economy, as Mrs. Stone has pointed out. One variation is where the people have become ladinoized; another is found outside of the area. Those are two factors. The third thing that has come out here is that in Yucatan (although I don't believe anyone would argue that they are ladinoized there), there is still the question whether they ever had as much of a market as in the highland areas. It was mentioned that when you get into the north of Mexico you get away from this also. Within the area itself there also are differences.

Paul: We might get nowhere if we talk about where we draw our limits. The question is: does it apply to the area to which it is supposed to apply? I don't think it's realistic to worry about drawing lines; we should discuss it in terms of the market economy. The area will define itself as we talk.

Stone: So far as I can see, it's only in Mexico and Guatemala.

Kelly: It doesn't even cover Mexico.

Beals: There is also the question of whether possibly, within whatever area we may be talking about, we may be describing differences between highland and lowland. As we go along we might question whether a great many of Mr. Tax's comments are not really trying to describe but to set forth general propositions for which he used Guatemala as an example.

Kirchhoff: Several speakers have commented on the fact that it is necessary to differentiate within Middle America. We should consider the relation between the highlands and lowlands. I have the feeling that markets are more strongly developed in areas in which highlands are close to lowlands, and that they have developed their specific characteristics as a result of this contrast. Where the lowlands are far away from the part of the highlands under consideration, you may not have strong development of markets.

Beals: I would agree with that; a good example is found in the Tarascan area where the Tarascans act as *entrepreneurs*. They collect highland products and take them to the lowlands, and vice versa.

Tax: I think that would go a long way toward explaining the Yucatan situation. This is something we should keep in mind.

(2)

Beals: I think you find comparable groups north of the Isthmus of Tehuantepec.

Tax: Are there groups in which there is an agricultural technology as primitive as that in Central America? How about the digging stick?

Kelly: Totonac agriculture is completely a digging stick economy.

Beals: Among the Mixe a considerable part of the agriculture is digging stick economy. A great deal of Mestizo Jalisco is also. Whether that's comparable or not, I'm not sure. I feel that the statement is too sweeping.

(3)

Beals: How accurate is the use of the term self-sufficiency? Are there any fully self-sufficient economic groups, even such a group as the Lacandon? How many groups could you find in the Mexican area which are really self sufficient?

Foster: It's not a question of *having* to import something; a lot of these groups could be self sufficient if necessary.

Tax: Obviously it's a relative term. I don't think any group in the world can be found that is self sufficient. The variations within the area of self sufficiency, however, are very great. Panajachel is far less self sufficient than any agricultural group in New England; they don't grow many of the things they use. They produce almost exclusively for the market. They make some of their clothing, but don't grow any of the materials for it. They buy almost all the food they eat. They are very much like the specialized farmers in the U.S. who have big wheat farms and who buy canned goods to eat. It seems to me to be a peculiar characteristic in a region which is so primitive in technology.

Camara: Self sufficiency can be divided into two phases: (1) subsistence economy for crops—anything they can cultivate—and (2) for the market, or that which is not included in the subsistence economy. The Lacandones or the X-Cacal groups cultivate, but still get many other things; even the Lacandones buy matches, etc.

(4)

Beals: I would like to make an observation from another area, Ecuador, where you have diminishing land resources plus an increase in population and a rapid expansion of commerce. The people in the village go over to the East from the coast, to Colombia and Peru; they are sometimes gone for six or seven months at a time. Growth in commercial activity is related to the land base and the population.

Tax: We have to recognize that what we say is not confined to Middle America but to a generalized situation of which Middle America is a part. I think you'll find this not only in Middle America but in the Andean area as well; I don't think you'll find it in all the other parts of the world.

(5)

Whetten: I am wondering whether the people working in Mexico wouldn't define specializations by the village, where you don't have this vacant town type of thing, rather than by municipio as you do in Guatemala.

De la Fuente: I would say that in Oaxaca you can substitute village for municipio.

Beals: If you use municipio in Michoacán you may get five villages in one municipio.

Tax: We would have to define the different political units in these countries. I know that in Mexico the municipio means something different from what it means in Guatemala.

Stone: The word village is better in the East.

Tax: Village doesn't mean much in Guatemala. What we can say is the local cultural unit.

Camara: We have to make the distinction again between highlands and lowlands. When we say Chiapas we are considering only the highlands; in the south coastal regions there is no such thing as the municipio as a cultural unit.

Beals: I think in Guatemala itself you have a nuclear center with a scattered population. There's a quite different situation in Michoacán; there the municipio includes the cabecera, which has about half the population of the municipio, and has a series of smaller villages which are about one-fifth to one-half the size of the cabecera. The smaller village may have a pattern of specialization which is not the same as that of the cabecera.

Paul: The village is a more constant unit.

Tax: I agree that if we are talking about Middle America we don't use municipio.*

Guiteras: In Chiapas sometimes you have specialization by *rancherías;* in other cases the whole municipio has the same specialization.

Tax: What's most interesting in Guatemala, to me, is that you find two rural districts with an imaginary boundary between them. On one side of the line the women make pottery, for example, and on the other side of the line they don't. Regardless of how the community is defined, is the specialization by communities or is it haphazard?

Guiteras: If the article is produced only for the use of the cultural group, one ranchería will produce it, but if it is to be taken outside, then all the women will make it.

Paul: Specialization is by the local community; the question is, how are you going to define the local community?

Tax: We could very profitably cooperate in defining the local community in Middle America as a whole.

(6)

De la Fuente: I think this statement is very strong. In Oaxaca three or four villages that happen to be the poorest tend to contradict this statement. There is a tendency for the people to work in other villages.

Tax: I would call this specialization; I would consider it a sign of poverty when people have to work for other people. If you get a whole community in which there are laborers, that's a sign of poverty.

*** In the remainder of the paper following this footnote, the term *municipio* has been changed to the more generalized term "community."—Ed.**

De la Fuente: These are recognized merchants, people trading in the city markets.

Tax: It's a kind of negative specialization.

Beals: I think you can find some good examples of people who are very poor and who have no specialization whatever. Sometimes they just sit and starve. They live many months of the year without having any crops. It may be related to some of this that a greater value is placed on maize cultivation as compared to other types of cultivation; I think this is generally true. The primary value of all these communities, regardless of specialization, is their maize farming. Is there a possibility of discovering the relative values of these other occupations? Does merchandising have a higher value than the cultivation of secondary crops, etc.? It isn't always true that merchandising is necessarily a poverty occupation; sometimes merchants are better off than the men who farm.

Goubaud: In a general survey of industries in Guatemala forty-two industries of the Indians were listed. It is interesting to note that there were various industries within the municipio. We got a ranking of at least three industries and left a fourth open. Here there seemed to be no specific preference. One community would have pottery as the main industry, with sandal making second and rocket making third; another community would have basket weaving, bread making, etc., so that we didn't find any specific ranking with regard to a preference within all the 194 communities.

Tumin: What about a hierarchy of workers?

Foster: In Tzintzuntzan the distinctions are between owning a store, as one basic category of enterprise, handicrafts, and farming. Of the latter there are two categories: (1) owning land; (2) share cropping. The person who gets enough money is apt to open a store. Very close behind him is the relatively large landowner, then you would have pottery making.

Tumin: What differences are there between the Indians who own their own land and those who do not? There are at least slight variations, partly due to the fact that the Indians are largely landless, or just trying to hold on to some land. Indians are now defining milpa, not as the land, as the produce.

Tax: The milpa is not only the cornfield but also the corn plant.

Tumin: They can't claim ownership to anything; 15% of the Indians own land, the rest don't.

Goubaud: Even if the Indians do not own land, do they consider that the preferred type of occupation?

Tumin: Yes.

Camara: That's just an ideal. If you need money, then you abandon the milpa.

De la Fuente: In Oaxaca the merchant is the person with the highest status, particularly if he is a shop-owner. Certain crafts like twisting *ixtle* don't demand much money, but they are crafts, so you have a general preference towards commerce.

Tumin: Isn't our problem that we're unable to define the hierarchy because there are syndromes of preference?

Tax: Nevertheless we started out by saying that the milpa is most preferred.

(7)

De la Fuente: I am wondering whether the phrase (a) doesn't imply, in English, a variety. It seems to me that "a variety of goods produced" would be better. Then I would be more in agreement.

(8)

De la Fuente: Regarding the statement "no interest in being self-sufficient." It seems to me that the growth of markets in Oaxaca is a tendency of the people to be self sufficient.

Tax: Is there a difference here in the definition of the term self sufficient?

De la Fuente: The tendency is to be self sufficient.

Kelly: De la Fuente is speaking in

terms of a larger unit. Tax is speaking in terms of the family.

Villa: It seems to me important to take into consideration that specialization in different items of the culture is one of the main features of the cultural patterns of the regions which we are talking about. We have specialization not only in production but in other aspects of the culture, specialization in dress, etc. This specialization is tied up with the cultural pattern.

Kelly: We have all noticed that in the North they are relaxed with regard to markets, etc.

Foster: Regarding this proposition about the relation of available milpa land to the market: in the Popoluca area there is no land hunger and there's no specialization whatever. There is agricultural activity the entire year.

Beals: We run into individuals who go into trade not because they have to but because it's a lot of fun; they're trading not because of economic pressure but because they like to trade. I think it's a cultural pattern. The whole question of specialization, and also the consumption of specialized goods, has some relation to values which people hold.

Paul: I think we're all agreed that the cause is multiple; certainly one determinant is the paucity or richness of the land but nobody would agree that this is the sole determinant. I was impressed in looking at McBryde's materials by whether they can farm or whether they can't farm; a determinant in this case is the milpa self sufficiency of the community.

Foster: Wouldn't there be people in Cherán who could not have land even if they wanted it?

Beals: Yes, but there are also those who can farm land but don't want to.

Kyte: In Guerrero the people want to be self sufficient.

Tax: Is there a difference in the degree to which security is important?

Kyte: These people were formerly nomadic pastoral people; now they are agricultural. The idea is: you might not be able to buy your corn, therefore you have to have the corn first.

Tax: In other words, they don't have a market system, so they'd better grow their own corn.

(9)

De la Fuente: Regarding points (3b) and (3e), there's a contradiction here. San Pedro is self sufficient to the extent that it raises its own maize. It seems to me that this may account for trade on the one hand, but on the other hand, we're presented with San Pedro as not self sufficient.

Tax: San Pedro doesn't grow all the things it uses. A community that happens to be self sufficient in maize has to buy less than a community that is not self sufficient in maize.

De la Fuente: There's a difference between the self sufficiency that is derived from growing maize and that derived from something else.

Goubaud: When you refer to self sufficiency in maize you would say that maize actually means money.

Tax: They don't have to spend money on maize. If they grow enough, then of course maize means money.

We haven't discussed the division of labor between the sexes. I think you have to take the community as a whole into account, or the household, and say that this family both grows milpa and makes pottery.

Paul: I think we have yet to define self sufficiency. Another thing that has come in here is the level of security; it is the extent to which you grow what you eat.

Tax: I mean by self-sufficiency simply the production of any or all items of consumption. A group (whether a family or a nation) is self-sufficient to the degree to which it produces the goods that it consumes.

(10)

De la Fuente: It seems to me that the most important thing is kinds of needs rather than kinds of people. This has to be tied up with points (1), (2) and (3) on the same page. These statements do not hold very well for the areas which I know. Peddling, for example; in Oaxaca this is carried on by Indians. Shops are owned mostly by Indians. We have an area in which the presence of Ladinos is not important in this market-shop economy.

Tax: But peddling exists and there are stores. You say that in both cases they're connected with Indians.

Beals: In Oaxaca you have a very tiny Ladino population. These Zapotec peddle, even to some extent among the Mixe. A lot of Mexican Indians live in town just as much as Mestizos do.

De la Fuente: But you will find a much larger number of Ladinos in the valleys.

Beals: In the valley the major function of the Ladino trader is to have a "wholesale house" from which the Indian trader can buy material to take back into the mountains.

Goubaud: Consider the large centers of population in the purely highland region of Guatemala; the door-to-door peddling is done by Indians.

Kyte: How about the quantity of Ladinos?

Beals: In those areas where the Indian population is not so heavy, if there is a Ladino population of any size in the town, then the stores tend to be run by Ladinos. I would also like to point out a basic difference. My impression is that the Indian has a fine time bargaining in most markets.

Tax: I think there is a difference between Guatemala and the few parts of Mexico that I have seen. I don't know whether this is a geographical and cultural difference or a difference between Indian and non-Indian.

Beals: Among Ladino markets in South America nowhere do you find the zestful bargaining that you find in Mexico. They quote a fixed price.

Foster: In Cuzco, if you haggle, the next price is higher.

De la Fuente: I have observed bargaining in quite a number of markets, timing it with my watch. My impression is that long bargaining is characteristic of a Ladino-Indian situation.

Guiteras: In Chiapas you don't have bargaining among the Indians; you only have it between Indians and Ladinos.

De la Fuente: This is tied up with the fact that the Ladino wants to drive a hard bargain.

(11)

Tumin: Local Indians who sell in the local markets are primarily women, but it's largely the men who come in from neighboring municipios; it's the Indian men who go out with their goods to other markets.

Beals: In Tarascan markets you find a majority of women selling but you will see women and men at the same spot, interchanging.

Tax: How about buying? Who goes out to buy the *panela,* salt and sugar?

Guiteras: It can be a man or a woman.

Wisdom: They sell what they make. If a man makes it he sells, and vice versa.

Camara: In the Sunday market in many cases, the man gives his wife money for her shopping, then when she returns, he goes to do his shopping.

Guiteras: The men sell the stools and tables; the women sell all the vegetables.

De la Fuente: The shift from women to men sellers begins to take place in the Ladino markets and in the permanent markets.

Tax: Obviously, when a man carries a large stock of something over a long distance, he will sell it. I didn't mean to suggest that men don't sell in the market; what I meant was that basically it's a woman's occupation.

Whetten: It's more true of that particular area than in central Mexico.

Kelly: If it's big merchandising, the man always does it. Chile, for example, is an important cash crop; if it is sold in small amounts the woman sells it, but if in large amounts then the man sells it.

Wisdom: In the Sunday market, or the fiesta market, you find men and women selling, but at the little markets held during the week you see only women selling, and they're not selling much.

Beals: Among the Tarascan you get a lot of joint activity. Even on trading expeditions the man often takes his wife along.

Foster: In the number of sales that are made women often participate in more individual transactions than do the men, but it is possible that men account for more than 50% of the gross income of the total sales.

Paul: That's much the same as in our own culture. I buy a car, but my wife buys the food, because she does the cooking. This can be balanced by the fact that women don't carry heavy objects.

Goubaud: Consider also markets for specialties, e.g., Momostenango, which has both a general market and a special market for blankets. In the latter all the selling is done by men.

Beals: You can multiply exceptions. In the Tarascan area the blankets are made by women but are sold by men.

Foster: At about what period in economic history did stores come in as a medium of effecting merchandising?

Beals: You'd have to analyze Sahagun's description of permanent markets in Mexico City.

Kelly: You seem to think that the market is not an Indian institution. There is a mass of information on markets in pre-Columbian times.

Tax: But how widespread were they? Whether or not it is an Indian institution in Guatemala is something on which we haven't any data.

Kelly: There were markets in Jalisco in 1525.

(12)

Wisdom: Is barter rare?

Tax: Where is it common?

Wisdom: They use corn for paying for things.

Guiteras: They even pay day laborers with corn in Chiapas.

Foster: There are two different aspects of barter: pure barter, and barter in terms of money.

De la Fuente: In Oaxaca barter has existed everywhere; in the mountain area it has largely disappeared. It has persisted in the village. Cultural objects are bartered for food.

Wisdom: Can you call this maize-money?

Tax: But there is real barter, such as among the Popoluca and in Santiago Chimaltenango.

Stone: That holds for the East also.

Villa: There is a secret market in Oxchuc where they barter; there is a traditional price for everything.

Whetten: The fact that markets existed prior to Cortes would be some indication that they were Indian.

De la Fuente: Markets have been growing constantly; it's the result of a large number of needs which have to be satisfied in the market.

Tax: I was saying not that the markets themselves but certain aspects of the market are the result of the presence of Ladinos.

(13)

Tumin: I am dismayed at how the tradition of separatism is overcome. In at least one case I know of, the Indian had a chance to make money, but local tradition prevented him from going into the enterprise.

Tax: We have many examples of that for this area. I certainly wasn't arguing that Indians are so economically minded that they can change all their plans at once in order to make a dime. There are these resistances and I think you take them for granted, but within the limits of their cultural ways I meant to indicate that they are economically minded.

Tumin: How about renting yourself out as a day laborer to a Ladino or Indian?

Tax: I think there we come into areas of race relations. There may be places where the feeling against Ladino is enough to override economic advantage.

(14)

Beals: In Mexico the major part of the market is Indian but held in a Mestizo town. There is a whole series of little Ladino towns which apparently live off the Indians.

(15)

Camara: Could you say that small towns are more dependent on subsistence economy, and large towns going into a market economy, since group activities are more related to religious activities? In this way you could explain the increase in the number of mayordomos in the small towns.

Tax: They tend to be specialized regardless of the size of the population.

Camara: Religious activities are more attached to agricultural activities.

Tax: In some places where the cult of the saints is present, they're connected with the fiesta calendar and not the agricultural calendar.

Goubaud: The communities that are mostly agricultural will have ten cofradías. Totonicapán is highly industrialized and has twelve; there doesn't seem to be much correlation.

(16)

Paul: McBryde says most of the land is communally owned.

Tax: McBryde doesn't say exactly that, and of course it isn't true.

Paul: It seems to me that if you have a communal land system the whole competitive situation changes. Competitiveness may come in more strongly with individual ownership of land.

Goubaud: In a survey of 80 communities in the western part of Guatemala we found only one community still holding land on a communal basis.

Paul: How old a pattern is this historically?

Goubaud: From about 1873 on.

Tax: We don't have figures; we know there was a movement to allot lands.

Goubaud: The first reform was in 1832; it didn't go very well. There is a difference in what is described here as communally owned land being given to the Indians; the Indian could keep it as long as he used it. He didn't own the land but had the use of it.

Tax: You might have a communal piece of land somewhere that isn't being used but there isn't much such land. People occupy all land except some mountain tops.

(17)

Tumin: How about the statement concerning the elders of the towns where land is communally held.

Tax: Where the elders have power to assign communally held land, isn't that a restraint?

(18)

Kelly: The remarks regarding the economic role of women give the impression that women don't participate in agriculture. Totonac women do participate in agriculture; they help in cultivating and harvesting. In Guatemala the milpa is primarily a man's work but women help out in various places.

(19)

Foster: This question of work cooperation interests me. It's pretty much the equivalent of the African pattern in which you can expect to call upon a greater or smaller number of men to help you and in return they can call upon you for a number of days of work. This is important among the Popoluca.

General agreement was that it is widespread.

Foster: I think Kirchhoff is pretty near right in his emphasis of the importance of the highland-lowland contrast, with respect to the market; I have in mind West Africa where you don't have a very significant variation between highland and lowland areas, where you have villages and cities and the market economy is very similar to that in this area.

Tax: There might be some other variation, for example, seacoast vs. inland.

Kirchhoff: I have been interested in

the great cities in Mexico and West Africa. In Africa there is the contrast between forest and savanna, and there is, as in ancient Mexico, a tremendous development in localized crafts with many little workshops and smiths. I think the degree of specialization—artificial division of labor rather than natural division of labor—seems to be much stronger.

Wisdom: What is the basis for this artificial division of labor?

Tax: Historical reasons? We come to a point where we don't explain.

chapter 4

ETHNIC AND COMMUNAL RELATIONS

by Julio de la Fuente

ETHNIC relations in Middle America were originally characterized by the domination of two groups—the native Indians and the transplanted Negroes—by a third group, the whites. Of the two groups which represent the largest part of the population today, one may be characterized as racially very mixed, tending toward the Caucasoid, literate or relatively so, of national-modern culture and predominantly Catholic; the other is basically Indian racially, tending to be illiterate, of primitive or backward culture, and pagan-Catholic. The first constitutes a great society of urban type, with social classes; the second consists of a series of ethnic and local sub-societies of rural type, without social classes, which may be described as tribes or as ethnic communities.

In addition to sources indicated in the bibliography, the documentation of this article is based on field work and the following sources:

Aguirre Beltran, Gonzalo, Xochistlahuaca (MS.) and personal communications concerning Guerrero. Camara Barbachano, F., Notas Sobre Clases Sociales en Tenejapa. (MS.). Guiteras Holmes, Calixta, MS. on Tantoyuca. Pozas Arciniegas, Ricardo, Personal information on Atlixco, San Cristóbal las Casas, Zinacantán

The social structure of these two principal groups in some regions approximates a caste system, and in other regions may be considered as a class system, the second of the two groups in both cases having a generally subordinate position with respect to the first. Cultural traits generally constitute the primary element of ethnic distinction and affiliation and their social consequences may often be greater than those of somatic traits. The assimilation of the subordinate group to the dominant culture, and the amalgamation of the two groups, alter the position of the subordinate group in the social order, permitting—with certain exceptions—vertical social mobility of its members into the superordinate group. In certain parts of the area relations between the two principal groups have changed from ethnic relations to class relations. In comparison with the United States, racial connotations are much less; in comparison with the United States, South Africa, and parts of the Caribbean, Middle America may be characterized by the absence of a "Negro problem."

The two principal groups are the Ladinos and the Indians.[1] Minority groups consist of Negroes and foreigners. Communities in Middle America may be classified into two principal types with regard to their ethnic composition: (1) mono-ethnic (totally Ladino, Indian, or Negro) and (2) mixed. However, there is much variation in the ethnic composition of communities. Some are preponderantly Indian with few Ladinos (for example, San Pedro la Laguna and Yalalag); some are the reverse (San Cristóbal las Casas); others have a more balanced proportion (San Luis Jilotepeque and Agua Escondida). There is scarcely any community whose inhabitants are unaware of the existence of groups different from their own.

Although ethnic distinctions are made primarily on the basis of cultural differences, somatic traits also constitute a basis of such distinctions. Emphasis on both kinds of traits sometimes results in the categorization into races. However, race is a construct derived predominantly out of cultural differences, racial terminology is vague or inconsistent, and many Ladinos are not categorized within any race.

---

and Chamula. Weitlaner, Robert, MSS. and personal communication concerning Ojitlán.

This paper was thoroughly revised by the author, incorporating results of the Seminar discussion on the original version. The revision was translated from Spanish, and edited, by Betty Starr. The extract from the discussion is included for its interest.

The degree to which one or another class of traits constitutes a basis for ethnic (or class) distinctions is illustrated by the following cases, in which Ia. and IIb. represent atypical "island" situations.

Ia. The very accentuated Caucasoid traits of the Ladinos cause their members to be defined in racial terms ("of Spanish race" or "white") in contrast with those groups somatically different ("of Indian race" or "mulattoes"); some members of the group, only slightly Caucasoid but of high social status, consider themselves and are considered by others as legitimate members of this group. (The situation in Arandas constitutes an example of this.)

Ib. There is a feeling that Ladinos ought to be Caucasoids and Indians (or Negroes) somehow different. Nevertheless, the use of cultural traits in making ethnic distinctions sometimes results in a double categorization by which an individual may be considered as racially Indian (or Ladino) but culturally Ladino (or Indian). Such is the case in the Distrito of Villa Alta.

IIa. In some areas where there are Negroes (notably the rural coast of Guerrero), "whites" are distinguished from *negraditas* by their color, and especially by the cultural traits of education and wealth. The *negraditas* may include individuals with slight or considerable color; they resemble the whites somewhat in economic and cultural characteristics. The *cuculustes* have very accentuated Negro traits and are rustic and poor. All these groups are distinguished from Indians by language, dress and custom.

IIb. Some individuals may be categorized as Negroes or mulattoes but their color is not noticed. Indians and foreigners are distinguished by dress and speech. (This is the situation along the coast of Veracruz.)

In culture, as in somatic traits, the various groups lack homogeneity. Ladino culture has certain variants—urban, rural, regional, etc.—but with certain exceptions, there is felt to be one national form of culture. No Negro culture is apparent and the use of Spanish by Negroes identifies them culturally as Ladinos. There are many Indian subcultures, more or less contrasting—and local—whose bearers consider them as one culture or as related cultures, by contrast with Ladino culture. Certain cultural traits are recognized as Ladino or Indian and not as peculiar to a specific group, except in detail. The substitution of Indian traits for Ladino traits results in their diminishing temporally and spatially as distinctive ethnic and even class elements. Urban Ladinos of high social status and rustic or primitive Indians offer the greatest cultural contrast, a lesser contrast being presented by rural Ladinos, who are similar in custom and way of life to Indians, and acculturated Indians.

The most important traits of distinction between Ladinos and Indians and their relative degree of importance are as follows: (1) The locality of birth or residence, generally urban (or central) for Ladinos. (2) Language spoken—Ladinos speaking Spanish and Indians speaking an Indian language. (There are many exceptions to this general rule: Spanish-speaking monolinguals may be categorized as Indians because of their way of life, as in Atlixco and Agua Escondida. Some bilinguals are not categorized as "Indians" but as members of a specific ethnic subgroup such as the Zapotec. In some communities, both groups are predominantly monolingual. This is the case among the Mixe. Ladinos may speak only Spanish and Indians may be bilingual, as in San Luis Jilotepeque; or, both groups may be bilingual, as in Agua Escondida and Dzitas.) (3) Illiteracy, which, although more general among Indians is great also among rural Ladinos. (4) The Indian surname, or the name composed of two names. Indians do not always have an Indian surname, as in Michoacán; and some Ladinos do have one, as in Agua Escondida. Furthermore, the origin of a surname is not always clear. (5) Costume, with few exceptions, is generally a differentiator of groups. It is of less significance when only the women of both groups dress differently, as in the Distrito of Villa Alta; when many individuals of both groups and sexes wear "Indian" costume, as in Dzitas; when Indian men and women wear "country" dress, as in Tantoyuca; or when men wear an urban costume and women wear a rural costume, as in Atlixco. (6) Various customs and beliefs, such as house type, method of cooking, method of burying the dead, celebration of fiestas and dances, etc. Existence of the *cofradía,* usually distinctive of Indians, may be present in both groups, as in Agua Escondida and Dzitas. Spirits may be dealt with in a similar manner by members of both groups, as in the Distrito of Villa Alta. And paganism, although more characteristic of Indians, may not be foreign to Ladinos, as in Dzitas.

Type of occupation and relative wealth also serve as group differentiating traits. Foreigners generally have urban occupations, with a high degree of remuneration or prestige, their economic position being high or intermediate. The economic position of

Ladinos varies from the highest to the lowest level. Negroes resemble middle or lower class Ladinos in occupation and wealth; Indians hold rural, backward, and artisan occupations, of little remuneration and prestige, their usual economic position being low. Some occupations may be categorized as Ladino and others as Indian; others are not ascribed to any one group. Although agriculture is practiced by nearly all, the practice of cultivating the fields oneself (not having another occupation) often distinguishes the Indian from the Ladino. Occupations exclusive to Indians are those of *chirimía*-players, *teponaxtle*-players, weavers (on pre-Columbian looms), or curers.

The enumeration which follows suggests degrees of contrast with regard to occupational differences, the greatest contrast being represented by (I), intermediate contrasts by (II) and (III), and the lowest degree of contrast represented by (IV):

I

Foreigners tend to be missionaries, storekeepers, merchants, and specialized workers, such as doctors or teachers. Ladinos tend to be storekeepers, travelling merchants, saloon-keepers, teachers, manufacturers and artisans. Indians tend to be common laborers, bearers, servants, and curers. The majority of the Indians are agriculturalists, other occupations being secondary. (In some areas, notably the Midwest Highlands of Guatemala, Indians are also travelling merchants.) Occupational differences listed here are particularly characteristic of communities in southeastern Chiapas and northwestern Guatemala.

II

Ladinos are agriculturalists, cattle-raisers and storekeepers; some, like the Indians, are day-laborers, servants, and sorcerers; Indians may be *chirimía*-players and only Indians are midwives. (This situation is found in Agua Escondida.) Here there is less contrast in occupations due to the presence of rustic Ladinos.

III

Indians, as well as Ladinos, are teachers and restaurant-keepers; only Indians are storekeepers. Indians may have a number of occupations as typically "Ladino" as "Indian." In certain places, such as San Pedro la Laguna, Ladinos, like the Indians, are agriculturalists and shamans. Here there is still less occupational contrast due to the ability of Indians to hold "Ladino" occupations.

IV

Ladinos and Indians tend to be occupied in the same forms of agriculture, commerce, modern craftsmanship, industry, teaching, music and the priesthood, although only Ladinos are doctors and Indians have many traditional occupations. (This is the situation in the Distrito de Villa Alta.)

Generally, Indians as a group are poorer than Ladinos; however, the opposite situation exists in Yalalag, Agua Escondida, and Papantla.

Foreigners, with respect to other groups; Ladinos, with respect to Negroes and Indians; and Negroes with respect to Indians, occupy a superior position in the social system. The social structure in particular communities may be described as that of caste, or something which approximates it, and in others as that of class. The fact that the principal distinctions tend to be cultural has led to the categorization of caste as cultural or social. Ladinos constitute a superordinate caste and Indians a subordinate caste in San Luis Jilotepeque, in Chiapas, and among the Chorti. In other areas, such as Oaxaca, Michoacán, and Veracruz, the structure is rather that of class. Negroes are subordinate to Ladinos. There is stratification into classes among foreigners and Ladinos, with little or no social stratification among Indians. Lower class rural Ladinos are considered by upper class Ladinos as similar to Indians, although according them a somewhat higher social value than that accorded Indians. (This is the case in Chiapas and in Agua Escondida.) There is an absence of well defined social stratification in some Ladino communities, in Tzintzuntzan for example; there is, likewise, little social stratification among Negroes in Veracruz.

Some foreigners (Spaniards), descendants without mixture from Spaniards, and Ladinos are ascribed superiority over Indians because of "race," blood, special qualities attributed to race or blood, and color. The valuation on the part of Ladinos of the white color of an individual, the desirability of the same, and contempt for dark color, exemplified somewhat sharply in Arandas, is common. The attributing to Indians of a lack of intelligent or rationality, retarded or infantile mind, incapacity to progress or to engage in certain occupations, possession of animal qualities or other degrading characteristics supposedly congenital is very common (in Oaxaca, Chiapas, Veracruz, and San Luis Jilotepeque, for example). It is not always clear when these characteristics are considered as truly congenital and when they are considered to be culturally determined. Inconsistency is indicated by the exceptions made for ladinoized Indians.

It is common for Ladinos to look down on particular customs and beliefs of the Indians—their general way of life, habits or speech—characterizing them as backward, coarse, or inferior, and looking down on Indians as a group. The most critical attitude is probably found among urban Ladinos. Indians are devaluated to a considerable extent in San Luis Jilotepeque, and in Chiapas, somewhat less devaluated in Agua Escondida, the Distrito of Villa Alta, and Zinacantán, and regarded with some esteem in Tehuantepec. Ladino ancestry, even though partial, is an important status symbol, supplemented by physical traits, as in Arandas; local origin, as in Villa Alta; and possession of a Spanish surname, as in Dzitas. In San Pedro la Laguna, physical superiority and inferiority are respectively linked with dark and light color, such evaluations being extended toward Indians and Negroes on the one hand and toward Ladinos on the other hand. Various superior qualities are attributed to foreigners and Ladinos, especially in the Distrito de Villa Alta. Caucasoids are considered to have superior characteristics in Quintana Roo and Chan Kom. Some ladinoized individuals of San Pedro la Leguna esteem Caucasoids sexually. Although some Indians depreciate Ladino customs, they tend to acknowledge their own inferiority in culture or language and accept their inferior status. In some places, their own customs afford sufficient satisfactions so that they pity the Ladino for not having them. This is the case among the Chorti. In most cases, attempts are made to escape from a position of inferior status, as in Quintana Roo, Cancuc, or San Pedro Chenalhó; in others, the feeling of vertical distance does not exist, as in Ojitlán or among the Huichol. The Zapotec and Nahua ascribe inferiority to the Mixe and Huave, on the one hand, and to the Huastec, on the other.

Social mobility takes the form of vertical, trans-ethnic "passing" and also vertical intra-ethnic "passing" (from one subgroup or Indian community to another). By "passing" is meant to acquire the status of a different group, whether or not members of the group know the original affiliation of the individual. Such original affiliation is not usually lost, so far as those who know the individual well are concerned. "Passing" involves assimilation, amalgamation, the breaking (sometimes) of relations with the individual's original group, the hiding of original traits which are retained, a change in mental attitude, or various of these processes in combination. Where the social structure approximates a caste situation, none of these processes, nor their combination, lead to "passing." The most frequent direction of "passing" is from Indian to Ladino.

Differences in social mobility exhibit variations as follows:

I

In some communities there is a complete absence of "passing."

a. Here no Indian is considered a Ladino, regardless of his degree of ladinoization or his occupation, and no child of a mixed marriage brought up as a Ladino is accepted socially as a Ladino; Ladino status is sought and achieved outside the local community. This is the case in San Luis Jilotepeque.

b. In some communities, a ladinoized individual would be considered to be a Ladino if raised or educated as such; or, he would be categorized as racially Indian and culturally Ladino, but there are no cases of passing. This is the case in Agua Escondida.

II

In other communities, there is a certain amount of "passing."

a. In these, ladinoized individuals, with long residence in Ladino communities and of artisan occupation, sometimes marry Ladino women and pretend to be Ladinos but they are either not recognized as such by the latter group or considered as Ladinos of the lower class. Few individuals (all male) try to pass; complete Ladino status is obtained only in the second generation. This situation is exemplified by the Chorti.

b. In still other communities, individuals ladinoized to a slight degree, some women raised as Ladinos, and children of formal and informal mixed unions raised in the same manner, are recognized as Ladinos. This is the case in Tenejapa.

III

More complete or total "passing" also exists in parts of the area:

a. In several communities, individuals ladinoized in language and custom, individuals of high status or children of mixed unions raised as Ladinos, of both sexes in both cases, are considered Ladinos. This is the case in Dzitas, Distrito of Villa Alta, Zaachila and Tantoyuca.

b. In Tzintzuntzan and Michoacán generally, marriage of an Indian woman with a Ladino man gives her his status; Ladino status is also obtained through processes already mentioned.

Substitution of a Spanish surname for an Indian surname by those who are becoming ladinoized is general. Costume acquires special emphasis in communities in Chiapas and Guatemala (but not in the Distrito of Villa Alta). In Tantoyuca, Yucatan, and Chiapas, an incomplete degree of ladinoization is indicated by the use of special terms such as *arrazonado,* but the status of the individual does not actually change much. In Cancuc, some Indians believe that an Indian cannot acquire Ladino customs or become a Ladino. In other communities, such as San Pedro la Laguna, Tenejapa, and San Pedro Chenalhó, ladinoized individuals tend to identify themselves with Ladinos, look down on Indians, conceal their tribal connections, and demand and obtain from Indians the status of Ladino. At the same time they still consider themselves as Indians. Sometimes these individuals find themselves in a social limbo, belonging neither to one group nor the other. Such is the case in San Pedro Chenalhó and Tenejapa. In the Distrito of Villa Alta, no ladinoized person is considered to be a genuine Ladino. Instead, he continues to be considered as a member of his original ethno-social unit.

The attitude of Ladinos toward ladinoization and toward "passing" varies from "punishment directly applied to Indians who try to practice Ladino customs" (reoprted by Gillin for San Luis Jilotepeque), some obstruction of the education of Indians—somewhat general in the area, to frank approval, as in Agua Escondida. The attitudes of the Indians include both extremes.

The most approved form of ladinoization, so far as both groups are concerned, is change in language (except, perhaps, in Quintana Roo). Although occupations are theoretically open to all, the rise of the Indian to many Ladino occupations is limited by his ignorance, poverty, lack of ambition or interest, and indirectly, rather than directly, by pressures exerted by Ladinos. However, the tendency of the Indian to rise to Ladino occupations may be considered general. The Indian who does so rise is considered for all practical purposes as a Ladino. As a result, there may be even in a small family both Ladino and Indian members. (This frequently occurs in the Distrito of Villa Alta and Zaachila.)

Passing from Ladino to Indian among adults occurs relatively infrequently, partly because of the disadvantage attached to it, but it is incidental to amalgamation, living in Indian communities, sentimental or social identification with Indians through marriage with an Indian, or other causes. The Indianized person is treated as an Indian by those of his original group, although he continues to be considered superior by the Indians themselves. If he is a lower class Ladino, he is not accorded so much respect on the part of the Indians, although commonly he retains his original affiliation. One form of passing is the acceptance on the part of the Ladino that he has obligations equal to those of the Indians with whom he lives (this occurs in the Distrito of Villa Alta).

The most general rule in inter-ethnic relations is that intimate contact and personal relations between Ladinos and Indians may be limited by differences in language, interests, customs and status, personal relations being less frequent than casual contacts and semi-personal or impersonal relations. A second rule is that in both kinds of relations there is an unequal distribution of privileges, generally favorable to the Ladinos. Divergences in patterns of association or separation and in distribution of privileges are large. Residential separation according to group, with central location for Ladinos, is typical of most of the mixed communities considered. Agua Escondida, San Pedro la Laguna, Tzintzuntzan and Yalalag constitute exceptions. Neither group obstructs the establishment of the other in their territory except in Quintana Roo, Cancuc, Tantoyuca and San Pedro la Laguna, where the Indians obstruct the Ladinos. With exceptions, there are no special services or public places for each group, although Indians may prefer some such (using a certain part of the cemetery in Agua Escondida, or being the sole operators of canoes in San Pedro la Laguna). For a Ladino to eat in a public restaurant with an Indian is improper in some places.

In San Luis Jilotepeque there is the greatest separate participation of the two groups in social activities, with greater exclusion by Ladinos of Indians from Ladino activities. At the same time, Ladinos attend Indian celebrations when they wish, without previous invitation. In Agua Escondida, there is no unwillingness on the part of Ladinos to associate personally with Indians, although joint participation of both groups is infrequent. But there is less social distance, and to the degree to which it exists, it is attributed to cultural differences. In San Pedro la Laguna, both groups dance separately (in public dances) and generally they eat separately. In these places, the rule is accepted by the Indians. In Dzitas and other communities mentioned in this paragraph, there also exists a rule almost entirely opposite from that of San Luis Jilotepeque, although Ladinos occasionally visit Indians (in Yalalag, for example), some Indians segregate themselves (Zaachila). Social distance is maintained to a considerable extent in the Distrito of Villa Alta, less so in Yalalag, and but slightly in Ojitlán. Ladinos are generally received as honored guests, especially in Guatemalan communities; Indians are not thus received by Ladinos. Chan Kom constitutes an example of decreasing honorary attention paid to Ladinos.

Racial prejudices do not appear to obstruct inter-ethnic sexual relations, although in Mexican villages, the presence of foreigners and Ladinos inhibits "crossing" which may take place; crossing is also rejected by the Huichol. "Crossing" of Ladino men with Indian women—but not of Ladino women with Indian men—is considered more or less seriously by some Ladinos as a form of improving the Indian race or of modifying the animal characteristics ascribed to Indians. This is the case in Oaxaca, Veracruz, and Tehuantepec. Similarly, some Indians permit this class of relations in order to counteract the sterility of women (as in northern Veracruz), to protect women (among the Mixe), or for other reasons. Casual Indian-Ladino sexual relations occur in a few cases in San Luis Jilotepeque and Agua Escondida, occur in greater number in San Pedro la Laguna and Villa Alta, assuming the form of violation or rape of Indian women in these two places, Santa Eulalia, among the Chorti and in San Pedro Chenalhó, and the rape of Ladino women in San Pedro la Laguna.

Informal and formal Indian-Ladino unions are limited because of differences in culture and status. Generally the Indian man tends to be a ladinoized individual and the Ladino woman of lower class or otherwise unattractive. The couple are looked down upon by Indians or by both Indians and Ladinos and they achieve recognition only if they achieve stability, a condition which is rare. In Dzitas, the Indian wife is not completely recognized by her Ladino husband's family. Mixed formal unions do not exist in San Luis Jilotepeque, whatever the occupation or degree of ladinoization of the Indian; nor do they exist in Agua Escondida. In Arandas such unions are objected to and in some cases subject a Ladino woman to denial by her family. But they are registered, in growing numbers, in many places. In the majority of such cases, the Indian man or woman is a ladinoized individual. Both types of relations are common among Ladinos and Negroes or mulattoes. Informal and formal unions between Indians of distinct subgroups and communities are marginal; those of Indians with Negroes and other groups not mentioned are also secondary.

Relations of ritual kinship through baptism (or similar relations) are frequently established between Ladinos and Indians or between Indians of different subgroups and communities, giving rise to a network of personal, social, sacred, and economic relations. Almost invariably it is the Indian who solicits the relationship, rather than the Ladino. Preference for a Ladino—when there is such preference—is due to particular qualities ascribed to Ladinos, the protection which a Ladino may provide, or because the Ladino is able to pay for the ceremony. The Ladino generally complies with his duties as a godfather although he does not take the relation very seriously. He extends to his Indian *compadre* certain courtesies which he does not give to common Indians, but yet not equal to those which he would give to a Ladino compadre.

Ordinary or professional work, commerce, educational institutions, religious and official activities permit frequent semipersonal or impersonal relations among the ethnic units considered. Differences in wealth, ability, education, and other qualities result in the situation that, with exceptions, foreigners with respect to the other groups, Ladinos with respect to Indians, and Indians of certain subgroups or communities with respect to other Indians have a superordinate role. In agriculture, the role mentioned for the first group is absolute and that of the second group almost absolute. Exceptions are encountered in Tantoyuca and in Agua Escondida, where Ladinos may work for Indians. Examples of Indians superordinate to other Indians are constituted by the Zapotec and Zinacantecos who are agricultural "bosses" of the Mixe and Chamulas respectively. Almost no exceptions are known to the rule that Indians with respect to Ladinos and Mixe and Chamulas with respect to Zapotec and Zinacantecos are their bearers, and not the reverse.

Traditional differential payment or differential treatment of the

Indian by his Ladino "boss" is common. Agua Escondida, where payment is not differentiated according to ethnic group, constitutes an exception to this general practice. The Indian "boss" does not treat the day laborer of a different subgroup differentially, except in Yalalag. In the performance of agricultural and artisan tasks, no separation is made of workers according to group or subgroup, when they co-participate.

The celebration of fiestas and the treatment of the sick bring about frequent more or less equalitarian relations. Indian dance masters and musicians are hired by Ladinos individually (or by organizations), musicians of both groups perform together, and Ladino musicians are hired by Indians. Each group tends to employ traditional curing methods. Indians frequently go to a Ladino doctor, or to the Ladino curer, although not as frequently as to the former. In spite of the lower status of the Indian, lower class Ladinos employ curers, midwives, sorcerers and other Indian specialists, some of whom cover wide areas in their treatment of clients of both groups.

Commercial activities bring about a large number of contacts based on mutual understanding and in places common to all groups. Numerous transactions are effected between members of all groups with relative social equality, all adjusting their actions to legitimate or illegitimate rules of the market (right of profit and bargaining; taking advantage of the situation or of the ignorant person), the latter practice frequently developing into abuse of the Indians, although Indians also take advantage of other Indians or Ladinos. Personalization of relations among those engaging in such transactions is common among merchants or individuals of different groups, subgroups or communities who are given food or lodging, although these relations may remain impersonal. Ethnic, sub-ethnic or local grouping is somewhat common in the market, such groupings being determined by kinship, by practical considerations. The segregation of travelling merchants in Cancuc, and the limiting of their stay in Quintana Roo, has more to do with the fact that they are Ladinos than with the fact that they are merchants.

There is joint participation of all groups in educational institutions. The Ladino education of the Indians is favored in some places, by both Ladinos and Indians, as a form of "civilizing" them, assimilating them, putting an end to their backwardness, or modifying their general inferiority. Nevertheless, some Ladinos tend to limit such education because of the profits which the Indians' ignorance affords. Some Indians reject schooling, or accept it nominally. (The first situation is exemplified in Quintana Roo; the second, in the Distrito of Villa Alta, among the Mixe, and in communities in Chiapas.) The education that the Indians receive is commonly inferior in quality and quantity to that which Ladinos receive, although frequently similar to that given rural Ladinos. Ladinos, and sometimes Indians, tend to look down on the Indian teacher, and Ladino teachers commonly have the same attitude toward Indian pupils. (This is the case in Oaxaca and Chiapas.) With the exception of a few Indian schools, there are no special educational institutions for each group. The Indian schools are not rigidly mono-ethnic and their orientation is assimilative. Generally, a teacher is assigned to any group, independently of his ethnic affiliation. In some parts of the area, teachers do not discriminate against students according to group nor are students thus segregated (Agua Escondida); in other places, there is a tendency toward such segregation (in San Luis Jilotepeque, for example). In Tantoyuca, there is a tendency to separate students according to group, outside the school; in San Pedro Chenalhó, Ladino teachers and students, and ladinoized students subject Indian students to various kinds of discrimination; the self-separation of "Huastecs" from "Mexicanos" in the performance of certain tasks and during recess periods is common.

With regard to religious activities, the greatest separate participation of Ladinos and Indians occurs in rituals and ceremonies considered pagan or unorthodox by Ladinos, in which only Indians participate (as in Santa Eulalia, the Distrito of Villa Alta, or San Luis Jilotepeque), although in certain other places, Ladinos attend such ceremonies as spectators (in Dzitas or in northern Veracruz). All groups participate jointly in Catholic festivities held in famous sanctuaries, titular fiestas of villages or church rituals conducted by a priest, differing according to kinds of organizations, types of celebrations, and the amount of social distance which is maintained. In San Luis Jilotepeque, for example, Ladinos consider cofradías and their celebrations unorthodox and do not attend such celebrations. Ladinos assume the principal roles in orthodox ceremonies, assigning secondary roles to Indians, and reserving for themselves the right to sit down in the church. In Agua Escondida, there is a tendency toward ethnic differentiation in the composition of cofradías. In Santa Eulalia, both Ladinos and Indians participate in church celebrations, and in processions. In San Pedro la Laguna, on the other hand, resident and "foreign" Ladinos participate in church rituals only during fiestas, when a priest officiates; they do not visit the Indian cofradías; and, during public fiestas, they keep apart from the Indians. In Cancuc, the pattern is similar, although Ladinos contribute economically to fiestas. In Yalalag, both groups participate in religious fiesta organizations, in church rituals and in processions, Ladinos and "foreign" Indians tending to form their own groups, apart from the local Indians. In Tantoyuca, there are two permanent organizations for the maintenance of the church, one consisting of Ladinos and the other of Indians. No apparent separation exists in Dzitas and Otatitlán. Ceremonial dancers in religious fiestas tend to be Indians, except in central Mexico, and parts of Veracruz, where they are Ladinos, and in Guerrero, where they may also be Negroes. In the latter area, Ladinos and Indians participate in the same dance. The celebration of titular fiestas leads to a close interaction between communities of different groups and includes the reciprocal granting of hospitality, interchange of musicians or reciprocal visits of authorities, the attentions which the Ladinos give to those of their own group differing from those which they give to Indians. Undifferentiated joint participation may be considered the rule among Protestants.

All groups are subject to a common national government and to laws which make no racial distinctions. Politico-administrative control—whether of the nation, state, or department—rests in the hands of Ladinos. Few or no Indians (ladinoized) and Negroes, in some areas (in Chiapas, Veracruz, and Guerrero) achieve superior elective positions. In areas predominantly Indian, Ladinos occupy positions of district or departmental nature, as administrative and judicial functionaries, although in Yucatan and Oaxaca, ladinoized Indians may hold such positions. In municipios with a relatively large proportion of Ladinos, the number still being less than that of the Indians, superior local elected or appointed authorities are Ladinos, the lower positions being given to Indians. A reversal has apparently occurred in such places as Dzitas, Tantoyuca, certain villages in Chiapas, and Agua Escondida. In most Indian villages, local authorities are elected from the group, and by the group. In communities in Chiapas, two functionaries are appointed. Both were formerly Ladinos; one (the *agente*) has been replaced by

Indians in a number of cases. In Yalalag, Ladinos may also hold lower positions, and in the Distrito of Villa Alta, there is a tendency not to give superior positions to "foreign" Indians. As a general rule, Indians do not have a political voice in non-local affairs, both because of their own disinterest and because of the small degree of social value accorded them by Ladinos. Indians are little interested in politics and they avoid or depreciate politicians. At the same time, in certain parts of the area—particularly in Mexico—Indians may apply to politicians in order to obtain benefits—predominantly for the community, or for the subgroup or individual. The feeling of local autonomy is common, with variations in regard to intensity. Nation and state are represented, so far as Indians are concerned, by superior or inferior functionaries or the army. The function of such functionaries is but vaguely understood, or referred only to immediate experience, and their interference in local matters is rejected, undesired, feared or tolerated. Ambivalence with regard to such functionaries is common.

Differences in rights and privileges among the various groups are often considerable. Indians frequently hold municipal offices without remuneration (contrary to law), but all Ladinos in similar offices are paid, except in Indian villages (such as the Distrito of Villa Alta). In appointive offices there are generally no such distinctions. Gratuitous enlistment of roadworkers and enlistment of men for military service, although theoretically applicable to all, falls heaviest upon Indians and upon poor Ladinos. Both groups participate jointly in roadwork, although in some places there is self-segregation by communities. Ladino functionaries commonly demand personal services of Indians or impose additional tasks upon them. An exceptional case is constituted by the situation in some Chiapas communities where two authorities preside—one Ladino, the other Indian—to which apply respectively Ladinos and ladinoized Indians on the one hand and Indians on the other. Preferential justice favorable to their own group is commonly administered by Ladinos, or by Indians favorable to Ladinos. The Indian, when in Ladino communities or in Indian communities distinct from his own, frequently behaves with caution in order to avoid differential justice which may be accorded him. He may claim and obtain from Indians of inferior status in his own subgroup or community certain privileges (as do the Zapotec, from the Mixe, and the Zinacantecos, from the Chamulas). Good mutual relations between Indian villages are reaffirmed in the form already mentioned with regard to fiestas.

The unequal status of Ladinos and Indians is frequently demonstrated in social expressions and modes of behavior, sometimes structured in a pattern which is mutually accepted. The strictness of rules, their number, and the situations in which they are applied have numerous variations. The term *indio,* or diminutives of it, and other descriptive or epithetical terms, are reserved for Indians, social inferiority or inferiority of other kinds being ascribed to the individual or to the group. The term *indio* is accepted in some places (as in Tantoyuca, Chan Kom, and among the Chorti), and is rejected in places where Indians apply distinctive terms to themselves, which Ladinos use because of custom or not to cause offense, even when some of these terms are paternalistic (as in Quintana Roo, the Distrito of Villa Alta, Ojitlán, and Tantoyuca). The names which Indians apply to Ladinos have superior connotations, but frequently are also derogatory. In different areas, both groups use special terms for persons who are culturally intermediate, such terms being either descriptive or disparaging.

Ladinos commonly call Indians by their proper name, without using *Don* or *Señor,* or their feminine equivalents, reserving such terms for members of their own group. They address Indians only as *tú,* and apply the same name to all Indian women (as in Veracruz). Ladinos do not remove their hats on greeting Indians, regard them condescendingly, and make demands upon them. Indians accept these forms of treatment in most places, remove their hats when greeting a Ladino, call him *Don,* employ the *usted* form in speaking to Ladinos (when they know the form), ask favors of Ladinos, and behave humbly, obliging, and grateful in speech and gesture. The most strict or elaborate pattern (existing in San Luis Jilotepeque) decreases spatially, changing into equalitarian treatment through the operation of personal relations, characterized by an absence of a feeling of social distance, among slightly acculturated Indians, the superior status of lower class Ladinos or Ladinos in general not being recognized. Examples of such less strict treatment are found in San Pedro la Laguna, where an Indian compadre has the right to be admitted to a Ladino house and to sit down; in the Distrito of Villa Alta, where an Indian storekeeper or an educated Indian may be called *Don* by Ladinos; in Ojitlán, where a similar individual or a compadre may have the same term applied to him; and in Dzitas, where a female curer may be called *Doña*. In some parts of the area, hostility toward the Ladino frequently leads to a situation in which only special members of this group are treated with respect. (This is the case in Quintana Roo, Cancuc, and San Pedro Chenalhó.) Finally, continuous contact with Ladinos (as in Chan Kom), or the knowledge that the Ladino's position is less important than in former times, results in the Indian consciously refraining from behaving in a respectful manner (as in Dzitas, the Distrito of Villa Alta, Oaxaca, and Michoacán).

Relations between the two groups are in some cases friendly and characterized by an absence of distrust, fear, resentment, hostility or serious friction, and by mutual tolerance of the customs of the group other than one's own. Similar relations exist between different Indian subgroups and communities despite former conflicts between them. In other cases, a conflict situation exists, temporarily or permanently, due to economic competition commonly concentrated about land, politics, religion, etc. Such conflict tends to be local, not extended to other Indian groups, nor toward Ladinos of a different community.

The following cases constitute a provisional typology of conflict areas:

I

A region characterized by greater conflict among Indians (resulting from land pressure and general economic competition) than among Indians and Ladinos. Indians exhibit some prejudice against unknown Ladinos and resent regional Ladinos, traditionally dominant, as well as those (generally governmental employees) who exercise political and general dominance. Regional Ladinos exhibit suspicion of Indians of particular villages. Political, occupational, and religious competition are not exclusively inter-ethnic and do not give rise to serious friction. The latter appears in Indian communities, in the form of legal and armed disputes over fractional limitations of land, predominance in the market, etc., causing the temporary cessation of all kinds of relations between the communities involved. The reluctance of a community for inhabitants of other communities to make use of their water supply, affiliation with protestantism, sorcery, or the economic authority which some groups exercise over others (as the Zapotec over the Mixe) have no serious consequences.

II

An area in which there is great hostility of Indians toward Ladinos (reciprocated in certain localities by Ladinos), a trauma of former violent conflicts because of the intrusion of Ladinos into the territory of the Indians and the plundering of their land. Examples of this type of conflict area are found in Quintana Roo, where there is a relative adjustment of Indian-Ladino relations and a shift of sympathy toward Anglo-saxons and Negroes. Conflict in Santa Eulalia is characterized by the desecration of pagan images and sacred places by Ladinos, contributing to the hostility of the Indians. The same situation occurs in certain Chiapas communities (in San Pedro Chenalhó, because of former outbreaks of hostility; in Cancuc, because of the transference of local political power to the Indians; and in San Pedro Chenalhó, where Indian women are violated by Ladinos).

III

A third type of conflict area occurs in places where Ladino-Indian relations, formerly peaceful, with superordination and subordination mutually accepted, have developed into a double conflict. (This is the case in Tantoyuca.) Here, Indians exhibit resentment and fear of Ladinos due to the recent plundering of Indian lands and destruction of Indian property, such resentment being directed toward Ladino authorities because of their protection of the exploiters. The latter, in turn, resent the relatively greater favor accorded the Indians in the regional organization. This conflict has been complicated by the breaking up of Indian lands into *ejidos.*

Relations between Ladinos and Negroes appear to be peaceful, as are those between Negroes and Indians, even when shaded by some fear of Indians by Negroes, because of sorcery, and fear of Negroes by Indians, because of violence ascribed to them.

DISCUSSION

(1)

Tax: We have a little trouble in defining the Indian and the non-Indian; we have to contrast the Indian with somebody. Usually there are local names for the people who aren't Indians; from Chiapas down through Central America the non-Indian group is usually called *Ladino,* but north of that area there doesn't seem to be one common term. So I think our major problem is to see whether there is a pattern, throughout the area, of two groups of people, one Indian, the other non-Indian.

Watkins: Can you define the non-Indian by defining the Indian?

Paul: An Indian is a person who considers himself, and is considered by others, an Indian; all others are considered non-Indian.

De la Fuente: This judgment is made mainly on the basis of outward appearances.

Beals: An Indian perhaps, can be defined as one who recognizes himself as an Indian. In the areas that I know, that would work. It would fit with my own judgment as to what is an Indian and what is not an Indian. Those who don't regard themselves as Indians have certain characteristics; they don't have an Indian language, most of them speak Spanish, buy store clothes, and have X pesos.

Tax: That would work in Guatemala. The chief trouble is that the characteristics of people who are known as Indians in some places are the same as characteristics of people who are not known as Indians in other places. There is this subjective definition.

Stone: Anyone is an Indian who lives in a community where they speak a language other than Spanish and follow the customs of that group.

Paul: I think this is an objective criterion and not just subjective; it's a social fact. I think it's the surest of all social facts. The fact that there are individuals in between shouldn't worry us.

De la Fuente: Some people who are Zapotec don't regard themselves as Indians. They have their own language. They know they are Indians because the Ladinos call them Indians sometimes. This brings up the question of the meaning of the term. These are members of a certain group.

Paul: Are they indígenas?

De la Fuente: Yes. They are members of a large group; they are members of a particular village; they are members of a linguistic and ethnic unit.

Beals: Those are special cases; there is no doubt about them. You have such a strong Indian area there; where you get closer contacts then you get a sharper definition.

Tax: If we're adopting this as our primary definition, we would have to say that people recognize themselves as Indians or as members of some local group.

De la Fuente: On the other hand there are people in this area that consider themselves neither Indian nor Ladino.

Tumin: How do they distinguish themselves?

De la Fuente: They are not Indians or Ladinos. They are "Zapotec," "Mixe," or "Chinantec."

Tumin: There are three groups then: Indians, Ladinos and Zapotec.

De la Fuente: There are Zapotec, Mixe and Chinantec, but not necessarily "Indians." Some people say the Mixe is an Indian.

Tumin: So you have several intermediate groups.

Paul: What do they call themselves —*indios?*

De la Fuente: Some call themselves "people of Castillian language."

Watkins: Then we start out with somebody who recognizes himself as an Indian.

Tax: Could we say that there is a tradition of being a member of the group that was there before the Spaniards came? An Indian is somebody who still recognizes cultural affiliation with the group that was there before the Conquest.

Foster: Do you mean that the Indians recognize the state of affairs that existed before . . .

Tax: No, they don't know any history. Where people call themselves Indians, where they recognize themselves as Indians, they are really carrying on a tradition that dates from the Conquest.

Wagley: What are you going to do with people who are really Ladinos but who call themselves Zapotec?

Paul: How do you know there are two groups there anyway?

De la Fuente: The difference is between Indians—Zapotec, Mixe and Chinantec on the one hand, and Castillians on the other hand. In other places there is a difference between mountain people and valley people. There is a difference between Indian groups and Castillians in the villages and cities. We have a distinction between *naturales* and *los que no son*. Parsons says there are no *correctos* and *tontos* in Mitla. We are beginning to find something of that sort in Yalalag. Something like that is more precise in speaking of towns. There are newcomers to these towns; you get people who are neither Indians nor Castillians.

Tax: The situation seems pretty complicated in that area, but I suggest that, for convenience at the moment, we assume there is a major distinction—however it is going to be defined—between Indians and non-Indians. We can worry about the relations between the two groups and whether there is an intermediate group as we go along. Then we can go on to some of these generalizations to see how far we get agreement on kinds of ethnic relations.

chapter 5

SOCIAL ORGANIZATION

by Calixta Guiteras Holmes

IN DISCUSSING social organization in Mesoamerica, I am referring especially to Indian groups; only in that which concerns *barrios* and ritual kinship is there participation by non-Indian groups. I shall describe (1) social organization as it is found at the present time; (2) variations in social organization; and (3) observable changes and the possible origin of Maya systems of social organization.

The kinship systems which have been studied can be classified as bilateral and patrilineal unilateral; in the first, descent is reckoned both in the father's and mother's line; in the second, descent is reckoned in one line only—the father's.

Using Lowie's classification of kinship systems into four types, it is found that three are present in Mesoamerica: the *lineal* and the *generation* systems, found among the bilateral groups, and the *bifurcate merging*, found among the unilateral patrilineal groups. The systems which belong to the generation type are those which were formerly unilateral. The fourth type, called *bifurcate col-*

lateral, is a transitional type, or one in process of change in Mesoamerica, in that it presents marked inconsistencies which indicate a change from one type of system to another, for example, the lack of uniform rules of ascent and descent. This transition always manifests itself in the form of a change from a unilateral to a bilateral system. Classification of these types is based on the terminology used for the first ascending generation.

In the lineal systems we find two different ways of grouping the relatives in Ego's generation: (1) the terms for cousins differ from those for siblings (Nahua, Sierra Totonac, Tarasco of Cherán, and Mazatec); (2) the terms for cousins and siblings are identical (Zapotec of Yalalag and Mitla, Mixteca Alta, Mixe, Otomí of Mesquital, Maya of Chan Kom, Popoluca, and Chorti of Guatemala).

In the generation systems the same term is used for cousins and siblings (Tzotzil of Zinacantán, Chamula, and Huistán).

In the bifurcate collateral systems we find two ways of classifying the relatives within Ego's generation: (1) the same term is used for siblings and cousins (Otomí of Oztotepec and the Huastec of Veracruz; (2) merging, i.e., one term is used for siblings and parallel cousins while another is used for cross cousins (Lacandon).

In the bifurcate merging we find three ways of classifying the relatives of Ego's generation: (1) bifurcate merging with overriding of generations, i.e., siblings and parallel cousins are called by one term but father's sister's son and daughter are called by the same terms as sister's son and daughter, while mother's brother's son and daughter are called mother's brother and mother's sister (Tzotzil of San Pablo Chalchihuitán and the Tzeltal of Oxchuc and Cancuc); (2) the same term used for both siblings and cousins (Maya of X-Cacal and some Tzotzil of Chenalhó); (3) one term used for siblings, parallel cousins and mother's brother's children, and another generation—overriding term for father's sister's children (other Tzotzil of Chenalhó). To make it clearer I have arranged all the groups mentioned, in the table which follows:

From the table it seems that at the present time the bifurcate merging type is found only among Maya speaking groups, the only groups which reflect a unilateral organization; therefore, bilateral systems predominate in the Mesoamerican area.

It may be said that in this area, regardless of the type of kinship system used, there exists an emphasis on age difference, observable

Type	Group	Terminology
Lineal	Nahua	One term for siblings, another term for cousins.
	Sierra Totonac	
	Tarasco (Cherán)	
	Mazatec	
	Zapotec (Yalalag)	One term for both siblings and cousins.
	Zapotec (Mitla)	
	Mixteca Alta	
	Mixe	
	Otomí (Mesquital)	
	Maya (Chan Kom)	
	Chorti (Guatemala)	
	Popoluca	
Generation	Tzotzil (Zinacantán)	
	Tzotzil (Chamula)	
	Tzotzil (Huistán)	
Bifurcate Collateral*	Otomí (Oztotepec)	
	Huastec (Veracruz)	
Bifurcate Merging	Maya (X-Cacal)	
	Tzotzil (Chenalhó)	
	Tzotzil (Chalchihuitán)	One term for sibling and parallel cousin, another term for cross cousin, with overriding of generations.
	Tzeltal (Cancuc)	
	Tzeltal (Oxchuc)	

both in kinship terminology and in behavior.[1] A distinction is made between older and younger brothers which is extended also to the parents' brothers. Only a few groups make these distinctions by the use of adjectives, although this practice seems to be of but a few years duration. The majority of the systems have special terms to indicate this age difference; the use of different terms according to whether Ego is masculine or feminine is almost general in Ego's generation, and less common in the first ascending generation.

There are two general tendencies in the whole area: bilateral and patrilineal. The first is evidenced by the following:

a. Taboos concerning incest are generally bilateral.

b. Few groups observe strict rules of unilateral residence.

c. Relations between spouses tend to be closer than between siblings.

* The Lacandon should be classified among the Bifurcate Collateral considering the first ascending generation, but they merge in Ego's generation, as has already been stated.

d. With few exceptions, both sexes have property rights, and both sons and daughters may inherit property.

e. The position of women is relatively high. Divorce is equally possible for the woman or the man. Women together with their husbands control the family purse-strings. On the marriage of a daughter both parents must give their consent. The counsel of an old woman is considered as much as that of an old man (both of whom are relatives). In the politico-religious organization there are offices filled by women, although not as many as those filled by men, and an office is considered to be held by a couple.[2]

Along with this bilateral tendency, nevertheless, a unilateral, patrilineal tendency is observed in the area,[3] for which there is the following evidence:

a. There is *no case* in which the opposite tendency may be observed. Whatever unilateral tendency exists is always patrilineal; for example, there is a tendency toward patrilocal residence, but none toward matrilocal residence.[4] In those cases in which inheritance and property rights favor one sex, it is always the male. There is bride-service and bride-price as well as polygamy, but never polyandry. Political control is in the hands of the men, and offices are considered to be filled by men rather than women.

b. There also exists throughout the whole area a certain vagueness concerning relations between relatives. No very definite patterns of conduct are found except for those concerning parents and children, older and younger brothers, etc. Geographic proximity and frequency of contact are the most influential factors in conduct. There are no avoidance patterns nor joking relationships; the institution of the avunculate is not present. In general there is a high degree of individualism and, therefore, variations within the same community.

c. There is little feeling of genealogy;[5] relatives beyond the second or third ascending generation are not remembered. Those on the paternal side are more likely to be remembered than those on the maternal side.[6] In the majority of the groups kinship terms are applied only to the children and grandchildren of the same grandparents.[7]

Ritual Kinship. This is the relationship established between god-parent and god-child and, what is equally important, that established between god-parent and the child's parents; the latter relationship is called *compadrazgo*.[8] These relations extend solidarity beyond the limits of the family and as Beals says, "weave a network of relationships over the whole community," and, according to de la Fuente, even beyond the community. It is safe to state that this is an institution that exists all over Middle America. However, as Foster puts it, "no two major Mexican areas have quite the same combination of compadrazgos." The one general to all is that established at baptism; it is also the most binding. There are also *padrinos* of marriage and of confirmation, which are quite general in the area, plus others that differ from place to place: of the candle, of the crown, of the gospel, etc. One instance in which a native ceremony persists within the Christian pattern is the *hetzmek* of Chan Kom.

Generally, it may be said that a group will have more occasions on which ceremonies of this sort are celebrated if it is more advanced or has more external contacts, with the exception of the upper social classes in the big cities. The more isolated and less acculturated groups usually practice only baptism; those groups which do not know these ceremonies are exceptional. It is also exceptional to find cases in which the compadrazgo relations are tenuous or almost non-existent, although the sacrament may be received by some who seek to take advantage of opportune occasions.

In the majority of cases the terms which designate godparents and godchildren consist of those for parents and children, with prefixes meaning God, sacred, church, etc. For the relations between compadres, the Spanish terms are used. In many cases the children of compadres are considered as brothers and to them are applied these terms with the prefixes mentioned above.

Taboos exist against incest between these ritual relatives, especially those of baptism. Nevertheless, in the majority of cases these ritual relatives perform the functions of the consanguineal family, such as digging the grave of a dead person, washing, dressing and carrying the corpse (Popoluca of Soteapan, Sierra Totonac, Tarasco, Tzeltal and Tzotzil).

There appear to be no rules which dictate who may be a godparent. As an exceptional case we have the Chorti of Honduras, where the rain priest and his wife are the godparents of the whole community. Among the Huastec of Veracruz, the individual chosen to be a godparent must *completar la mano,* that is, be the godfather of five brothers. Here also, these relations until a few years ago established a different status in the life of a man; one could drink or smoke in public only after doing these things for the first time while in the company of one's compadre.

Godparents are chosen from among relatives or non-relatives; within the ethnic group or from outside of it; within the same economic level or from a higher economic level. In some cases marriage sets up a compadrazgo relationship between two households (Cherán, Tehuantepec). In this case it seems only to label a relationship which is established in places where the term compadre is not used for it. The soul of a child seems to be connected in some way with its godparent. In Chenalhó, for example, after long consideration I was not decided upon as a proper *madrina* because I lived far away, and in illness the child's soul might wander in search of me.

Another relationship concerning which I lack data is that which is established with a person who receives the name of *reposición*. This is initiated by giving to a child the name of a specific person; the persons seek an individual whom they estimate possesses those qualities which they would like to see in their child, and the person chosen is advised that the child is his reposición. Apparently they hold the idea of the transmission or extension of virtues from one person to another.

Lineages. These are exogamic, patrilineal groups which are distinguished by bearing the same Indian name.[9] In some Tzeltal and Tzotzil groups the land belongs to the lineage and may not be transferred. In those groups in which land is inherited exclusively by male children, the masculine members of a lineage live in houses either contiguous or near one another. The dead are buried in the land belonging to the lineage. Their members cooperate with one another. Their milpas are not separated by *bardas*. A woman continues to belong to her paternal lineage.

There are groups in which the members of the lineage are dispersed. Generally, these are groups in which land may be sold to outsiders, in which the woman may acquire a piece of land with the product of her labor for her sons, or in which land is inherited by both sexes.

The above lineages—localized and non-localized—are found in Chiapas, where in the case of dispersion of members of lineages, one also finds patrilineal groups of consanguineal relatives. These patrilineal groups may be the same as the *chinamit* of Northwest Guatemala. We know that they once existed among the Mixe, and among the majority of the peoples of Mesoamerica, according to the ancient chronicles.[10]

Clans and Name-Groups. The clan is unusual in the Mesoamerican area; it is found only among two Tzeltal groups in Chiapas—in Oxchuc and Cancuc—and among the Lacandon. The Tzeltal clans are patrilineal, matri-patrilocal (patrilocal with temporary matrilocal residence), exogamous, and non-localized. Each clan is composed of an indefinite number of lineages, whose members originated from or came out of four caves (the clans in Oxchuc and Cancuc are four in number) in which at the present time still live the *lab* of each of their members. A woman does not become a member of her husband's clan. The lineage lands belong to the clan. The members of the clan, and to a greater extent those of the lineage, stand in a relation of brothers to one another and are designated as such. Social control through the medium of witchcraft is exercised among members of the clan. The head of the clan is the oldest man, who is respected and feared; in recent years this headship has disappeared in Cancuc, thus originating conflicts that at times break out in violence (members of the clan who occupy offices in the regional government try to assume rights, in certain aspects of internal organization, which were the prerogative of the ancient clan head). The clans are equitably represented in the politico-religious organization.

The clans in Oxchuc and Cancuc lack insignia, tutelary god or saint, and special fiestas or ceremonies. In Oxchuc they are known by a Spanish name which precedes the Indian lineage surname, although generally the first is not used; the second by itself indicates the clan, since a particular native surname belongs to a particular clan as well. In Cancuc, nevertheless, although a Spanish surname exists, it does not mean anything, as each clan has its own name and specific lineages.

All the above applies to the clans of the Lacandon, which are totemic. In some groups where clans are not found, there are lineages grouped together under certain Spanish surnames, forming name-groups of which the majority are exogamous and non-localized. There is a tendency toward the disappearance of name-groups as regulators of matrimony, the lineages conserving this function, although these are also tending to disappear, giving place to smaller consanguineal groups.[11]

It is my opinion that, although lineages at the present time are not localized, they were localized in former times, since generally the surnames refer to specific places (in spite of being found at present in different places[12]) and that the name-groups are remnants of ancient clans.

Of the Mixe it is said that formerly families related by marriage lived in small settlements and that these settlements were exogamous. The same situation exists today in Chenalhó. The Mixe could not marry a person of the same name-group. This we find also among the Chinantec of Ojitlán, Veracruz. It appears that the following groups were formerly organized into patrilineal lineages or clans: the Tarascan, Otomí, Totonac, Maya of Yucatan, etc.

The larger divisions; that is, those in which a greater number of persons are grouped together, seem to be the first to disappear, the lineage persisting, for example, in places where the clan or name-group has disappeared. Uni-local residence gives way to bi-local or neo-local residence (isolated bilateral families).

The place where one lives is of great importance throughout the area; feeling oneself to be an integral part of the *barrio* and the *municipio* is of primary importance. Territorial subdivisions play a predominant part in religion as well as in social and political organization, as may be observed in all that concerns patron saints, local gods, etc.

Division into barrios is found in the greater part of the area, with the exception of a considerable part of the Maya area. Barrios are localized and non-localized, the former predominating. There are barrios which subdivide towns, and barrios which subdivide the lands of a whole municipio, the former predominating. The number of barrios varies and it appears that the number is in direct relation to the size of the community. There are barrios with a patron saint and others without one. There are barrios which, although they bear the name of a saint, do not have tutelary fiestas. Membership in the barrio is through inheritance or residence; the first is always the case with non-localized barrios, both types of membership being found in the localized barrios. In the majority of cases the barrio does not regulate matrimony, although the ancient chronicles referred to exogamous and endogamous barrios.

The function of the barrio is almost always evident in the religion (organization of *mayordomías*, brotherhoods, prayermakers for the *milpa*, etc.), and in the organization of *tequio* or communal labor. The majority of barrios have a "chief" or *principal*. Barrios are sometimes distinguished by ethnic differences, differences in occupation, etc.; there is generally a more "backward" barrio, the barrio of the *inditos;* barrio of potters, weavers, tanners, etc. At times there is rivalry between barrios. In many cases the barrio has been displaced by more modern subdivisions, such as sections, demarcations, blocks, which sometimes, but not always, coincide with the boundaries of the ancient barrio.[13]

The non-localized barrios must have originated from the localized barrios. The *santos* and the religion tend to be concentrated in a single church, the chapels losing importance. Communal labor is also losing its ancient function, which in the majority of the groups has come to be a function of the municipal government. We frequently find a division into two barrios or halves, which suggests the moiety, called in many cases *arriba* and *abajo*. These halves correspond to the barrio formerly described. At times a half is a grouping together of old barrios as between the Chinantec of Ojitlán and the Mexicanos of Chiconamel. In the first case the halves are endogamous.

The *calpules* that we find in a Tzotzil group (Chalchihuitán) are five endogamous subdivisions of the municipio. Within each *calpul* live the exogamous patrilineal lineages (the latter group is that which possesses the perfect Omaha system). The old men of the calpul are its representatives in the presence of the authorities of the municipio. Members of the calpules make up the political and religious organization. The endogamy of the calpul refers solely to the first marriage.

As a special group which is found in a great part of the area we have that which is formed by the old men or principales, who fulfill a religious role, a political role, and exercise social control. This organization is tending to disappear.

If we take into account the predominant tendencies within the area the variations are not great, since the majority of the communities follow a general pattern, but we have to take them into account in considering the extreme crystallizations. These, in general, point in two directions: (1) that of the bilateral extended family, such as has occurred among the Chorti of Guatemala, where indeterminate kinship institutions have been replaced by a system of large bilateral families which cooperate, with sibling exchange and a kinship system in accordance with these institutions; and (2) that of patrilineal families, lineages, and even totemic clans.

Proceeding from the least to the most unilateral we have the following examples:

a. Chichicastenango, where patrilineal extended families are tempered considerably by locality considerations (i.e., the wife probably loses her kin affiliation to take on her husband's kin-locality affiliation; and in cases of reversed residence, the contrary is to some degree true.

b. Santiago Chimaltenango (Huehuetenango) where there are patrilineal extended families, but it seems that the wife does not lose her affiliation in her father's household.

c. The Tzotzil and Tzeltal area, particularly Oxchuc and Cancuc, where clans and name-groups are found, with the type of kinship system that accompanies clans.

d. The Lacandon, with totemic, patrilineal clans.[14]

In order to deal with observable changes we refer to the types of systems which we have called transitional. We can speak of a transition from the bifurcate merging to the lineal, i.e., from a unilateral, patrilineal organization to a bilateral organization with descent reckoned through the paternal line. This is illustrated by what we have observed in the Tzotzil of Chiapas. The Tzotzil of San Pablo Chalchihuitán have bifurcate merging with overriding of generations, using one term for siblings and parallel cousins and different terms for father's sister's children and mother's brother's children. Those from Chenalhó, belonging to the same system as those from Chalchihuitán, are found to have made changes in Ego's generation; one of these groups has extended the use of the term for siblings and parallel cousins to maternal cross cousins, while preserving the overriding of generations for the paternal cross cousins.

Meanwhile, another group, from Chenalhó also, has lost all distinction between parallel and cross cousins, having extended the sibling term to all cousins, as have also, for example, the Maya of X-Cacal. Other Tzotzil groups (Zinacantán, Chamula, and Huistán) not only use the sibling term for all relatives of Ego's generation, but have extended the use of the terms for mother and father to include the siblings of these, having changed to a generation system.

The kinship system of the Huastec of Veracruz, at present bifurcate collateral, is apparently derived from the bifurcate merging. The same change seems to have occurred in the system of the

Lacandon; here, however, siblings and parallel cousins are still distinguished from cross cousins.

Relying on more or less ancient data we can also say that the following changes have occurred in the kinship systems of the Tarasco, Otomí and Mixe:

Tarasco—from bifurcate collateral to lineal.

Otomí—from bifurcate collateral to lineal.

Mixe—from bifurcate merging to lineal.

For the kinship systems of the Nahua, Zapotec, Totonac and Mixtec, we lack the data which might indicate the nature of earlier kinship systems. The last two have not been fully studied up to now.

The change of systems in Chiapas has been accompanied by changes in inheritance and property rights and by changes in residence. The nuclear family is acquiring more and more importance, permitting and practicing marriage between cross cousins, real and classificatory. The influence of the Catholic church and bilaterality extend taboos in both lines. In general, marriage is monogamous. Polygyny is infrequent; when it occurs it may be sororal or nonsororal. The Lacandon are exceptional in having sororal polygyny in the majority of cases and a system of relationship which indicates marriage between cross cousins.

For an explanation of that which we have called extreme crystallizations among Maya-speaking peoples, we have to go farther back in time. Regarding the Maya kinship system, we have data only from the time of first contact with Europeans, in which the system of the Maya of Yucatan was typically a unilateral organization. It seems impossible that the extended bilateral family of the Chorti could have arisen from this system without intermediate stages. Now, according to data which we have for some Maya groups, alongside an organization into patrilineal lineages, persisted a name which was inherited from the mother through the feminine line. This may have been a cultural lag which could indicate a stage of double descent, with patrilocal or matri-patrilocal residence, with a progressive emphasis on patrilocal residence, and, following this, inheritance through the paternal line by male children. The stage of double descent must have been preceded by a matrilineal stage. The sororal polygyny of the Lacandon, the exceptionally privileged position of women among them, the Iroquois terminology, and perhaps temporary matrilocal residence that we find in Tzeltal and Tzotzil groups suggests a possible matrilineal organization in former times. In these systems of Maya-speaking groups which have not lost the bifurcation in the first ascending generation (and in many groups, also in the descending generation), separated from the Maya trunk for some two thousand years, we find the same terms, or phonetic modifications of these, to designate the mother's brother and the sister's son; this is true even among the Huastec. Terms for the paternal line vary from one group to another, but the terms mentioned have persisted and in the present system of the Zutugil of San Pedro la Laguna these terms have been extended to the father's brother and the brother's son.

The extended bilateral family of the Chorti could have proceeded from the matrilineal stage without passing through the double descent stage and through that which gives way to the crystallization of the perfect patrilineal system which we find among the Tzeltal and among some Tzotzil. Nor did all of the Maya groups have to pass through the double descent stage; some may have passed directly (or with short bilateral stages) from the matrilineal to the patrilineal, especially if they were already in contact with groups which were already in this latter stage.

The changes which we have been able to observe, which represent the passage of systems which indicate a unilateral organization to those which indicate a bilateral organization, or a tendency toward the latter, I believe are due largely to the stimulus of contact with European civilization. The Indians have not copied the European system (lineal with a distinction between cousins and siblings);[15] instead the new ways of life have brought them to a reorganization of their ancient systems, always toward the bilateral; but, as we have been able to see, the terminology for Ego's generation in the majority of cases uses the same term for siblings and cousins. Spoehr has found the same situation in his studies of the Muscogee.[16]

DISCUSSION

(1)

Foster: Is there a distinction between older and younger sister? In the systems I know best—the Mixe, Zoque and Popoluca—there is a distinction between older brother and older sister, distinct terms are used; but the term is the same for younger brother and younger sister. This is not extended to the siblings of the first ascending generation.

Paul: The tendency is to distinguish

between older and younger uncle and aunt.

Tax: Compared with some areas, where it's a major tendency, I suppose this is a minor tendency. Throughout the area there is a considerable tendency to differentiate. Father's older brother is frequently distinguished, if not in terminology certainly in behavior, from the younger brother. To a lesser degree the mother's sisters are distinguished by age. There's something that doesn't come out in the formal kinship terminology. You get the vocative terminology, but what do they actually call these people? Frequently they call the father's older brother father, and they may call older brother father if the father is dead. I don't know how widespread this is. In Chichicastenango in the vocative system, older sister is mother (although the younger sister is not daughter).

Paul: Father's older brother is father, even if father is living.

Foster: These are characteristics primarily limited to the Maya-speaking peoples.

Tax: I think this is tied to systems where you have extended families, where the family is important, the brothers living together and inheriting land, etc.

Paul: How about Santiago Chimaltenango in the Cuchumatanes? Is there a tendency to distinguish the father's brother by age?

Wagley: No. I don't think so.

Paul: Even within the Maya area, it's a minor pattern.

Guiteras: The distinction between older and younger is mainly between siblings.

Paul: What you get is an age-sex distinction in the Ego generation.

Foster: That would hold for the Popoluca and, I believe, the Mixe and Zoque. Where they are younger than Ego, sex is not important. Younger sisters are classified with nieces and nephews. In the ascending generation, rather than classifying older sister with the parents, or older brother with the parents, older brother is called by the same term as uncle and older sister by the same term as aunt.

Guiteras: Among the Otomí older brother is called *tío,* even among groups using Spanish terms.

(2)

De la Fuente: This statement should be qualified; there are very large differences in the position of women. The Huastec and the Tzeltal are examples of this. I would suggest modification of the sentence in which you speak of *divorcio* in a legal way, for what is really indicated is separation, in the common use of the term. Also, the reference to *cargos* being fulfilled by women must be to the religious organization rather than the politico-religious organization. The women simply share in the latter somehow.

Guiteras: Religious offices are filled by women.

(3)

Tax: I take it that the opposition set up between bilateral tendencies, on the one hand, and unilateral tendencies on the other is intended to speak for Middle America as a whole. The Chorti are the extreme of bilaterality, so you would find all these things applying to the Chorti; the Tzeltal are the extreme of patrilineal tendencies.

Paul: Is the position of women generally higher in bilateral systems than it is in unilateral systems in Chiapas?

Guiteras: No. I'm not referring to the kinship system.

Tax: There may be some counteracting tendencies. I think these comparisons are of the area as a whole with other places in the world. There are patrilineal tendencies in Middle America, but not as there are in Arabia.

Foster: The comparisons we've been making are within the area. It seems to me that in laying down the major propositions we'd better stick to Middle America.

Guiteras: None of these refer to the kinship system; they refer to behavior tendencies in general. The answer to

Mr. Paul's question is No. We have a high position of women among the very patrilineal peoples of Cancuc, who have an Omaha kinship system.

Kelly: We have overlapping terminology: bilateral kinship system and bilateral tendencies.

Watkins: It is also somewhat confusing to use bilateral to refer to both the terminology and behavior.

(4)

De la Fuente: The statement that there is no tendency towards matrilocal residence seems too strong.

Paul: There *is* a lot of patrilocal residence; in San Pedro, for example, more than half are patrilocal. We should say there are no cases in which the matrilocal principle predominates; what matrilocal tendencies exist are minor.

De la Fuente: This would be true of San Pedro and Yalalag.

Watkins: How about temporary matrilocal residence?

Guiteras: That would make residence bilocal.

Tax: Do we agree that whatever unilateral tendencies there are, are in the direction of patrilocal rather than matrilocal; patrilineal rather than matrilineal?

Foster: There is agreement among us that it holds good for the entire area. It seems significant to me because when the question comes up of reconsidering kinship systems, it is a highly useful guide when there are indications of a unilineal kinship system having existed at an earlier date.

(5)

Kirchhoff: In ancient Mexico one section of the population was extremely interested in genealogical bookkeeping.

Guiteras: I haven't found this anywhere.

Kirchhoff: This has a bearing on the question of to what extent the internal stratification in Indian groups today is traceable to an older stratification.

Lasker: As a physical anthropologist working in the Tarascan region, I accumulated vast amounts of genealogical data, working with some more or less Indian groups and observing which ones knew most about their families; there was no tendency for the Mestizos to know any more about their family than the Indians.

Tax: In contrast to North American tribes with whom I have worked, where almost anybody in the community could trace back not only his own family but that of everybody else.

(6)

De la Fuente: What I have obtained indicates that they remember both equally well. In San Pedro it is about the same.

Paul: You might qualify that to say that they remember the patrilineal line better when residence tends to be patrilocal.

Wagley: Parsons mentions in Mitla the tendency to recognize relationships through the surname. How would that work out?

Gillin: The ancient Maya had cross-cousin marriage; the Eastern Pokoman don't show it.

Paul: Informants in San Pedro said that "in a place nearby" they marry cousins.

Tax: They always gossip about another town. In Panajachel they say the Indians of Santa Catarina are always matrilocal; they attribute opposite attributes to the people of another town.

Gillin: The Pokoman marry cross-cousins but it isn't preferential.

Foster: There is one term for brother-in-law, another term for sister-in-law, and another term for sibling of the same sex. Isn't that frequently associated with cross-cousin marriage?

Tax: This terminology could be accounted for by a system of sibling exchange. You find sibling exchange; I don't think there's any known case of cross-cousin marriage.

Villa: There is classificatory cross-cousin marriage.

(7)

Tax: What about the relationship between grandparent and grandchild?

Kyte: It is stronger on the compadre level.

Paul: You can't have a very strong relationship between a child and an adult.

Tax: It can be quite strong when the child is brought up by a grandparent.

Paul: The much closer relationship is the compadre one.

(8)

Tax: There are some variations in ritual kinship about which I would like to know more. In Chichicastenango, for example, there's a kind of ritual and non-social relationship: one man, acting as ritual godfather, will baptize thousands of children. Obviously, there can't be many social relationships established between him and many of the others.

Toor: I have never heard of cases in Mexico where only one man is padrino.

Paul: The Chorti have specialized godfathers.

Wisdom: Anybody can be a godfather among the Chorti.

Guiteras: Among the Chorti of Honduras rain priests are the padrinos for the whole village.

De la Fuente: Is it possible to establish a hierarchy of padrinos?

Guiteras: Sometimes the baptismal one is the more important.

Paul: They're always the most important.

Stone: How much of this is pre-Spanish and how much of it is Catholic practice introduced by the Spanish? They don't baptize in parts of Costa Rica. It loses its importance when you get out of Middle America. The compadre, however, is very important in the non-Indian groups.

Foster: I think we're dealing here with a Spanish trait. The question, as I see it, is to what extent is the proliferation of the compadrazgo system in Mexico and Guatemala something which developed in the New World. Is it perhaps a substitute for an earlier type of social organization with interfamilial relations which has disappeared?

Paul: I think this is what Parsons states as an hypothesis for Mitla: it is a substitute for what was once a more proliferated true kinship system—now a ritual kinship system. In San Pedro they do have the compadre system but it's very weak. If it were to be eliminated it wouldn't make much difference; yet theoretically they would have a need for it, because they have a very attenuated kinship system.

Foster: In Spain the system is far less developed than in most places in the New World. It's not a particularly important system.

Wisdom: In any of these Indian languages do we get native names for compadres?

Guiteras: I haven't found any. They're all derived from the Spanish. *Padrino* is always the word for father with the Indian word for church or God added.

De la Fuente: What about the hetzmek?

Paul: There were group baptisms at adolescence for which they had native sponsors—an approach to the godparent pattern, but they are sponsors for the event rather than for the individuals.

In some communities people who have different kinds of compadres and compadres seem to feel related in more than a kinship way. Certainly this is the case with the Yaqui. How about Cherán?

Beals: It's true there also.

Paul: It is interesting to see what types of groups are formed on the basis of the compadre relationship.

Foster: They may take care of burials.

Paul: In San Pedro the dead are buried by an impersonal, objective organization. There are six cofradías and whichever cofradía is working at that time buries the man.

Foster: Perhaps that's why the compadrazgo system hasn't developed there.

Tax: In Guatemala, the overriding social institution is not the family but the politico-religious organization.

Paul: I'd say it's a socio-ceremonial system.

Foster: In Michoacán you can see the great importance of the compadre system. There you have traders who go over a very wide area and make it a point to have compadres in each village through which they pass.

Paul: When you have personalized relationships among so-called primitive peoples, they tend to be on a genealogical basis. The compadre system forms the same type of personalized relationships. It therefore serves the purpose of linking trade partners—linking Ladino and Indian, linking *patrón* and worker. It has the benefits of the kinship system without the liabilities of it. This makes it a wonderful mechanism for introducing personalized relations.

Beals: You get a compadrazgo system in Ecuador; although it is not as elaborate it is well developed.

Gillin: This is true of Moche in Peru.

Wagley: It has great proliferation throughout the Amazon valley.

Paul: This is also true of the Yaqui.

Gillin: As Paul points out, it's impossible to get a true genealogical relationship under caste conditions, but this provides a linkage.

Paul: There are many communities where you tend to pick somebody from the other group. This is very much like what you get among blood brothers in other parts of the world. You have the need for personalized links. I think the whole theory of ritual kinship for connecting vertical groups is very interesting.

Gillin: There is also a prevalence of compadrazgo in the cities; there is a lot of this in Lima, Peru. In some ways it looks like a pretty good idea; it breaks down the impersonalization that you get in the big cities.

Paul: In Merida it gets pretty secularized; it tends to be weakened by the total city pattern.

Gillin: It's incompatible with a high degree of vertical mobility.

(9)

Tax: I'd like to ask Wagley how close the Chimaltenango family groups come to being lineage groups?

Wagley: I feel that in the past there was a considerable amount of solidarity in the surname group, without any of the clanlike characteristics. If it was like that, it was so far in the past that I couldn't prove it. Added to that, one gets a picture from LaFarge of the large family in this general area, which does not appear in Chimaltenango. It is my feeling that in Northwest Guatemala you have a tendency toward very strong and large lineages which may in the past have been something like the Tzeltal.

Tax: Are they exogamous?

Wagley: Definitely.

Paul: Regardless of known relationship, there is name exogamy.

Wagley: It's the name that carries the recognition of kinship.

Paul: In San Pedro people will marry people bearing the same name; name exogamy means nothing in this area.

Kelly: I'd like to have Dr. Kirchhoff comment on this.

(10)

Kirchhoff: This is a question that not only refers to the past but also to the evaluation of the conceptual understanding of the present situation; it goes back to the definition of a clan. We all realize that one important group of people has not been mentioned so far—the Nahuatl. In the old literature we have relatively few descriptions; Las Casas described an exogamous patrilineal clan very clearly. This has been described equally clearly for the Nahuatl of Mexico, where I would also speak of a clan. I feel that any group that considers itself to be of common descent—not a temporary grouping like a small family which says "we're related"—but a group which continues to exist generation after generation and traces its origin back to a common ancestor, should be called a clan. The Scotch clan, according to our typical definition that a clan is exogamous, is not a clan. I would now say that there is a second type of permanent kin organization based on a belief in common descent, in many parts of the world, represented by the *calpul* or the *ayllu*. Even here in the Maya area you find a place where you have a combination of the division of the whole group into a number of sections within which they marry, and in each of these groups you have a subdivision along exogamic lines. That combination has never been described for Nahuatl peoples. It seems to me that we have perhaps three different situations: one is clearly the exogamic patrilineal clan. On the other extreme we have the non-exogamous clan, which is what I would call the Scotch clan. And we would have here, in this case, a border situation—a combination of the *calpulli* and the old, characteristically Maya, exogamous clan. I do not mean that everywhere the word calpul is used to refer to a non-exogamous Aztec type institution.

Recently I discussed the situation with Rowe and Tschopik. For a long time they struggled with an apparent contradiction in that the ayllu looks so much like a landed clan, but it looks entirely endogamous; it has no rule of endogamy however, but a strong tendency toward it. We have all been taught that a clan is, by definition, exogamous. We anthropologists have taken a term from an institution which we didn't analyze too well and then associated a clan so definitely with the idea of exogamy that we can't go back and say that a Scotch clan is a clan.

It's important to remember that not all the peoples of Mesoamerica must have had an exogamous patrilineal clan; some may have had definite clans of the Aztec type calpul.

Gillin: You're presenting an intermediate type.

Kirchhoff: No, I wouldn't say it was intermediate. I would simply make a contrast between two types of one fundamental institution, the group based on kinship and the idea of common descent, and the idea of a line leading back into the past.

Tax: By this definition even the Chorti have clans! Their extended family consists of those people, either matrilineal or patrilineal, who become part of a local group. It's certainly a descent group, it's certainly a local group, and it's endogamous. (Two intermarrying families.) It's obviously not unilateral. Now we would call this a clan too; it's not unlike the old calpulli as a landed clan.

Beals: Then the word clan is entirely useless. You're getting to the point where you can say that almost anybody has a clan, the word clan embraces such a wide range of phenomena.

Paul: We need a name for a kinship group, yet we have two types. I think we ought to now use the word clan for a unilateral patriliny or matriliny. We have patriclans in the Maya area.

Kirchhoff: I don't object to that at all. The reasons why I think it is useful to include these two types—the exogamous and the non-exogamous—is that they are never found among very primitive peoples.

Gillin: I would like to ask about bilateral kindreds.

Kirchhoff: That term comes from the study of Germanic institutions; that is a different thing. You can have, with or without clans, the recognition of a whole body of relatives in both directions, to whom you have specific relations, but they don't constitute a group with boundaries. They have a certain relation to you which shifts with Ego.

Beals: The difference between Kirchhoff and me is that we have a fundamentally different viewpoint about what these organizations consist of. I submit that the calpulli organization had nothing to do with kinship, that it arose out of an organization which had a local base.

Villa: The calpulli in Chiapas, and also among the Chinantec, is as follows: In both places the whole community is divided into five subdivisions. The divisions are for political and religious functions, and regulate marriage in the sense that they are endogamous, but they have exogamous clans within the larger endogamous divisions.

Guiteras: There are five calpules; in each calpul there are a certain number of exogamous lineages.

Paul: Are they scattered through the divisions?

Guiteras: They should live in one division but now they have scattered somewhat. The names of lineages always refer to one place. They may marry outside of the lineage but within the division.

Villa: The endogamy only exists for the first marriage. After that, following marriages can be made in different calpules. I don't know about the calpules in Oaxaca.

Guiteras: In the Chinantec region there are also five; an endogamy of three and an endogamy of two. There are two moieties.

Kirchhoff: In one valley in Colombia the situation would be described without anything about exogamy. It is likely that we have here a situation which combined the two.

Paul: Do these endogamous divisions go by a particular name?

Guiteras: First the Spanish then the Indian surname. Each section has a particular Indian name.

Paul: So you have both the concept of what this type is—the *calpulli*—and specific names for each example of it.

Kirchhoff: From this material, I can't see any difference between clans and name groups. The lineage is a sub-clan, a closer, more recognizable section of a clan.

(11)

Guiteras: I didn't know how to apply the term name-group. It is a lineage because it has one name; then it corresponds to a lineage.

Tax: In a lineage you have to be able to trace the relationship.

Guiteras: I'm using the basic name groups. We have name groups with an Indian surname, these I call lineages. The clans and name groups with a Spanish name I call clans.

Paul: In principle, an exogamous unilateral organization is implied here.

Guiteras: But I can't put the two of them together. The larger group is breaking down while we still have the exogamy of the smaller group.

Kirchhoff: I'm still not clear about the name group. Is it a group of people with the same name—*apellido?*

Guiteras: I would have to call the Indian surname apellido also.

Kirchhoff: A lot of members of an earlier clan might have taken over a Spanish name. Why not operate simply with clan and lineage and recognize that in most cases the members of larger and smaller groups have what would have been originally one name, one apellido. Then we would have two terms rather than three.

Villa: Regarding the importance of the surname, in the old Maya systems that was very important. According to Landa, the Maya names were the mother's and father's surnames, so that a man would be named Chan Kan, each name being the surname of the respective parents; only the father's name was transmitted however. According to recent studies by Roys, both names were transmitted but that of the father was perpetuated in a different way. The name of the mother was used as a first name and that of the father was characteristically transmitted as that of the lineage. They wanted to perpetuate both lines, but they put the emphasis on the male line; they had words to explain the order of importance—first, second, and so on,—and that system still exists among the Lacandon.

Tax: There is a survival of this in

Huehuetenango. If a man is named Juan Martin, his first son would be Martin Juan.

Guiteras: This is found also among the Chinantec.

Villa: I would like to say a few words about the clan, the lineage and name groups. The old Maya system existed until recently among the Lacandon Indians. They had clan names and lineages. This old system was diversified in local variations which we can see in different municipios or communities of Chiapas. If you stay with this hypothesis, you discover that among the different groups in the northern part of Oaxaca the clans, as we define them for Chiapas, are not functioning in the same way, but have surnames which regulate marriage; the latter group is what I call a name group, not as crystallized as the clans that we find in Chiapas. The Mazatec region proves to be another area characterized by this same old pattern; this is very common in most parts of Northern Oaxaca. There are two first names; the second one is always transmitted through the male line and is the one that regulates marriage. Thus it is not possible to marry a girl who possesses your name. They use an apellido so it is possible to recognize immediately whether an individual is an Indian or not. If they want to pass over to the Ladino group they have to change their names.

Paul: Does this name group have any other functions than exogamy?

Villa: Yes, cooperation and hospitality.

Tax: Why aren't they to be considered clans?

Villa: I don't consider them clan groups because in the communities where I have found them there are dozens of men with these surnames.

Paul: You're spoiled by an ideal system. It's a clan system, but it's watered down.

Villa: It's not so crystallized. It's more amorphous than the ones we found in Chiapas.

Paul: But I think it's a clan.

Villa: They don't have a place to gather together and meet as a group.

Paul: If a girl called Elena José marries somebody from another name group. . . .

Villa: She continues to belong to the José group.

Paul: Then you have a clan there.

Tax: I think we'll confuse our terminology if we give a different name to every group that's a little different.

Wagley: The situation in Chimaltenango is exactly that described by Mr. Villa. I also hesitated to call it a clan, perhaps feeling that a clan ought to have some semblance of organization.

Paul: It has a name, exogamy and similar functions.

King: It doesn't go back to a common ancestor. You're dealing with a breaking down, an attenuation. You're loosening the classical definition of a clan.

Paul: What's the classical definition? You can use Murdock's definition, which is generally recognized; you can use clan as Linton uses it, or sib as Lowie has used it.

Gillin: I'd like to bring up the point of the meaning of the apellidos; how are they to be translated? The Pokoman apellidos always turn out to be the names of plants and animals.

Villa: For the Maya, according to Roys, almost all the Maya surnames corresponded to names of animals and plants.

Guiteras: Tzeltal surnames are names of plants and animals also.

(12)

Villa: In the Maya system of Yucatan and Northern Guatemala surnames were localized as they are now, so that by just knowing the name of an individual you could say to what community he belongs. There are well known surnames that belong to certain sections of Yucatan. It is the same pattern that we find now in the most Indian regions.

Tax: You find it in Western Guatemala. You could show that each community has its set of surnames. All the lake towns have typical surnames.

Villa: The recognition of the place of origin just through surnames is more emphasized in the more Indian regions.

Paul: If we do not use the word clan for what you find among the Mazatec, in Linton's sense of the word clan, then all the literature of what we call clans in anthropology should be thrown out. Totemism and clans are not necessarily correlated.

(13)

Kirchhoff: Regarding the barrio organization, we really know next to nothing of the historical origin of the present geographic subdivisions of Indian towns throughout Middle America, and I wonder whether people have really looked for this type of evidence. Guiteras makes the point that there are groups of ethnic differences. Years ago I was fascinated by something I found in Tepoztlan; of the seven barrios, three had different dialects of Nahuatl from the other four, and also a difference in costumes. I think that Tepoztlan, and possibly many other places which we know of as composed of several geographic subunits, may be the result of pre-Columbian concentration of groups in larger settlements. On the basis of saying that in ancient Middle America, and in its surviving Indian cultures, there are two basic kin groups or descent groups patterns—one of the exogamous unilateral type and another—non-exogamous—we might be dealing in this case with a geographic concentration in one settlement of a number of independent units.

Guiteras: There is no tradition of the coming together of two different groups. Among the Chinantec they have the tradition of three on one side and two on the other; the other two seem to have been from far away, and they came to live with these people, near them.

Stone: You don't find this to the south of Guatemala.

De la Fuente: For Yalalag I have many cases of this sort, a differentiation of the community and some indication that groups were brought in. So on the one hand we have this sort of phenomenon and on the other hand we have the splitting up of pueblos. It seems to me that this internal differentiation is extremely common in Oaxaca.

Guiteras: We read in the chronicles that among the Mixtec there were barrios.

Tax: Are we leaning toward the interpretation that wherever you find barrios they are the result of the coming together of different peoples? In some cases the origin may have been in the way you suggested.

Kirchhoff: I hope I didn't give the impression that barrios are always the result of fusion of different groups. I have made a survey of the ancient literature and have noticed the appearance of certain numbers. The seven pattern, as in Tepoztlan, has a very definite distribution. Other patterns are based on the figures three, nine, or two, four, etc.

Beals: I think the true object of our discussion is the origin of kinds of segmentation of societies. I am inclined to believe that you have segmentation of societies in some parts of Middle America which may have had their origin in terms of politico-ceremonial assignment of functions, into which was assimilated this pattern of the settling of groups from other places. This discussion could go on for a long time. The question is: Is there a fundamental distinction between different parts of Middle America? I think we can agree on this.

Kirchhoff: I just wanted to say that I wasn't interested in the theoretical problem. I simply brought it in to pull together what I believe belongs together. I am convinced that both in ancient Mexico and in the present survivals, all geographic subdivisions had a common descent basis, irrespective of their being associated with political functions. The present town of Tepoztlan, divided into seven barrios, has a cleavage running through it, a difference, strongly felt by the people, that three barrios are one group and four are another group.

I would like to ask what is meant by "non-localized barrios."

Güiteras: In the vacant-town municipio of Chamula, there are three barrios in town, but the people live in the rancherías. Membership in the barrio is inherited.

Beals: The typical Mixe town is divided into three sections.

De la Fuente: I would like to comment further on the variation in the number of barrios, and the relation of the number to the size of the community. I know of two or three communities where there are non-localized *barrios*. There are eighty barrios; it seems to be something like a *cofradía;* no localization.

With reference to the statement as to the number of barrios and the size, the statement would be true if Guiteras refers to the number of localized barrios. She does not specify which type of barrio she means; I would say this is true for localized barrios.

Kirchhoff: On localized barrios, I would urge very strongly that workers in the field pay attention to the number of units actually found. I have become convinced that all over Middle America in ancient times there were a number of geographical patterns. This has a very important bearing on field work to discover the changes. If one is not aware of a numerical pattern existing, one could not get the changes. If one knew it should be seventeen, and it was sixteen or eighteen, then one could look around for another division, or see if one has disappeared. Carrasco told me recently that in going through the Spanish sources on highland Guatemala, he found the same list of numbers that I have given, almost without exception. You might find one with twenty sections, another seven, another four, but it always seems to go back to some ethnic differences. The numbers two, four, eight and sixteen, are widespread.

Beals: Does each ethnic group have the same number of kin groups?

Kirchhoff: You notice a frequency of correlation between certain ethnic groups and certain numerical principles of distribution. This is very important in social groupings and actual human relations. In such complex regions as Middle America you are bound to find an intermingling.

(14)

Paul: How about totemic clans?

Guiteras: I think we can consider the Tzeltal as a bit totemic.

Paul: Even when you get out of the Chiapas area?

Villa: The Lacandon are totemic in the sense that all clans have an animal as a pet.

Paul: Just because they have animals as pets doesn't make them totemic.

Villa: They feel attached to these animals and it was prohibited to eat the animals.

(15)

Watkins: In regard to Spanish influence, wasn't it greater than you imply?

Guiteras: In no case did we find an exact copy of the Spanish terminology even translated into their own language.

(16)

Wagley: In general the paper treats the breakdown of the community as such; one of the things that I think would be useful here is a study of the breakdown of the municipio as an ethnic unit, as a group, for example, the Guatemalan municipio and the equivalent Mexican ethnic groups.

Tax: We could ask the question: what are the major forms of social organization in this area. I would say that in Middle America as a whole, kinship is not an important thing. You get the compadrazgo system, and the politico-religious system in certain areas, as the most important part of the organization. We ought to take into account the whole organization in Middle America.

De la Fuente: I wonder whether the Zapotec case fits in; there is a sense of kinship between all Zapotec and the relationship is pointed out in the term for brother. It is this sense of affinity of some kind which goes from the northwest Zapotec to the Isthmus.

Wagley: What is the ethnic unit of which this is a study of the breakdown? In Guatemala, Dr. Tax has pointed out the strength of the municipio. Was the municipio selected by the Spaniards to divide up the Indians or did they divide up the Indians with the result that the municipio became the ethnic unit? If we have in the Zapotec a sense of unity among people, this is quite different from Guatemala, where there is no unity among people who speak Mam, for example.

Paul: Are there different Zapotec dialects?

De la Fuente: Yes.

Guiteras: In Chiapas the municipio is the ethnic group.

Beals: In cases where you get an "upper" barrio and a "lower" barrio, the barrios don't belong to the people, but belong to one of the saints.

Kirchhoff: Do you have Indian settlements where one barrio has one occupation and another barrio has another occupation?

Guiteras: Not in completely Indian communities. In Indian communities you get specialization by rancherías or by the municipios.

chapt[illegible]

THE SUPERNATURAL WORLD AND CURING[1]

by Charles Wisdom

PRESENT-DAY Middle American supernaturalism is an end product of the combination of Spanish Roman Catholicism (especially that of the 16th, 17th, and 18th centuries) and the indigenous religion and magic of the ancient Maya and Mexicans. This latter has persisted in varying degree in different localities. In some areas (Mexico especially) it is accepted today as mere *creencias,* beliefs which one may hold or not, with the Catholic element having become the essential core of supernatural belief and practice. In other areas (Yucatan, E. Guatemala) the native supernaturalism is still considered important and necessary. Here the native deities retain their ancient role as the controllers, owners, and embodiments of all the universe useful to the Indians (soil, plants and animals, natural phenomena), and are requested in an annual cycle of ceremonies to give a portion of their goods for human consumption, as well as to bring about favorable conditions (richness of soil, rain, good harvest, absence of strong or evil winds, etc.). The saints in these same areas, and especially the patrons (who have no native counterparts), are perhaps no less important in the total religious life, but simply perform at a different level.

Generally, however, the early Catholic and native ideologies have become interwoven so that what we have is not a mere combining of two elements, a grafting of one upon another, but rather what might be called a complete fusion to the extent that the Indians themselves are unaware that any such historical process has taken place. An important point to make is that this has resulted in a new and distinct supernatural system, neither Maya, Mexican, nor Catholic, all the aspects of which are closely integrated to one another and to the remainder of the cultures of which they are a part. The system must, then, be studied among each Indian group as a functioning whole rather than as a combination of independent and disparate parts.

The *sacra* include a large number of supernatural beings, as well as sacred objects, places, and concepts. The supernaturals are loosely classified into six categories:[2] (1) God and Christ; (2) native supernaturals playing a double role of active deities (with saintly counterparts) and essence spirits, all associated with agriculture and its attendant earth and sky phenomena, as well as with celestial bodies and phenomena connected with them; (3) native patron supernaturals, also in the same double role and with saintly counterparts, who serve as guardians and protectors of specific localities, topographical features, plant and animal life, etc.; (4) active spirits associated with individuals, which include spirits of the dead and the half-spirit animal protectors called *naguals;* (5) apparitions; and (6) community and familial patron saints. Some of these fall into more than a single category.

God, usually a Christian name, is generally considered the chief of the hierarchy. Christ is somewhat identified with God; there is no clear distinction between the two, no doubt because of a lack of precise knowledge of the New Testament.[3] God (or Christ) is only vaguely thought of; he is all-powerful and pre-eminent, but is too distant and too little known to influence man's affairs directly. Prayers are often directed to him, in which he is asked to influence lesser deities to intervene in man's behalf.

The second group, the most important of the native deities, are usually said to be subservient to God, and to be his "ministers," or "helpers" in producing earth and sky phenomena.[4] They are generally of snake form, are thought to have some relation to real snakes, and are associated always with water, as that in rain, streams, lakes, springs, etc. They reside in both the earth and sky, and their activities account for rainfall, rainbows, lightning flashes, the striking of lightning, and thunder. The earth group, who usually live in lakes, large streams, and hills, account for hurricanes, the swelling of streams (as at the beginning of the rainy season), floods, and earthquakes. They are associated with ancient stone and clay artifacts, especially axes. They are located in the four world directions, the one at the North usually being pre-eminent. In their active role they directly cause the phenomena of earth and sky, and in their passive role they are the mere spirits, essences, or embodiments of nature. Most have saintly counterparts.

The native deities which represent and control celestial bodies are also associated with rain, crops, etc. The earth is looked upon theistically, and is generally personified, being approached ritually as the giver of life, good crops, and plenty. This deity is in some cases the patron of maize and milpas. The sun is also personified as a male deity, thought of as the giver of life (Mexico) or as the source of all esoteric knowledge (East Guatemala).[5] The moon is personified, being associated with childbirth, agriculture, and fruition in general. This is a female deity, called *la virgen,* and is generally thought of as the companion, or consort of the sun.[6] Both sun and moon are associated with eclipses, which are generally considered dangerous for pregnant women, young crops, and anything else in process of growth.

The third group, the native patron supernaturals, are active deities in their role as guardians and conservers of the segments of nature with which they are associated, and are passive essence spirits, or embodiments, of those same segments. In the passive role they also account for growth and increase. A few, in the active role, also appear as malevolent apparitions, no doubt for the purpose of preventing man from entering their precincts and from taking what belongs to them only. Examples of this third group are the patron protectors of deer, wild animals, fish, mountains and their produce, forests and their produce, precipices, dark and secluded areas in the forests, milpas and maize, cattle and other domestic animals, remedial plants, etc. Generally, they have both Spanish and native names, being paired off with various saints.

Spirits of the dead, of the fourth group, are sometimes malevolent, bedeviling and pursuing the living.[7] They are honored immediately after death, usually on the anniversary, and sometimes for several years thereafter. On the Day of the Dead they are annually given food to eat, and their graves decorated. They are further propitiated by the avoidance of personal names, especially of the recently dead and of one's enemies, and by the use of the affectionate terms *compadre* and *comadre* when referring to them.[8] This concern is motivated by the desire to both honor the dead and to express continuing affection for them, but also to mollify them and to persuade them to quit the area of the living. The nagual, an individual animal, half real and half spirit, which attaches itself to a person at birth and protects him throughout life, is only imperfectly understood by the Indians today.[9] Its identity is discovered by its footprints in ashes laid out for that purpose, or this may be done by divining. Upon injury to or the death of one's nagual, one suffers a like fate. Nagualism has by now got confused with the animal transformation of sorcerers and witches.[10] It is relatively unimportant anywhere, and seems to be confined to Mexico and the Guatemala highlands.

The apparitions, comprising the fifth group of supernaturals, are without exception malevolent.[11] They are mainly night-walking, and encountered by single individuals in lonely places. One now called the devil (but who may have had native counterparts) is associated with, or disguised in whirlwinds, and travels about giving sickness. In some areas he is the chief of all the apparitions, being responsible for all evil, black magic, and the arm of maledictions. He is especially characterized by a hairy black hand, very ugly, the sight of which may cause insanity. Other apparitions (*Siguanaba* and *Sisimite* in Guatemala, *Matlasiwa* in Mexico, *Xtabay* in Yucatan) are extremely ugly in appearance, and serve as nursery bogies as well as enforcers of the moral code. To achieve the latter they appear before single travellers, especially wrongdoers, on lonely trails at night, and in the guise of a sweetheart. They attempt to embrace the victim, then assume their true appearance, and the fear thus caused results in insanity. Most of the apparitions are said to carry off children to eat, and to capture lone adults. Insanity is often explained as the result of encounter with an apparition. As previously stated, some of the patron deities (of the third group) play a secondary role as apparitions, sometimes capriciously, at other times to frighten away people who come to take from that part of nature which the apparitions themselves own and control.

General is the belief in a number of dwarf apparitions (as *Duende* and Big Hat), probably of Spanish origin and varying in characteristics. Some are always on horseback, and others are dressed in green and with long hair (probably associated with vegetation). One wears an enormous hat. They make Faust-like pacts with people who wish to increase in wealth, and attempt to persuade young married women to go off and live with them as concubines. They are visible only to the woman approached. Also general is belief in doglike apparitions called *cadejos*.

The sixth group, the patron saints *(los patrones, los santos)*, are without doubt the most highly regarded and the least dispensable of all the supernaturals. They have steadily gained in competition with the native deities, who have lost in importance and prestige as the Indians themselves have come more and more into contact with non-Indian culture. It is probably safe to predict that the patron saints will eventually take over entirely.[12] As previously stated, there are saintly counterparts for nearly all the native deities, which are either mere additions to the native religions (existing only in name) or represent the beneficial aspect of the deities with whom they are paired. The patron saints, however, have real existence, being carved in wood and suitably dressed, although for lesser saints a mere picture may suffice. They serve as community patrons for families. Saint worship is general throughout the area, and seems to be the most important aspect of the religion of any group. In fact, Middle Americans might almost be characterized as saint worshippers.

Each patron saint, whether communal or personal, has a character, name, and special reputation of its own, as distinct from all other saints.[13] Those of the same name are related, usually as brothers, but in some cases are considered different aspects of the same saint. The patron's beneficence extends over a particular locale or community of people, and it is asked for help in times of special danger and hardship. Each church contains the effigies of a number of saints, the most important being always the patron of that community. The others have differing degrees of power, i.e., ability to help man, and reputations for power may be built up and lost over a period of years. Some are said to have a mysterious origin, in the distant past, and this accounts for their greater power. Some are more "miraculous" than others, having performed well in the past. The family patron effigy is housed in a small temple near the other houses, and sometimes in a sleeping house.[14] He may be kept in a box or case, stood up on a square altar. Along with the effigy are candles and other paraphernalia.

The most important of the ceremonies to the native deities are performed at fairly regular times throughout the year, thus comprising an annual ceremonial cycle, and are especially concerned with milpa agriculture and favorable natural phenomena.[15] They are performed when clearing the milpas in February and March, for the first rains in May, for planting, for rain during the growing season, for harvest, and for protection of stored maize and other produce. Other ceremonies, usually not calendric, are given to propitiate the wind gods, to "pay" the deer god for animals taken, and to propitiate malevolent deities of the forest, streams, hills, etc. Elements in these ceremonies are prayer, sacrifice (either as a payment or as a return of part of what one has taken), incensing, candle-burning, avoidance of sexual intercourse (but in some cases the engaging in intercourse in a prescribed manner for its effect on plant growth), the avoidance of certain foods (but in some cases, fasting on one or two special foods only, especially maize), and use of intoxicating liquors.

Community patron saint worship includes the "great festival" (celebrated by the entire community once each year on the saint's day), parading of the effigy through the streets both on its day and at times of community concern and misfortune, burning of candles and incense before the effigy by individual petitioners, and praying. Candles are burned before other effigies in the church, as well. Family patrons are likewise celebrated on their days, and at times of family sickness and misfortune. Generally the patron saints are included in many of the agricultural and other ceremonies directed to the native deities, on the theory that the more supernatural aid the better.[16]

Several specific notions regarding the supernaturals and the supernatural practices may be mentioned. Characteristic in varying degree of the supernaturals are: (1) neutrality toward man; (2) duality, which is moral, sexual, personal, and local; and (3) multiplicity. Apparently all the native deities are morally unconcerned with man, there being a few who have no contacts with him whatsoever, but those on whom he depends in his struggle with nature are willing to cooperate with him in return for the proper performance of ceremonial duty on his part. Failing this, they may become malevolent. The patron and other saints may become malevolent also, if not properly worshipped, but they are not considered in any sense neutral.[17]

The general concept of duality is especially strong. Many of the native deities are looked upon as morally dual, in the sense that they are both beneficial and harmful to man. Although they have no actual concern for him, they may, at different times and in different guises, work to his good or detriment. Thus, in one aspect the rain gods produce beneficial rain, but in another the same gods cause floods, death and destruction by lightning, and so on. Sexual duality is an ancient concept, extended now even to the saints. A given supernatural may be sexually dual, appearing or performing now as a male, again as a female, depending upon its relation to nature and upon the presumed character of the natural phenomena with which it is associated. An extension of this is the consort relationship, in which a supernatural of one sex is allied in a sort of marriage relation with one of the opposite sex. This is usually an expression or symbol of a close relationship, real or supposed, in nature itself. Another extension of sexual duality, especially in the case of apparitions, is shown in the cross-sexual relation between supernatural and man, in which the male aspect is concerned with living women, and the female aspect, with living men.

The concept of dual personality is illustrated by the duality of deity and essence spirit (or apparition) and the duality of deity and saint. The deity aspect of a supernatural is always active, while its spirit aspect (the mere embodiment or life principle of a part of nature) is passive. The apparition aspect is, of course, active, and in every case malevolent. Most of the supernaturals are paired with saints. In some cases these saint aspects merely provide another name for a native deity, while in others the saint aspect is beneficial and the deity aspect, harmful. Local dualism is illustrated in the bi-locality of many of the supernaturals in both earth and sky, especially in the case of those ancient deities responsible for earth and sky phenomena. Here again is an expression of a close relationship in nature.

Multiplicity is evident in the belief that a native deity singly inhabits a specific locality or part of nature, and may even be seen individually, but that the same deity is innumerable, and everywhere at once. Wherever that aspect of nature with which he is associated is to be found, there he may be found also.

The role of the native supernaturals as controllers and embodiments of all natural phenomena is explained by their resemblance, in varying degree, to the phenomena they represent, as well as by the fact that they are always present in such phenomena. They are still the principal controllers of natural phenomena (especially in Yucatan and Eastern Guatemala), since prayers are addressed to them to exercise their control. But, as previously stated, they are distant from man, and are totally uninterested in his welfare. They can exist without him. They are universal, and therefore only partially individualized, although they probably were more individualized in the past before saint worship had achieved its present importance, and they are more or less lacking in human character. In contrast, the community and family patron saints have now come to control natural phenomena to some extent, but only at odd times of the year and outside the annual ceremonial cycle, as when drought and other misfortunes are prolonged.[18] In such cases the saint, who loves his people and is near to them, can be directly and intimately approached, as man to man, and asked for aid. This man-to-man relationship is very real, since the saint is essentially human, lives with the people whom he serves as patron, and may even be carried around to see for himself the calamities he is asked to avert. The patron saint, unlike the native deities, has no significance, therefore, except in his relation to man.

The notion that the native supernaturals own the world and the produce and phenomena in it seems general. They are thus really being paid, in ceremonies, sacrifice, and first-fruits, for what man is about to take or has already taken from them, as well as for producing favorable conditions. This no doubt accounts for the commercial tone so evident in native ceremonies (the reference to and naming of ceremonies as "payments" to this or that deity, the use of ritual money as sacrifice, the contractual nature of ceremonies, etc.). The patron saint "owns" nothing and embodies no natural phenomena. He merely helps man, out of compassion and because he has power to work miracles. This power is felt to be derived from God, but is also inherent, especially if he has to his credit a series of miracles, and if his effigy is old and of mysterious origin.

The sacred objects include: (1) crosses; (2) such paraphernalia as musical instruments, masks, crowns, candles, incensarios, etc.; and (3) certain plants and animals. The Christian cross, the most important of the sacred objects, is closely associated with the patron saints. Each cross has some uniqueness from all others; in some areas they are individually named, and even dealt with as deities (Jacaltenango, Chan Kom). In most cases they are made only from the wood of a certain tree. The principal cross of a community (village or *municipio*) is the tall one in front of the church, while lesser crosses are set up on some of the roads (usually four) at the points where the latter enter the pueblos, along the important roads as wayside crosses, along the trails at dangerous spots, and in the family courtyards and temples. The cross is a powerful and universal symbol, being both protective and curative, and so figures prominently in religion, curing, and magic. All the crosses are celebrated annually on May third *(día de la Cruz)*, when they are adorned with a variety of plants, milpa produce, and flowers.[19] Family and community crosses are also adorned at other times during the year, as with maize and stalks in July when the first crop comes in, during the harvest, and at times of sickness and misfortune.

Musical instruments used in ceremonies probably have little sacred value in the area as a whole, but there is a general feeling that most of them must not be used for purely secular purposes, and that they have a close relation to the saints and saint worship.[20] The *tun* drum of Guatemala is the best example, since it is used only ceremonially, and since each has a unique origin and history. Ceremonial masks and crowns are also somewhat sacred, especially the former, which, like the tun drums, have unique histories and are said not to be replaceable. Candles are indispensable in saint worship, as well as in certain magical practices. Black candles, or tapers, are especially sacred, being generally used in the more native ceremonies, while white ones are considered fitting for saint worship.[21] Very general is the belief that candles partially burned before saints acquire some power or additional sacredness, and may be used medicinally. Censers seem also to be irreplaceable, or at best can acquire sacredness only after very long use in ceremonies and on altars. To this list may be added intoxicating liquors, which are generally considered indispensable in performing ceremonies and curing.

The sacred food plants, especially maize, cocoa, and pumpkin seeds, are used as sacrifices to deities (as a food for them to eat or as a "payment" to them), as special foods to be eaten at ceremonies and festivals, and as foods for persons in a "delicate" state (as women in menopause and during childbirth, persons with magical sickness, etc.).[22] Of the sacred nonfood plants, *copal* is the most important, being used in a ceremonial sacrifice, to remove ritual uncleanliness, etc. Pine needles are especially used for altar and cross adornment and for covering the ground around sacred objects. There is much use of flowers for ritual adornment. Certain trees have ritual value (*ceiba* in Yucatan, *palo jiote* in Eastern Guatemala) as protective symbols, for the making of living crosses, etc. Tobacco has some ritual quality, as in curing and divining.

The animals having supernatural value or association include turkeys and their eggs (also chickens in some cases), deer, snakes, frogs, owls, and vulture. Turkey flesh and blood is used as a sacrifice, and *tamales* of turkey and chicken meat are especially eaten on festal occasions. All deer belong to a deer patron god, who must be "paid" for the animals hunted. The snake has great symbolic value, being closely associated with rain, rain-making deities, and lightning. Frogs are also associated with water and rain, and owls and vultures are associated with death and sorcery.

The sacred places consist of topographical features inhabited by supernatural beings, as well as places where ritual objects are kept and ceremonies performed. The latter include the church, to some extent the pueblo *cofradía,* sites where wayside crosses are set up, and the small family temples in which saint effigies and altars are housed. Topographical features include all hills and mountains, mountain crests, caves, springs, and large bodies of water. Some of these are especially sacred, as known abodes of supernaturals; others are only presumed to be so.[23] In every case sacredness derives from their being inhabited by deities, spirits, and apparitions. Dark and secluded places in forests, as well as dangerous spots along mountain trails, are also abodes of apparitions, and so approached with caution.

The sacred concepts are those pertaining to time, direction, number, form, and color. The days associated with saints and with calendric ceremonies and festivals are considered beneficial to man. Thursday (sometimes Friday also) is generally considered a bad day, the day when one is vulnerable to sorcery and liable to meet apparitions. Very general is the belief that the native sky deities inhabit the four world directions. The East is a good direction. The West is considered bad, being the abode of the souls of the dead, as well as the source of many evil winds. The upward direction is considered good, and the downward, bad. Candles, for example, are burned right side up in praying for good, but upside down when sending curses and sorcery. In some cases the right side of the body is good, and the left, bad. The number three is generally of ritual significance for women, while four is significant for men, possibly by association with the three stones of the fireplace (woman's sphere) and the four corners of the milpa (man's sphere). Eight is important in curing. Nine is generally used, and may be of Catholic origin.[24] Thirteen, an ancient native concept, is important in Yucatan, but seems unimportant elsewhere.

The conventional sacred forms are the zigzag line, the square, and the cross.[25] Zigzag lines are in some cases associated with snakes, and so with lightning and rain. The square seems to be the only sacred plane, being considered the ideal shape for the milpa and the altar, and, by extension, for the universe. The cross is the most sacred of all forms, and plants the parts of which are cross-shaped are considered appropriate for ritual adornment and curing. Of the colors, white is generally associated with death, and is especially used in saint worship. Black is the appropriate color in agricultural ceremonies. Red is considered powerful and protective, as against magical sickness.[26] Yellow in some cases represents value, sustenance, and fruition, while green denotes growth and propagation.

Sickness is generally said to be caused by: (1) frights *(espantos)*, (2) evil air or wind *(viento, aire, aigre)*, (3) contamination by the ritually unclean, and (4) magical seizure by sorcery. Less general are such causes as nocturnal birds which bring death (Yucatan) and the magical use of plants to cause sickness and death (Eastern Guatemala). The causing of harm and sickness by maledictions (a generalized form of sorcery) is general.[27]

Two complexes of ideas relating to bodily condition, aside from sickness itself, may be mentioned. The first is susceptibility to sickness. This is determined by mental and physical condition, the "weak" *(delicado)* being susceptible, while the "strong" *(fuerte)* are comparatively safe. Weakness has four general causes: (1) abnormal bodily condition, as lack of vigor, over-exertion, excessive sweating, body exposure, wounds and blows, any sickness, and conditions of childbirth, pregnancy, menstruation, and menopause; (2) disturbed emotional states, as fear, anger, jealousy, hysteria; (3) lack of full development, as youth and infancy in persons, animals, and plants, old age, and unfinished condition, as an object in process of manufacture; and (4) possession of bland and pleasing qualities, as beauty, tameness, domestication. The opposites of these make for "strength."

The second complex of ideas is that of "hot" and "cold" (especially in Yucatan, but weaker or more generalized elsewhere). Many bodily conditions are described as hot or cold, and many plants, animals, and minerals, as well as foods and remedies made from these, are also hot and cold. A hot condition is treated with a cold remedy, and vice versa. Sickness may result from eating too many cold or hot things. Coldness is generally associated with water, dampness, vegetation, etc.; and hotness with piquancy and similar qualities. In some cases there is observable relation between hot and cold and actual warmth and coldness, but in many others such relation is entirely lacking. Good health and normal relations between man and nature (aside from sickness and other sources of ill-being) depend to a large extent upon maintaining a proper equilibrium between hot and cold with himself and in his contacts with things outside himself.

Frights are caused by: (1) actual fear, usually sudden, of one kind or another, resulting from serious accidents and from encounters and contact with the ritually unclean (described below); (2) hysteria, in varying degree and especially in women, induced by witnessing violence and destruction of any kind; and (3) extreme upset, usually sudden and unexpected, in one's normal condition and equilibrium. Thus, thunder- and electric-storms, near-drowning, slipping on high cliffs, sudden encounters with dangerous animals and apparitions, seeing blood and wounds, witnessing fights with machetes, conflagrations, etc., all cause frights. Some of the causes of weakness, previously mentioned, such as over-exposure to the elements, wounds and body blows, also can cause frights, since these upset one's equilibrium. In such cases there may be fear of resulting illness, as well as sudden bodily upset. The intensity of a fright depends on how delicado or fuerte one is. It may be accidental, as from a body blow, or intentional, i.e., arranged by sorcery. Actual symptoms of fright are generally said to be sleeplessness, paleness, apathy and loss of ambition, loss of appetite, and general weakness.

The cause of fright merge somewhat with those of weakness, the relation of cause and effect being somewhat unclear in the native mind. Thus, a fright renders one weak, and therefore susceptible to other forms of sickness, but a precondition of weakness also renders one more susceptible to fright and other sickness.

Evil wind is related to air or winds in general, but is specifically a harmful vapor which enters the body, especially through the openings and through wounds and open sores, to cause pain and malfunctioning. Animals and plants, as well as persons, are subject to it. Those with frights are especially subject, since the fright causes weakness. An evil wind may lodge in any part of the body, and this is the usual explanation for any pain or ache. Most winds remain fixed in a body part, but some can spread, causing more serious illness. Another form of wind, called windiness *(ventosidad)*, moves about violently. It is restricted to the head, and causes dizziness, insanity, etc. Still another, called *hijillo* (Eastern Guatemala), is described as a dangerous gas, and is said to be exuded from the ritually unclean, especially corpses.

Belief in ritual contamination as a cause of illness is general. Perhaps the most important and universal of its causes is evil eye *(ojo)*. Persons with staring, unusually bright, or hypnotic eyes come to be considered contaminating, causing sickness and other harm merely by looking at another person, animal, or plant, or even at objects. Those in a delicate condition are very susceptible, especially the sick, infants, and young animals. Plants wither and die from it, and objects in process of manufacture (being also delicate) are harmed. In evil eye there are no winds which penetrate the body, but simply sickness (manifested in sores, rash, pains, withering in plants, etc.) resulting from being stared at by the "eye," especially if at close range.

Similar to evil eye is the condition of "strong blood" (possibly related to "hot blood" in Yucatan), which seems to have a like harmful effect, and from coming in too close contact with a person possessed of it. Both evil eye and strong blood are permanent conditions in the agents. There are cures for both sorts of contamination, as well as preventives, such as the color red, the cross, plant remedies, etc. In some cases the agent is asked to bring about the cure, an illustration of the native idea that he who can cause harm can also cure it, and vice versa.

A third cause of contamination is that by persons who are ritually unclean by reason of some abnormal change or condition in the body. An example is women in pregnancy, during menstruation, and at menopause. One who is overtired, hysterical, angry, feebleminded, or insane may contaminate. Corpses, especially if touched, seem to contaminate, apart from their exuding a very harmful wind.

A fourth cause is encounter, especially when alone and on lonely trails at night or in the forest, with an apparition, evil deity or spirit, or spirit of the dead.

There seems to be no sharp distinction between fright, evil winds, and contamination as causes of sickness, since any or all three may operate in a given case. Thus, the person with evil eye is not only contaminating but may cause a fright, from fear of a close encounter with him, and further, he is a kind of "carrier" of evil winds which can "jump" to another person on close contact. Similarly, corpses, menstruating women, apparitions, and the like, are contaminating, and also have evil winds either in them or hovering about them.

Sickness by sorcery includes frights and evil winds magically sent, "filth" *(suciedad)* sent into the body, and pain and illness sent by sympathetic magic. Allied with this are maledictions sent by nonsorcerers upon their enemies by continuous wishing of harm, and by burning candles upside down at the church door. General statements concerning sorcery are difficult to make, as too little is known of it. The maltreating and burying of an image of the victim occurs in some areas. This is probably of Spanish origin, although other examples of similar sympathetic magic, of probably native origin, are reported. For example, the burning of the victim's seed cobs to cause crop failure, maltreating of the umbilical cord to harm a newborn infant, and burying of wax and candles, etc. Such magic is avoided by burying or hiding objects which might be thus used.

Appearing before the victim in the guise of a harmless animal, usually a domestic one, so as to get close and unsuspected and for the purpose of "throwing" the sickness, is general. Sorcerers are said to also transform themselves into owls or vultures for this purpose, for which reason the owl especially is a symbol of sickness and death. The use of mustard seed to catch and kill such an owl appears in both Guatemala and Mexico. Sorcerers also send sickness by insect messengers, either by their own control over these insects (Yucatan) or by praying to a maleficent deity that they be sent upon the victim (Guatemala). Belief in the sending of slimy and revolting substances, and even animals such as frogs, into the victim's body is general.

Curing is the responsibility of such professionals as diviners, curers *(curanderos)*, herbalists, massagers and "surgeons," and midwives. The diviners and curers, in some cases the same individuals, make great use of ceremony and magic, and usually receive their knowledge and power from a patron deity. Being involved with the esoteric and supernatural, they are often suspected of sorcery, as well. There is often no clear distinction between the curers and herbalists, though in some cases there is, the former using magic and prayer, and the latter merely administering remedies. Many of the midwives are also herbalists. Massaging and surgery, together with bone-setting, are often performed by the same individual, as well.

The diviners diagnose ailments, determine if they are magical or natural in cause, point out sorcerers, locate lost objects, and look into the future. They examine the contents of eggs, feel the pulse,[28] look into "crystals" (bits of glass), toss grains of maize into the air, etc. The curers treat for frights, evil winds, "filth" in the body, maledictions, and ritual uncleanliness. Both they and the diviners work in semidarkness.

Curing technics include: (1) "seizing," in which live turkeys, frogs, eggs, etc., are passed over the patient's body, thus taking the sickness into themselves; (2) "pulling," in which the curer imitates a pulling motion over the patient until he has pulled the "filth," evil wind, or other cause of sickness out through an opening or extremity; (3) spitting, in which the curer chews tobacco, rue, and other plants and sprays his saliva over the patient's body; (4) incensing, in which the patient is stood over burning wax, made often of copal, and fumigated; (5) magical injection of sustenance into weak patients by poultices of eggs, maize, limes, etc., generally attached to the wrists, ankles, and neck; (6) exhortation and prayer, in which the sickness is ordered to leave the patient and to come into its "home" or "house" (the curative agent), and in which the patron of medicine (San Antonio), as well as other saints, is asked to drive the sickness out; and (7) the use of objects and shapes having ritual potency (the cross, charms, candles which are burned, candle stubs from altars, plants and plant parts having resemblance to the body part affected, etc.). There may be also mentioned sucking, bleeding, and cupping, but these are not general. Several of these technics may be used simultaneously, or following one another in the same cure. The curers very generally manufacture charms and heartbalms, using certain flies, tobacco, tiny birds, and certain plants. These are sold for individual use. They also advise concerning little acts of magic which work as charms and heartbalms.

The massagers rub the patient's body, towards openings and extremities, to remove winds, filth, etc. Pinching of the flesh, as a means of "breaking loose" the sickness, is employed along with massage. They sometimes use exhortation, as well, though not prayer. As surgeons they may specialize in binding and resetting broken bones, but also treat wounds and staunch bleeding.

Remedies are mainly of plants, and are prepared by being beaten in small gourds or pestles, ground on the metate, toasted, baked, or dried in the sun, or reduced to ashes. These are made into hot and cold teas and lotions (which are drunk and applied locally), used externally in powder or ash form, or made into pastes to be applied locally as poultices. Animal remedies are less important, since the peoples, themselves are much more familiar with and dependent upon the plant world. Several such remedies are general: baked and powdered rattlesnake flesh to cure venereal disease, the rubbing of a live frog (a "cold" animal) over the affected part to reduce the swelling and inflammation.

DISCUSSION

(1)

Beals: This paper by Wisdom on the supernatural world and curing in Middle America, or Mesoamerica gives quite a particularized summary of certain aspects of ceremonialism and curing. In the discussion of detail, the question is raised of the degree to which he describes the area which he knows best, Eastern Guatemala and Yucatan, as compared with more northern parts of Middle America. I have the personal impression that it applies best to Eastern Guatemala, and less to Western Guatemala and Chiapas, the Yaqui in northern Mexico and the plateau peoples of central Mexico, in that order. It's possible that there are suggestions of such areas in the generalizations. These differences perhaps reflect differences in level of acculturation, and perhaps more than that, they represent differences in aboriginal cultures. These are problems that might occur again in the discussion of detail.

It also occurs to me that if we had a concrete distribution of some of these things it would be more illuminating. One difficulty in establishing such distributions is in evaluating the difference in the function of a trait, or the difference of its significance in a particular culture. How do we evaluate these things in terms of a generalization about Middle America?

It seems to me that what could be most generally accepted in the paper are the comments on the cult of the saints. In what way does this development of the cult of the saints differ from Mestizo Latin America?

De la Fuente: The statements as to the localization of a number of features, as here presented, seem to be correct. On the other hand, this paper poses the problem that we are here more concerned with the Indian population than with the rest of the population; this leaves the picture of Middle America incomplete. It is true that the cult of the saints is a part of the non-Indian culture, but still we have seen only half of the whole picture.

Beals: The suggestion was made that this deals primarily with the Indian groups, and leaves the Mestizo aspect out of consideration.

Tax: In the Midwest Highlands, all the way to Huehuetenango, the cult of the saints is so strong that it overshadows everything else. I think Wisdom's description begins to apply again in Huehuetenango and also in Yucatan. I think it's rather curious that the same traits are there but the emphasis is so different between the Chorti and Chichicastenango, for example.

(2)

Tax: Regarding the statement, "Supernaturals are loosely classified into six categories," do you mean the Indians themselves classify them?

Wisdom: I suppose I do. There is a distinction here; there are six categories but there is an overlapping. The same being can play more than one role. There are about six roles.

Tax: There are also things here that from experience in other parts of Guatemala just don't ring true. I would say that the saints are images; they are supernatural objects, the *sacra,* considered to have power.

I would say that in Midwest Guatemala there is no class one at all, that Christ or God is one of these saints. God is different from one town to another because there is a different saint. On the other hand I think it's clear that there is some interplay of natural phenomena. The sun is at the head of it; the moon is also important, the stars are auxiliary. The classification would be quite different.

Guiteras: But if you want to include the Ladino culture then you'd have to include God and Christ.

Tax: We have to draw the line somewhere.

Beals: If we are going to apply this to the Tarascans, they would have classes: (1) God and Christ; (5) Apparitions; (6) Community and familial patron saints.

Tax: You could set up a classification like this and use the categories as part of a trait list. Number one would not fit into the Midwest Highlands, however, in the sense that you have it there.

Beals: In Central Mexico, I think you would start with number six. Among the Mixe, I think all six categories would be present.

Whetten: The order would be increasingly vague.

Wisdom: The arrangement here is not in order of importance.

Paul: God and Christ are not in the native minds in many of the areas.

Whetten: In many of the churches of Central Mexico, the local saint is important, but the people are seldom interested in God or Christ.

Foster: How about *la Virgen* as a separate category?

Beals: You might consider her a superior saint.

I think the discussion rather indicates that the nature of category number one, God and Christ, varies considerably throughout the area. They are more often present where the native has abandoned his supernaturals —the native supernaturals, in general, are a group that is limited. They don't occur in all areas of Middle America.

(3)

Tax: In Midwest Guatemala Christ (meaning the figure in the church) is God and the sun is God. The thing isn't straight in anybody's mind, but there is this identification.

Beals: They have no idea of the Trinity.

Kelly: Don't they pray directly to minor saints?

Tax: They go to the patron saint of the power they want.

Guiteras: In Chiapas they pray to the saints; they never pray to Christ.

Kelly: We once tried to make a good

impression on an old woman by giving her a crucifix; she didn't even recognize the figure of Christ.

Tax: This is one of our big differences. In Yucatan and among the Chorti, there's a conception of all these gods, whereas in most of the area, it's either the cross or the cult of the saint. I am saying that if there is a notion of Christ, it is just another vague idea.

Paul: Among other things, the religion is a projection of their social and cultural system. To the extent that you have a disciplinarian family you get a disciplinarian system of gods. In one community, when God is seen in the volcano he is a Ladino and since the Ladinos are dominant politically or in a social status, there's a projection.

Tax: The god in the volcano is also associated with the Devil.

Whetten: In Chichicastenango does the local santo act by influencing higher ones, or does he have some direct authority?

Tax: Where people are doing rituals before a minor image I should think that they expect somehow or other that the image is going to get them what they want. Theologians may rationalize, but simple people neither rationalize individually nor do they have a cultural rationalization for it.

(4)

Tax: I would think that this represents the remains of the ancient priestly religion that was characteristic of the Maya.

Guiteras: It could be Catholic also.

Wisdom: How much of this idea would you find in Mexico?

Beals: How many native gods are there in Mexico?

De la Fuente: I would like to know where the idols are going to be fitted into these six categories? I cannot fit these so-called idols into them. We find idols among the Mixe and Zapotec, while in San Pedro la Laguna we find only stones which have a more supernatural meaning.

(5)

Beals: How about the belief that the sun is male and the moon female?

Tax: That's found in Guatemala.

De la Fuente: I would find it difficult to say that the Zapotec consider the sun male and the moon female.

Mason: Is there no stress laid on the Morning Star? It is very important in the mountains of Mexico.

Wisdom: It is in Honduras.

Tax: It's one of the very few stars recognized in Panajachel.

Beals: It's one of the few that they recognize, but no particular significance is attached to it.

(6)

De la Fuente: How about calling the moon by the name of *la Virgen?*

Beals: This is medieval European and goes back into Platonic philosophy.

(7)

Beals: The emphasis on spirits of the dead can vary considerably.

Kelly: Aren't they always malevolent?

Beals: No. Among the Yaqui they are part of the family.

Guiteras: The only fear about them in Chiapas is that they might come for somebody that they love.

(8)

Paul: How general is avoidance of personal names of the dead?

Beals: It's weak in plateau Mexico.

Wisdom: It does occur in the East.

Guiteras: You have it in Chiapas. If you are taking genealogies they won't give you these names.

Villa: They don't like to give you *any* names. I wish to clarify this. The idea is not especially connected with the dead; it is a general idea that they do not want to give any names.

Toor: Don't you think that they are afraid that their names would be used in witchcraft?

Tax: Most of the people of Guatemala have two names; they don't tell you their real name.

(9)

Foster: I don't like naguales included here. It seems to me that you're mixing up two concepts. Two different phenomena are called by the same term, nagual. In some parts of the area, the nagual is the guardian or associated spirit animal which is closely linked with the individual from birth, for example, as in Chiapas. Elsewhere the nagual is a transforming witch, which transforms himself into an animal. This is known in Guatemala as a *characotel*. What we've got here is the associated or guardian spirit linked with the spirit of the dead.

Villa: I would like to make a point about the nagual. Among the present-day Tzeltal Indians, the nagual is not attached at death. In Oaxaca you have something else that seems to be attached to the individual at death. Among the Tzeltal the nagual is acquired when the individual is about fifty years old. That was not the case in the old days, because we have reports from Nuñez de la Vega that the nagual was attached to the individual at death. Then we have documents coming in at the end of the 17th century expressing the same condition that we have at the present day among the Tzeltal: the nagual is used for social control.

Paul: This would modify the last sentence;—that it's unimportant. It is very important if it's used for social control.

Villa: It's very important. This was an old trait.

(10)

Beals: How general is the animal transformation of sorcerers and witches and is there any place where it doesn't occur?

Gillin: This concept as set forth here fades out in proportion to the ladinoization of the group. You don't find anything of this sort among the Ladino Catholics. Where we operated, in San Luis, the Ladinos don't believe in the soul of the dead, except for purgatory.

MacNeish: In Tamaulipas they think the soul comes back.

Paul: I would like to suggest that the attitude toward them is that they are malevolent.

Beals: It's ambivalent.

(11)

Beals: Regarding the fifth group of supernaturals: apparitions, are we in agreement that this is a general type in the area?

Foster: Not just in the area; in the world.

Beals: It's a certain kind of supernatural and I believe in Middle America it's rather general.

Foster: Do water spirits fit into this category?

Beals: In some areas they do.

Foster: Among the Popoluca they appear above water; they may appear in the shape of a beautiful woman who seduces a man.

Tax: You find that in Guatemala and Chiapas.

Guiteras: Not only do you have beautiful women; you may also have a strange animal, or a mixture of the two. These are all also water spirits.

Foster: Have any of you run into the idea of a person turning into a skeleton? We could, perhaps, get a list of rather similar apparitions.

De la Fuente: I find two items here which seem to me to pertain only to Guatemala: this conception of the Devil, and this general belief in apparitions; these are not Mexican.

Beals: I have the impression that the duende is a useful Spanish-American trait.

Kelly: I'm not sure it is introduced. We have deities that control the thunder.

(12)

Beals: If I interpret this material correctly, Wisdom has suggested that the patron saints are types of supernaturals that are gaining in importance. If we say that in certain areas they have gained more than in others, how much then remains in the generalized statements about the cult of the saints?

Whetten: Are we sure it's a process of gaining? Might it not be the reverse? Do you mean that they were not important previously and that now their importance is gaining?

Wisdom: In general they have gained.

Paul: You mean because the others are diminishing in importance?

Wisdom: The saints are taking over more and more functions.

(13)

Beals: How about the statement that each saint differs from all other saints, even those with the same name.

Foster: Is there ever rivalry between the saints of two villages?

Beals: There's no warfare which centers around the competition of saints. I think there is competition of saints but I would have difficulty in producing an example.

Tax: We know of cases of rivalry between towns but I don't think we have a case where the important rivalry between towns is due to the rivalry between the saints.

Paul: In Guatemala they may say "The San Miguel here is kind of weak, but over there he is stronger."

Beals: You also get this migration of the saint from one place to another; the image left one place because it wasn't happy there.

Camara: I would like to know if we have to make a distinction between the patron saint and the patron cross.

Beals: I have the impression that the usual treatment of the cross is as a saint.

Kurath: Is the cross necessarily a Christian concept?

Tax: I don't think anybody has suggested that it is necessarily Catholic.

Beals: The ideology associated with it is Catholic at the present time.

Wisdom: What we call the santo is something different from a saint. There are certain characteristics attached to saints in Middle America that you might not find attached to saints in general.

Beals: I would question that for Latin America. In a particular place you might find particular characteristics attributed to them.

Beals: How far is it true that there's a fair degree of interchangeability between Mestizos and Indians, Mestizos visiting Indian shrines in the Indian community, and vice versa?

Tax: That's a part of my experience.

Guiteras: You have that in Tenejapa.

Gillin: It's my impression that the Indians usually approach the saints as a group, whereas Ladinos usually approach them as individuals.

Beals: Not in my experience; the Indian approaches a particular saint for a particular purpose. He goes to the church and leaves an offering.

Tax: There are two things involved here. Gillin is thinking of the elaborate organization that surrounds the saint.

Gillin: There appears to be more organization among groups with which I've worked.

Beals: The organized group exists but that doesn't interfere with the Indian, as an individual, approaching the saint.

Tax: I don't know what the distribution is but I think that in Mexico, as opposed to Guatemala, you will find many more individual Indians going to saints for their own purposes. I think there's much less of that in Guatemala. It isn't a very common practice.

Guiteras: We find that in Mexico what is being prayed for is for the benefit of the whole community, unless it's for illness in one's family or something like that.

(14)

Kyte: I wonder how general the family patron saint is.

Beals: What is general is the house altar.

Guiteras: When a peddler goes through an area selling saints, the people will buy whatever saint he happens to be selling; then they pray to that particular saint, but that doesn't necessarily mean that he is the family patron saint.

Tax: It differs by areas; in some places there are saints and in others crosses.

Guiteras: Among the Huastec, the hunters of deer would always have a saint that has a little deer with him; they will always try to get that special saint.

(15)

Beals: We agree that there is a limited distribution in Middle America of native deities.

Tax: I think there is a real areal difference and I'd like to get some notion of where it exists. In the Midwest Highlands of Guatemala there is nothing in the way of having a real agricultural ceremony, compared to that of Yucatan, the Chorti and Chiapas. Western Guatemala is an island surrounded by peoples who have communal ceremonies connected with rain and agriculture. You can say that what is an island in the Maya area is common through the rest of Mexico.

Beals: I would agree with that.

Paul: To the extent that Western Guatemala differs from the Cuchumatanes; a complementary distribution is the development of the cofradía. In the Midwest Highlands you have a well developed cofradía system and exclusion of the milpa deities. Mayordomía is important.

Tax: We have a peculiar distribution. The Maya area is an exception.

Paul: If you divide the Maya area into two parts it works better.

Tax: That's right.

Mason: You certainly had communal agricultural ceremonies in pre-Columbian days.

Kurath: May I ask whether there is dancing in these cycles? I think we would all agree that the well organized dancing in this area is in connection with the cofradía system or at least with the Catholic calendrical ceremonies. What kind of dancing is there?

Tax: Both sacred and secular.

Villa: In Quintana Roo there is a sacred dance around an altar; it is a special dance for all agricultural ceremonies and for the patron saint also. It is not exclusively agricultural. In Yucatan there is also a dance exclusively for agricultural ceremonies. These are all old dances.

(16)

Beals: One point that isn't handled in this treatment of the saints is the pattern of making a pilgrimage to a shrine.

Tax: What is the distribution of that? It isn't common in Guatemala.

Camara: It is in the Ladino communities.

Beals: You can also have pre-Columbian patterns of pilgrimages. You get this in Michoacán.

De la Fuente: Weitlaner is tracing the pilgrimage route to the coast.

Toor: In Guatemala, don't they go to Esquipulas?

Tax: Not very often.

Guiteras: We find the practice of visiting neighboring towns on the days of their fiestas.

Kyte: Do you consider the *promesa* as a pilgrimage?

Beals: I had that in mind as a part of the pilgrimage. One makes a vow.

Tax: The promesa is found everywhere.

Gillin: In San Luis there is a commission of men sent every spring to get holy water for planting.

Kyte: Is this parading of the saint through the street very common?

Toor: It's not permitted in Mexico.

Gillin: In Eastern Guatemala they parade them.

(17)

Beals: Concerning some of the specific notions regarding the supernaturals. The first of these is the question of the neutrality of the deity toward man; to some extent this applies both to the native and the patron saint context. The contrast is that the native deity is neutral toward man whereas the patron saint is not. This may be true for Guatemala but is there any case where the saints who are universal in the area are neutral?

Paul: I think you could reverse it.

Tax: Do you have to keep propitiating saints so they don't do you any harm?

Paul: If you don't do the *costumbres* you may get sick. The other supernaturals, like the spirits of the dead, are moral. They'll come down to punish you if you quarrel in the family or sell your property. I would say that the supernaturals who are not saints are the guardians of morality; they're not neutral at all.

(18)

Beals: The point is made that community and family patron saints have come to control natural phenomena to some extent. Is this a general observation, that you may get control of natural phenomena through the patron saint?

Tax: I think we agreed before that it was a general thing.

(19)

Beals: What days in the Catholic calendar are most important?

De la Fuente: Carnaval is not important in Oaxaca.

Foster: The day of the patron saint is not important in Tzintzuntzan.

De la Fuente: How about *candelaria?*

Foster: It is mildly important in Tzintzuntzan.

Tax: I would like to suggest that the one universal fiesta, *semana santa,* ought to vary the most. On the patron saint's days they go and visit each other's fiestas; on Good Friday all are at home, and diffusion doesn't have a chance.

Beals: In the Yaqui area semana santa lasts about six weeks. In this case you have a representation of a European mystery play; it isn't literary, but was taught by the missionaries. The form became more or less fixed.

General agreement that: semana santa is general except for the Totonac; Christmas is not important; *Día de los Reyes* is more important; the Day of the Patron Saint varies in importance; carnaval is important in Chiapas.

(20)

De la Fuente: Regarding the statement that musical instruments used in ceremonies probably have little sacred value: I note that there is a general feeling that certain kinds of music must not be used for secular purposes. The chirimía and drum are used in secular performances.

Tax: In Chiapas they are sacred.

Camara: The rattle is sacred and is considered an important object.

Gillin: At San Luis Jilotepeque the chirimía and tun are used only in sacred affairs.

Watkins: Is the marimba secular?

Tax: But it's used on sacred occasions.

Paul: It's both sacred and secular.

Gillin: They never play it in church.

Paul: They play it in religious processions.

(21)

Kelly: Are black candles made of the wax of a native bee?

Paul: The black candle is a part of European black magic.

Beals: I think from a number of areas you have the black candle associated with black magic.

Tax: There are differences also in types of incense used.

Mason: Do you have any prayer sticks or any metal objects?

Tax: Metal objects are used by shamans.

(22)

Kelly: Corn is placed on the altar, but that does not seem to me to indicate that maize itself is sacred.

Tax: What do the Totonacs drink?

Kelly: Quite a variety of fermented drinks. *Rafina* is one, which is just straight alcohol. There is no ritual drink.

Foster: The only time the Popoluca drink cacao is the night before they bury a person; the soul of the deceased can pass only if the survivors have drunk it.

Villa: The same thing is found in Quintana Roo.

Gillin: Is the use of *chilata* as a ceremonial drink general?

Tax: It's made of corn; corn gruels are found all through the area.

Kelly: The tamale is pretty well confined to ritual occasions.

Tax: Is there any place in the area where corn foods or drinks aren't sacred?

Gillin: Is there any place where beans are sacred?

Paul: They are used in divining.

Tax: It's also one of the ceremonial foods.

Gillin: What I'm thinking of are foods that are prepared in a certain way.

Wisdom: . . . and must be eaten on a special occasion.

Beals: In Cheran there is a special kind of tamale that is used.

(23)

Beals: Does Cancuc perhaps afford an exception to the statement about cemeteries and sacred places?

Guiteras: In Cancuc, people are buried in the lineage grounds.

Tax: In Chichicastenango they bring the body to the town cemetery.

(24)

Villa: The number nine is generally used. Among the Maya we have two groups that were always fighting—the nine gods and the thirteen gods. This is pre-Hispanic and now is very important in the ceremonies of the Maya of Yucatan.

Foster: But that doesn't exclude the possibility that this was reinforced by Catholicism.

Villa: I mean only that it was not necessarily of Catholic origin.

Kelly: Seven is very strong in the Totonac area.

Foster: Also among the Popoluca.

Tax: Are there any numbers that are universal in Middle America?

Paul: Three and four: three is a female conception and appears on grinding stones; four is a male conception and stands for the four walls of the house.

Beals: In what other context is the number three important?

Paul: Three months, for the ideal hetzmek for a girl; four months for a boy.

De la Fuente: It seems to me that this paragraph has to be broken up. There are sentences which refer exclusively to certain parts of Guatemala only.

Paul: Do we at least have the statement that there are sacred numbers?

Tax: We also have good and bad days.

Guiteras: In Chiapas you can't even bury the dead on certain days.

(25)

Tax: I haven't encountered the zigzag line as a sacred form.

(26)

Paul: How about red being a strong color?

Kelly: I find that red is associated with death.

(27)

Villa: This is not complete. In the case of Chiapas, unless you comply with the customs or the moral good of the community, you are susceptible to receive, as punishment, some form of disease.

Paul: That's widespread.

Tax: Regarding the notion of sin: the particular form it takes in Chiapas may be unique.

(28)

Tax: This is found in Eastern Guatemala, Chiapas, Oaxaca, Michoacán and Sonora.

chapter 7

RELIGIOUS AND POLITICAL ORGANIZATION*

by Fernando Cámara

Introduction

THE present paper is an attempt to describe, classify, and interpret the structure and function of religious and political organization in a number of Mesoamerican communities with the purpose of discovering common characteristics and significant differences. In the discussion, both Indian and non-Indian communities are considered. I am assuming the existence of three "cultural levels": Pre-Columbian, European, and Contemporaneous. I am also making use of the concept which postulates a constant modification of structure, content, and meaning of religious and political organization from a type which is "primitive," traditional, ancient, rural, or "Folk" toward another type which is contemporaneous, modern, and semi-urban, due to contact with the city.

My working hypothesis is that it is possible to classify and interpret religious and political characteristics in such a way as to estab-

* Translated from the Spanish, and edited, by Betty Starr.

lish two ideal types, to which I am applying the terms *Centripetal Organization* and *Centrifugal Organization*.[1] Pre-Columbian elements are included in the first type, and also elements of European derivation (of the sixteenth to the nineteenth centuries); the second type contains basically these European forms as well as contemporary and modern elements.

A Centripetal Organization has a structure the content and symbolism of which is oriented toward the conservation of an already established socio-cultural order; this order is traditional, homogeneous, collectivistic, well-integrated, and obligatory. In it, theoretically at least, the well-being of the community tends to be placed before that of the individual. A religious and political organization of this type is found in communities where the emotional and utilitarian needs of their members are homogeneous and reciprocal, and where a great majority of the cultural stimuli appear to be determined by tradition and by the community. The community (generally the *municipio*) is considered, theoretically—and practically, by its members—as the social and cultural unit.

A Centrifugal Organization has a structure the content and symbolism of which is not oriented toward the conservation of any traditional order of beliefs and practices; it is changing, heterogeneous, weakly integrated, and voluntary. In it, theoretically, the well-being of the individual, or of a specific group, is placed before that of the community. In communities with this type of organization, the emotional and utilitarian needs of their members are variable; cultural stimuli tend to be selected and modified in terms of benefit to, first, the individual, then his family circle, and third, the pueblo, village, local community, or *cabecera* (the most important social and political unit in the municipio). It is this third level that is considered the social and cultural unit, that can and sometimes must change.

Two problems arise in connection with the above classification. The first concerns the nature of the available material, which varies in quantity and quality according to: (a) the purposes and interests of the authors; (b) the period in which the investigation was made; (c) the amount of time available to the investigator; and (d) the conditions under which the field-work was done. The second concerns the difficulty of distinguishing, in many instances, between an ideal structure or function and that which exists in actual practice. As a consequence, the authors may have given too great emphasis to certain aspects of the culture and may have underestimated others. However, in spite of these difficulties, certain primary tendencies in religious and political organization in Mesoamerica may be noted.

The use of similar terms with different meanings and of dissimilar words with the same meaning presents another problem, particularly in the use of terms such as *indio, nativo, ladino, blanco, mexicano,* etc. A partial solution consists in emphasizing the functional characteristics of ethnic elements, according to their correspondence with one of the two ideal types.

The communities are classified in the table below.

TABLE 1

Location	*Centripetal*		*Centrifugal*	
Mexico	Ayutla	Mitontic*	Chacaltianguis*	Mitla
	Cancuc*	Oxchuc	Chan Kom	Soteapan
	Chamula	Tenejapa*	Cherán	Tehuantepec
	Chenalhó	X-Cacal	Chilchota	Tepoztlán
	Zinacantan*		Dzitás	Tzintzuntzan
			Yalalag	
British Honduras	San Antonio Socotz			
Guatemala	Chichicastenango	San Pedro Carchá	San Luis Jilotepeque	
	Jacaltenango	San Pedro la Laguna		
	Jocotán	Santa Catarina Palopó		
	Nebaj	Santa Eulalia		
	Panajachel			
	San Juan Chamelco			

* Communities where the author has done field work.

In some communities, certain aspects of the politico-religious organization are such that they do not fit into the classification. These variations and exceptions will be indicated.

Characteristics of religious and political organization in Mesoamerica

The communities studied, usually municipios or "districts," form units within larger geographic and political areas: "states" or "departments." X-Cacal and Socotz, organized in tribal form, are exceptions.

The municipios or districts consist of sub-units known by such names as *parajes, congregaciones, aldeas, cantones, calebales, rancherías,* and *ranchos* on the one hand, and on the other, of a *cabecera, villa,* or *pueblo,* the proper name of which is extended to the whole municipio. Among exceptions are San Pedro la Laguna, Tzintzuntzan and Yalalag; each has only a cabecera.

Most of the population is engaged in agriculture, although a tendency toward specialization is becoming noticeable. Significant variations are found in communities with a Centrifugal Organization, where artisans, officials, and employees form an important socio-economic group. Soteapan and Chan Kom are the least specialized. On the other hand, such centripetal communities as Chamula and Chichicastenango are distinguished by a strong nucleus of travelling merchants.

In a municipio with Centripetal Organization, almost all of the people—homogeneous in occupation and culture as they are—constitute a single community; in a municipio with Centrifugal Organization, the people who live in the cabecera tend to form a community by themselves.

Two types of people, culturally speaking, live in the municipios: Indians who live in scattered huts in the parajes; and Mestizos or Ladinos* who live in the cabeceras.[2] However, important variations occur in almost all the municipios according to whether or not Indians live in the cabecera, permanently or temporarily, as well as in the total number of Ladinos living there. Exceptions occur in X-Cacal and Socotz where there are no Mestizos and in Chacaltianguis where there are no Indians.

The Indian inhabitants of each municipio consider themselves related to and identified with it by a series of homogeneous cultural characteristics (type of dress, accent in speech, patron saint, agricultural products, etc.) which differentiate them from the inhabitants of other communities, even from those in neighboring municipios. Variations and exceptions occur in communities with a Centrifugal Organization; "ladinoization" reduces the identification of the cultural group with the municipio, although people still think in terms of local differentiation.

The cabeceras are social centers, principal foci of commercial, religious, and political activities, in which converge paths and roads

* The term Ladino is applied in Chiapas and Central America, Mestizo in some places in Mexico (see p. 94). Although a distinction may be made on the basis of origin of the terms as related to the groups to which they are applied, in this paper they will be used interchangeably.

from parajes, other cabeceras, and urban centers. X-Cacal and Socotz constitute exceptions since neither has a specific center for commercial transactions, although each does have a center for the expression of socio-ceremonial life.

The cabeceras have such subdivisions as *barrios, calpules, secciones,* and *mitades,* which delimit, differentiate, and select the ceremonial activities of the political and religious functionaries, and perhaps contribute as well to the creation of economic and social classes. Important changes may be noticed in the cabeceras of the centrifugal communities where the plan of streets and blocks with names and numbers has been influential in the loss of the feeling of belonging to, or having obligations toward, a certain barrio, section, etc., where socio-economic groups and classes are already important.

The structures of the religious and political organizations are, basically, replicas of old European forms and contemporaneous models, although the number and kind of their officials vary. Nevertheless, in communities with centripetal organization, and in some centrifugal communities, there still may be found political posts and religious offices of a type existing in pre-Hispanic times. In communities with a centripetal organization, the number and kind of officials is greater and more heterogeneous than in those with a centrifugal organization. Cherán, Mitla, and Yalalag are exceptional centrifugal communities each of which has more than forty officials.

Theoretically, the religious and political organizations have as their principal end the maintenance of an already established sociocultural order. However, in communities with centripetal organization, communal cohesion is being rendered more and more difficult by the assimilation of elements of semi-urban life through the presence of Ladinos or Mestizos. In the centrifugal communities, economic competition and the uncertainty of status have already undermined cohesion to such an extent that the members of the political and religious organisms promote change. Forms of control basically of pre-Hispanic character still persist in Cancuc and Oxchuc, where direction of the native group remains in the hands of individuals with powerful capabilities for esoteric practices (witchcraft).

Religious and political organizations provide for the moral and material well-being of the community. In the centripetal communities, the political and religious functions are carried out on the basis of cooperation and mutual aid, in which the whole native community is supposed to participate, directly or indirectly, and emphasis is placed upon moral objectives. Apparently these objectives are becoming difficult to carry out. In the centrifugal communities, the objective consists rather in the material betterment of the cabecera and of some of its inhabitants; cooperation and mutual aid have decreased.

All of the posts in the political organizations and a great majority of the higher offices in the religious organizations are filled by individuals of the male sex. In the centripetal communities, the direction and execution of formal rites and practices are in the hands of men, while some women—generally the officials' wives—are subject to certain restrictions, receive deference, act as assistants in the externalized cult, and prepare various offerings. Extreme variations are found in the religious organizations of Chamelco, Nebaj, and Tenejapa, where there are *mayordomas,* and in X-Cacal, where, in pagan ceremonies, women are excluded, even from performing culinary activities. In the centrifugal communities, and in the Mestizo or Ladino groups of the centripetal communities, where religious organizations are preponderantly Catholic, women act as leaders together with their husbands; even unmarried women and girls may participate formally. Variations are found in Chacaltianguis and Soteapan where the Catholic organizations lack importance, and in Chan Kom, Cherán and Soteapan also, where pagan-Catholic rites are practiced and women are excluded.

In communities with centripetal organization, where the number of Ladinos or Mestizos is small or practically nonexistent in comparison with the total native population, the religious and political organizations are structurally and functionally integrated and constitute *a single body* formed of native elements. In this organization, an hierarchical system is followed; theoretically it is expected that each member of the male population will fill various posts and offices as an obligation (ascribed status) or *servicio* which he has toward the community (municipio, cantón, or tribal group) and through which he identifies himself with it.[3] Only in such small communities as X-Cacal and Socotz do the possibilities of such service actually extend to the whole masculine population; in other communities the possible number of officials greatly exceeds the number of posts and offices. Ladinos or Mestizos may or may not have their own organization.

In the communities with centrifugal organization, where the number of Ladinos and Mestizos is significant in proportion to the total native population, the religious and political organizations are structurally and functionally independent of each other, although on certain occasions they collaborate closely. In the political bodies, the Indians occupy inferior posts, if any, and as for religious offices, they are exclusively non-Indian or Indian.[4] In both organizations, the hierarchical system is becoming less important and the individual who fills a political post or religious office does it voluntarily (achieved status) and without formal compulsion on the part of the local community (cabecera, villa, or pueblo). In these communities, the possible officials surpass the number of available offices. Mitla and Yalalag constitute exceptions since each has *a single religious and political body,* which is hierarchical, and posts and offices are considered as a servicio; in Cherán and Chilchota there is selection and grading for some religious offices.[5]

In none of the communities studied do special families inherit rights to specific posts and offices; in general these are of temporary character and theoretically open to any individual. Nevertheless, for at least the more important posts and offices, such qualities as honesty, judgment, speaking facility, energy, available time, economic solvency, and knowledge of the function to be performed are ideally required.[6]

In the centripetal communities there is a given time interval between the performance of a specific servicio and the one following it; however, the ability to speak Spanish, the knowledge of arithmetic, or the paying out of money permit one to discharge one's duties rapidly and facilitate irregular promotion. Important variations are found in Oxchuc, where the possession of supernatural powers is important; in X-Cacal and Oxchuc the office of *jefe supremo* is held for life; in Socotz the "stewardship of the saint" is also a lifetime office. In communities with specialized musicians and dancers, these act, theoretically, for life.

In communities with centrifugal organization, and in the Mestizo or Ladino groups of the centripetal communities, personal desire and economic solvency are more important than other qualities and thus only a few achieve their objectives. In some of these communities, certain actors in Catholic ceremonies or festivities perform their roles for life; masters or specialists in dances, dramatizations, and organization of ceremonial are losing status, and musicians perform commercially. In Chacaltianguis, Chan Kom, and Soteapan there are variations due to the slight interest in Catholic ceremonies.

In all of the communities, tasks of a material nature have to be carried out for the benefit of the municipio or the cabecera. These temporary occupations, which may or may not be paid for in money, are also considered as a servicio and include vigilance and cleaning of plazas, streets, and public buildings, labor on constructions of communal use such as irrigation works, opening of paths and roads, care of telegraph and telephone lines, etc. Those individuals holding important posts or offices and those of more than 45-50 years of age are exempt from these duties. In both groups of communities, officials of inferior rank, and others purposely selected, are charged with such duties; but they perform these tasks unwillingly since they consider them outside of their obligations, even when pay is received for them. In the centrifugal communities, these works are executed, nearly always, on the basis of a fixed salary paid with funds obtained through contributions and taxes on the population; on occasion the work is gratuitous and is done by those whose income is not subject to tax.

In both groups of organizations, new officers of the political body tend to be chosen by those individuals who are about to terminate, or have terminated, their post. Nominations may be personally brought about, but final decisions are in the hands of a small group with effective power. In communities with centripetal organization, physical, political, and moral force is employed in securing replacements in the superior ranks as well as in the inferior ones. Thus is constituted the *ayuntamiento regional,* which is generally integrated with the constitutional organization of the state or department, and, finally, with the national government. In the nomination or election of men to important posts, Mestizos or Ladinos who may, or may not, be members in the constitutional organization, are often influential. X-Cacal and Socotz are excepted since they have neither constitutional organizations, nor Mestizos or Ladinos. In communities with centrifugal organization, nomination of new officials is the work of local, regional, or state leaders. In these communities there exists only the constitutional body, except for Mitla and Yalalag.

In both the centripetal and centrifugal organizations, individuals ask the suitable authorities to be permitted to hold religious offices. In general, the holding of office involves expenditures of money (sometimes in considerable amounts, taking into account the total income of the individual) and the participation of family members and friends as assistants in ceremonies or tasks inherent in the office. In the centripetal communities, in many cases religious offices for the Indians are compulsory, as are also the political posts. The former are but rarely integrated with state organizations and never with those of national scope.[7] In the centrifugal communities, the offices, although recognized as local, form part of an organization of greater range which may, or may not, include neighboring pueblos. In general, Catholic canons are complied with, and the primary differentiation of religious offices concerns the amount of money expended by the office-holder. Cherán, Chilchota and Tzintzuntzan are unique in having "hospital" functionaries. In Chacaltianguis, Chan Kom, and Soteapan little interest is shown in Catholic offices and ceremonies.

In both types of organization there exists a group of individuals who, on account of having held political posts and religious offices, or through personal attributes such as being economically powerful, or being social figures in the community, are distinguished, respected, and obeyed. Generally they are men of maturity and experience. In communities with centripetal organization (except for X-Cacal), and in some centrifugal communities, this group of natives is known, generally, as the *principales, pasados* or *cabildos;* practically, they constitute a gerontocracy and their status is due to wide knowledge of politico-religious (and at times magical) ritual which they carry out for the benefit of the community. In other centrifugal communities (Chacaltianguis, Chan Kom, Dzitás, and Soteapan), a principal is valued, primarily, because he has achieved economic success, has special attributes of leadership, or is learned.[8] These same characteristics are beginning to be emphasized in the centripetal groups in substitution for knowledge of ritual and magic, and life experience.

In general, factors of age and civil status play an important part in the selection, election, and advancement of an individual in the hierarchy of posts and offices. This tendency is observed more strongly in the centripetal communities, since, in the centrifugal communities, personal interest is more important than traditionally established requirements. Services considered as inferior—police, messengers, bearers, cleaners of the public center, and secondary assistants in ceremonial—are occupied, principally, by youths. Posts and offices of considerable religious or political significance—*regidores, jueces, capitanes* and *mayordomos*—are filled by adults, generally married, who organize and direct administrative tasks of political nature such as the carrying out of religious ceremonies. Finally, functions considered as of greater responsibility (decisions in secular and religious justice and the planning and execution of appropriate ceremonial) are reserved for *alcaldes, jueces, gobernadores* or *jefes,* who almost always constitute a group of mature age and are married. The centrifugal organizations show significant exceptions in this respect.

In all the communities there is a tendency to ascribe social prestige to the official or to the post or office he holds, which increases according to position in the hierarchy.[9] The religious offices, because they are considered to be of sacred character and because the quantity of money necessary to defray the expenses of office is greater, are considered better than the corresponding political posts, although the latter offer greater opportunities for practical authority.[10] Nevertheless, in the centripetal organizations there is a tendency for the individual to evade or refuse offices and posts, claiming poverty, disinterest, incapacity, lack of time, or his rights as a free citizen.[11] Extreme cases are found in Oxchuc where the highest Indian functionaries are completely impoverished, and in Nebaj, where the "new rich" fill the highest posts and offices. In all the communities the political and religious bodies evidence insecurity and inefficiency, and lack of systematic organization, due, perhaps, to the confusion of past and present values and ideals.[12] Irresponsibility with regard to the needs of the community and disobedience of traditional and legal rules are frequent. This inefficiency and lack of organization has probably existed since the sixteenth century, and in the last few decades has become more intensified.

Possibly due to the greater influence of Mestizos or Ladinos in the political organization, or to a greater ladinoization of the community, conflicts which take place in the family group are ceasing to be resolved privately by the complaining parties and family heads.[13] There is now a tendency to take complaints before the authorities in the cabeceras, especially on festive days. This practice is less common for people who live in the parajes, but even these people are beginning to realize that the decisions of family heads are invalid because of others made by the constitutional political bodies. In addition, at many occasions family heads don't show enough interest to settle these disputes. In the centrifugal communities, it is difficult to find cases of family counsels, and justice theoretically rests in local and state organizations. The forms of reverence and etiquette still followed in centripetal communities, in which *aguardiente* is offered during the resolution of a conflict have ceased to have meaning or function in the centrifugal group. Disagreements between family groups are more common in the centripetal communities, while conflicts between persons outside of family groups are more common in the centrifugal communities.

Dependence upon the supernatural appears to be general in both groups of communities, although the following variations are noted: In Ayutla and X-Cacal there are basic differentiations between the Catholic and pagan; in the rest of the centripetal communities, and in Chan Kom, Cherán, Jilotepec, and Soteapan, cult practices are, in the majority, intimate mixtures of Catholic and pagan,[14] while in other centrifugal communities dependence on the supernatural is emphasized primarily in Catholic ceremonies. Magical beliefs and practices (witchcraft), although supposed general for the whole area, are more important in Ayutla, Oxchuc, Chacaltianguis, and Dzitás.

Veneration of a patron saint (Catholic image which is the "patron" of the community) is general in all the communities, as well as veneration directed toward other images of the Catholic pantheon and toward crosses. Significant differences are found, however, according to the relative importance given one or another image, and distinctions which may be made between the patron saint and the supreme God. In the centripetal communities, except for those of northwest Guatemala and X-Cacal, where more prayers are offered to the cross, the cult of the images has pre-eminence over that of the cross. In the majority of these communities, the patron saint appears to be considered as the supreme God; there may be a dichotomy in places where the patron image is a "Virgin" and not a "Santo." It appears that the practice of attributing greater importance to the patron saint results in the loss of the cult of other images. In almost the entire centrifugal group, the patron saint is ceasing to be the central figure, if we except the festivals on his calendric day; other images are very important for certain groups of inhabitants; the veneration of the cross is included in the general context of the cult; the distinction between the patron saint and the supreme God is more generalized.

Special centers for religious ceremonial such as churches, shrines, and other places considered sacred exist in all the communities, in the cabeceras as well as outside of them, although variations may be found according to the functions for which the sacred place is used. In the centripetal group, some ten to twenty images, including that of the patron saint, are kept in the church; there are private shrines, such as the chapels in the calebales of Chamelco and Nebaj, and the villages of X-Cacal; domestic or family altars are not general and lack images; certain caves, springs, crossroads, and other natural or artificial places with an esoteric meaning constitute sites where petitions are rendered and offerings made to the controlling beings of the lightning, rain, winds, sun, etc. In the churches, chapels, and altars the cult activity is more Catholic and less magical, but in other sacred places, on occasion, the contrary results; for the former places greater care and cleanliness is necessary; flowers constitute the most usual decoration. In the centrifugal communities, except for Chan Kom and Soteapan, the church is the principal center of the Catholic cult and the number of images kept there is almost always more than twenty; chapels exist primarily in pueblos where there are barrios, and in them are kept the image of the patron saint or virgin (of the barrio), as well as other images. Family altars are common, with or without images; they may contain offset pictures, prints, candles, and, generally, flowers.[15] Sacred places may exist, but with pagan-Catholic or magical function.

When there is no permanent Catholic priest in the community, the direction and execution of religious ritual is in the hands of specialists (*rezadores, cantores, sacristanes, maestros, capellanes, cabildos,* or *principales*), while administrative tasks are assigned to *topilillos, semaneros, sacristanes, "bishcales," acolitos, campaneros, mayordomos,* etc. In the centripetal group, except for the resident Catholic priest in Chichicastenango, specialists hold office permanently or temporarily, they do not receive pay for their services, and they are experts of Catholic and pagan ritual, offering prayers, rosaries and "masses" for the purpose of ingratiating the supernatural beings (both Catholic and pagan) which control their world. Catholic priests visit these communities two or three times a year, performing masses, baptisms, and, sometimes, a wedding.[16] X-Cacal is an exception since here the pagan and Catholic cults are strictly separated. The Ladino groups may have their own specialists. In the few centrifugal communities where there is a permanent Catholic priest, he is in charge of the orthodox cult; nevertheless, there are rezadores and other assistants named for a specific period, who, in the cabeceras without a priest, acquire permanent office, receive payment in money and hence may be considered as employees. The pagan ritual tends to remain completely outside of this organization.

The persons in charge of Catholic-pagan ceremonial, considered in many places as the "native" group, are principally occupied in supplicating or repelling the effects of natural phenomena for the benefit of the community as well as for the specific family or local groups by which they are called for this purpose. In general, these ceremonies are losing their meaning. Their performers—almost always possessors of supernatural powers, of mystic temperament and experts in magic ritual—are occupied in acts of witchcraft saturated with practices and elements of Catholic ritual. In the native centripetal communities of Midwest Guatemala and Ayutla, acts for the benefit of the whole group are not performed; in the Ixil area and in Northwest Guatemala the observation of the aboriginal calendar *(tzolkin)* is unique; in the rest, except for X-Cacal, those in charge of pagan-Catholic ceremonial and *brujos, zahorines, H-men,* etc. (who come to be such because of dreams and visions), may be the same individuals; the latter may remain outside of the formal religious organization, although exercising control and power over a large part of its members.[17] In the majority of the centrifugal communities, prayers for the presence or absence of certain natural phenomena (especially rain), and similar ceremonies in which good harvests and occupational success are requested, conform, almost entirely, to Catholic ritual; their performers, theoretically, form a part of the formal religious organization. Cherán, Chilchota, Mitla, and Tehuantepec are distinguished by retaining "brotherhoods" or societies which carry out this type of ceremony. Acts of witchcraft are executed by other individuals, who acquire knowledge through instruction and observation, and there are no ceremonies governed by any native calendar.

There is a general tendency for Ladinos and those in the process of ladinoization to ridicule, as a group, the religious ceremonies of the Indians, as well as their magical practices and acts of witchcraft. This may be due to ethical and moral values through which their basically European type of culture is symbolized, and the greater orthodoxy followed in the performance of Catholic ceremonies. On the other hand, although the Indians consider the ceremonies of the Ladinos as different from their own practices, they tend each day to imitate them more. Individually, the Ladino probably carries out religious practices of the Indians and submits to magical acts of native type when these are convenient to his interests, although he usually does so in secret or "by way of experimentation."

All religious ceremonies which take place in the communities studied are basically of utilitarian character although they differ quantitatively according to the emphasis manifested in final ends and in the number of participants responsible. In the centripetal groups, with the exception of Ladino elements, it is theoretically expected that ceremonies performed will benefit the whole community. For certain kinds of acts the performance of a specialist is necessary but the majority of the inhabitants cooperate economically; in a second type, performance of the acts and monetary expense are restricted to groups or individuals. In the first class belong prayers and "masses," in which rain, good harvests, health, and abatement of epidemics or other forms of misfortune are asked for, and such acts have a sufficiently binding character. In the second class are included cult acts and festivities directed toward Catholic symbols. People not economically responsible may participate and enjoy themselves due to the secular character that generally permeates these festivities. In the centrifugal communities and in the Ladino groups of the centripetal communities, religious ceremonies are not necessarily supposed to produce physical and economic benefits for the whole community, but rather for the small group which bears the cost; nevertheless, when economic help is asked for a majority of the inhabitants, such communal benefit is taken for granted. In general, the first group of ceremonies and festivities have a more restrictive character than the second, although in both secularized elements are more numerous than in the centripetal communities.

The existence of individuals responsible for the material care and festivities of Catholic images, including that of the patron saint, is general. Differences may be found with regard to the degree of compulsion as compared with voluntary undertakings, and in the kinds and number of responsible persons. Thus in the Indian communities with centripetal organization, except for Socotz and X-Cacal, the coercive force which is occasionally employed has been noted, although there are also individuals who ask for these offices in order to entertain, or to fulfill this traditional obligation once and for all, or both. The responsible persons are designated as mayordomos, cargueros, and capitanes. Although in Mexican communities the first are charged almost exclusively with the material care of images, vestments, decorations, and processions, and the others supply food and drink during the fiesta, in the Guatemalan communities a unique group known as a cofradía carries out both activities. The number of responsible individuals varies annually from a minimum of from two to five in parts of Guatemala, to near 100 in Nebaj and Chamelco, and a maximum of 350 in Tenejapa. In the group with centrifugal organization (except for Mitla) and among the Ladinos of the centripetal group, the care of, and the fiesta for, the image are generally undertaken voluntarily or in fulfilment of a promise. The responsibilities fall to a single individual (mayordomo or carguero), who is aided by his family and some of his friends. Nevertheless, in worship and festivity significant differences are found in the various communities: in Chacaltianguis and Yalalag prayers and candles are offered but there are no fiestas; in Soteapan they are almost without importance; and in the other communities, material care and fiestas are practiced. Cherán and Chilchota are distinguished by having, in addition, mayordomías independent of the church images and even one for family property.

In the Catholic cult, in both groups of communities, it is believed necessary to respect the images and to pay them attention so as to save one's soul, to be on good terms with them and to ask from them that which may be believed just, or even unjust. Carrying out a fiesta, or taking care of an image, is a personal duty. It is also possible that the individual, or family, desire to change the daily routine of life, to promote social contacts, and to be considered important—given the social prestige which individuals acquire after having held some of these offices—may be influential in the motivation of the individual and his family to carry out such activities.

In the native groups with centripetal organization, men hold several offices before being recognized as important by the community; such a succession of inferior offices and, later, the mayordomías or capitanías implies monetary expense and the employment of considerable time and energy. Generally, the higher offices in the hierarchy are the most costly, and economic ruin, at least temporarily, accompanies the acquired social prestige.[18] However, occasionally, the waste of money seems to stimulate the individual, afterwards, to engage him in another work the earnings from which permit him to cancel debts incurred while in office, and/or to hold another cargo for the securing of higher prestige. Although this concerns Indians primarily, money passes into the hands of Ladinos who are the controllers of aguardiente, which represents the greatest expense in any festivity.

In the centrifugal groups where there are mayordomías, the holding of one office is generally sufficient in order to acquire some social prestige since these offices are assumed voluntarily. In places where there are barrios, there may be a certain amount of coercion since here the individual maintains a more intimate relation with his saint and with his neighbors. The fulfilment of such offices does not lead to economc ruin, but it does, at times, lead to uncertainty regarding social status.

There is a tendency to assign the images to a hierarchy, as well as to make evaluative judgments relative to the greater or lesser importance of their respective fiestas, and, therefore, to the importance of the persons responsible. Nevertheless, the ranking conferred on various images is almost always in conflict and frequently the hierarchical rank of an image is established or even changed in accordance with the success of its fiesta. The latter is appraised by taking into account the number of formal participants, amount of money spent, and possibility for recreation and fulfilment of religious duty, for those directly responsible as well as for other participants. In communities where mayordomos and capitanes form a single group, the wife of an official also acquires office and the accompanying obligations and deference; when mayordomos and capitanes form distinct groups, only the wives of the former are considered as officials (mayordomas). In the groups with centripetal organization, the evaluation of the images has greater homogeneity, being closely related to the hierarchical system still maintained. In the centrifugal communities, with the exception of Mitla, and among the Mestizos or Ladinos of the centripetal communities, the religious office here being a voluntary character, hierarchical stratification of images, of their fiestas, and of those responsible for them, is a matter of importance to only a small number of persons. Exceptions are found in places which have barrios since here conflicts are originated on account of the rank attributed to the various images, and to those responsible for them.

The presence, in all communities, during fiestas, of individuals who are masked, groups of buffoons, actors of pantomime, and musicians is general. In the majority of the native communities with centripetal organization, those responsible for religious fiestas, at least on some occasions, are distinguished by special dress and adornment; in addition, there are groups or individuals who, because of personal motivation, masquerade as Ladinos, women (Indian or Mestiza), soldiers, or animals, while others play at *toros* and *vaqueros*. These maskers may or may not act permanently. When they do, they are relieved from occupying politico-religious office, unless they may decide voluntarily to do so. The musicians play reed flutes, drums, horns, violins, guitars, and, at times, harps in accordance with specific occasions and ceremonies. Their work constitutes an office in the organization and their service to the community; they are distinguished and respected. The competition for professional prestige and economic advancement in the musical bands of Ayutla constitutes an unusual case in the centripetal communities. There are no specialized dancers; on occasion, buffoons and maskers perform rhythmic movements to musical accompaniment.

In the majority of the centrifugal communities, those responsible for religious festivities do not wear special dresses or adornments. Groups of maskers, buffoons, and actors of pantomime may or may not be organized and paid by the mayordomos; at times, this organization requires the services of specialists. In general, their number is much greater than in the centripetal communities. *Negros, europeos, viejos* and *indios* represent the principal groups, even in the secular fiestas. The dances are more general. The bands, in economic competition, are professionals and their songs are of the Mexican and foreign contemporaneous popular type; but the players of the flute and the *teponaxtle,* particularly in communities where barrios function as religious units, still maintain their semi-sacred character.

In all the communities where ceremonies to the images are performed, including that of the patron saint, a triple character may be found in these ceremonies: religious, festive, and commercial. Visits to the church and to the houses of colleagues and authorities, offerings, prayers, processions of images and the interchange of drinks and meals are general; fights, group drunkenness, and extramarital sexual acts constitute the festive climax, but fasts, abstinence, and confession of sins are also practiced. The images are "humanized" and some individuals speak to them, complain and weep before them, and adore them seriously and with passion, while others shout, laugh, drink, and even fight near them. Moments of silence and restriction are followed by the noise and emotional relaxation that the fiesta also demands; the shooting off of rockets, explosion of powder, music, games, shouting and races alternate with prayers, benedictions, temperance, and tranquility.

In the native communities with centripetal organization, the character of the ceremonies appears to be more religious, and festive and commercial aspects take second place. The most common drinks are *atoles, chichas* and *aguardiente,* and food consists of tamales made of corn or beans, soups, and a little meat scarcely seasoned. Prayers are made by specialists who half recite and half sing them with gestures. Offerings consist of candles, pine needles, flowers, incense, food, etc., and acquire a sacred character after having been oriented and blessed according to ritual formulas and appropriate prayers.

In the centrifugal communities, festive and commercial interests are placed before religious interests and thus popular fairs arise; entirely secular forms of amusement predominate, and, in general, people tend to hail their pueblo; occasionally, the great number of foreigners and "tourists" determines the kind of festivity, and aspects of religious character are converted into many other attractions. Aside from intoxicants, there are soft drinks and sodas; food is varied, and seasoned with various spices, according to custom and regional dishes. Orientation of offerings is not practiced. In general, ceremonies performed in the interior of the church, or before domestic altars, are attended by seriousness and temperance.

In all the communities studied, fiestas and ceremonies have a duration of several days which are designated according to the principal action carried on during that period. In general, small, poor communities tend to have a greater number of fiestas than those which are larger and less poor, although there are exceptions. Those directly responsible, participants, and spectators, vary in number according to the significance of the specific image or fiesta. Fiestas for the patron saint are most important; those for other images assume secondary importance. The ceremonies of *carnaval* and *Navidad* are more important in Mexico; Lent is kept regularly; and *semana santa,* in certain places in Mexico, consists of spectacular dramatizations. In the communities with centripetal organization, festivities for the images may represent the integration of the inhabitants with the gods. Rarely, help is sought from the few outcomers from whom might be received economic benefits which may be used in material improvements for the pueblo. In the centrifugal communities, the latter practice increases the status of the pueblo; in addition, of course, there are possible profits for certain authorities. The centripetal groups may carry on a greater number of fiestas and spend more in money and time on religious ceremonies if the total profits of the population are considered. Apparently there are also differences in the centripetal groups according to whether natives live in the cabeceras, whether festivities coincide with important market days—or vice versa—and whether the success of a fiesta is correlated with a special period of the agricultural cycle. The ceremonies of *noche buena* and *año nuevo* are more common among Ladinos, who perform them in the family group or with friends.

Celebrations of a religious character take place, also, in the parajes, congregaciones, or rancherías. They involve much fewer people, although the expenses may be considerable. Nevertheless, the celebration, although less ritualistic, less externalized, and never spectacular, conforms to a great extent to patterns already described. Change of both political and religious office in the centripetal communities, and in Mitla and Cherán, is also a reason for ceremony and religious fiestas; in them participate the members of the constitutional body and the hierarchs of ritual, since their interrelation with the other groups is as much structural as functional. In the centrifugal communities, changes of office may or may not be accompanied by fiestas. Pilgrimages and visits to sanctuaries outside of the municipio acquire importance in the centrifugal communities and in X-Cacal, although in the latter place these practices already seem to be on the decline.

Only small groups in the centrifugal communities appear to be interested in state and national celebrations and patriotic festivities, and an even smaller number understand their significance. In native communities, those individuals who participate in occasions of this sort are generally compelled to do so by political or physical force on the part of Ladino or Mestizo authorities. On the other hand, participation of the population in the centrifugal communities in these celebrations is almost always in terms of personal benefit.

Conclusions

The data that have been presented here may be brought together to form a general picture of the types of religious and political organization which are found in Mesoamerica. There has been no attempt to analyze the provenience or origin of cultural elements and complexes. Such a problem involves the use of other kinds of materials and demands different analytical techniques. In general, the monographs used do not have historical reconstruction as their primary aim. The problem was that of making comparisons (with data from specific communities) which permit the visualization of the totality of Mesoamerican culture, so far as its religious and political organization is concerned, always keeping in mind that the religious and political organization is part of a total social and cultural system.

A number of problems arose due to differences in the time at which the original studies were made. For example, the data on Socotz and Tepoztlan were gathered more than twenty years ago; those of Chan Kom, Dzitás, Mitla, Jacaltenango, Jocotán, Santa Eulalia, and X-Cacal were collected more than fifteen years ago; and the great majority of studies have been made during the past decade. Thus, some of the specific situations described for an earlier time may have ceased to be or may have been considerably modified.

Another difficulty concerns the precise delimitation of the community, taking into consideration the presence of Mestizos or Ladinos in the centripetal communities, as well as the existence of Indians in the centrifugal communities. In isolating "Indians" from "Mestizos," with the aim of making the materials homogeneous for the purpose of classification, the resulting abstraction negates the socio-cultural reality in which Indians and non-Indians share many vital experiences.

A multiplicity of facts may constitute causal factors in bringing about differences or similarities of religious and political organization in Mesoamerica. In this paper, for example, only passing reference has been made to certain economic characteristics which are significant to the full understanding of religious and political organization. Tax mentions, among other factors, ownership and use of land; geographic localization of communities in highland or lowland regions; the distance that separates local communities from large centers (cities) and markets, existing from former times or of contemporaneous development; differences in natural resources, technology, and specialization. (See p. 56.) For example, a large part of the religious and political life of a community may change in accordance with the new importance that a product may acquire in the local, state, national, or world market.

With regard to similarities and differences in structure and function of the religious and political bodies in Mesoamerica, it is possible that Mestizos or Ladinos living in a municipio may be, in many ways, responsible for a change toward patterns already present in modern society. If the politico-religious organization possesses a good number of pre-Hispanic cultural complexes, the distinction between Indians and non-Indians is great, and the fewer Mestizos or Ladinos there are, the greater the native communal participation in religious and political activities. Nevertheless, the size of the community, its ecology and number of inhabitants, their social relations, production, economic contacts, standard of living, and their conception of the world would modify this generalization.

The greater number of cofradías and mayordomías, although appearing in communities which are preponderantly "native" is not always associated with agricultural activities; festivals and cult activities may be carried out in lesser number by certain groups, but undertaken with greater elaboration, pecuniary expense, active and passive participation, etc., and may have more or less significant consequences in the orientation of the community. Smaller and poorer communities have, proportionally, a greater number of fiestas and responsible officials in the political organization as well as in the religious; this generalization may be invalid when the community regularly performs Catholic ceremonies, according to stages of the life cycle such as baptism, communion, marriages, and funerals, or have other pecuniary expense in ritual relations, secular recreation, trips, and non-subsistence consumption.

Taking into consideration the present structure and function of political and religious organizations of the communities studied, it is probable that the pre-Hispanic form may have been a single body, some of whose officials were recruited and others of which selected and appointed, according to their function and their place in the hierarchy, theoretically considering all the members of the community for these positions. Those dedicated to esoteric and magical practices may have been within, or outside of, the organization. This particular situation has not as yet been found anywhere, but the group of communities with centripetal organization is most similar to it.

The process of acculturation in Mesoamerica consisting of "mestizoization" or "ladinoization" has accelerated in the last few years. Where this occurs, it is possible to point out the following changes in religious and political organization: (a) formal and functional separation of the native religious and political bodies; (b) greater acceptance and significance of religious events than of political events; (c) substitution in the political organization of native officials by Ladino or Mestizo officials; (d) pre-eminence of festivities in the cabecera over those of other ecological units; (e) subordination of native religious and political organization to the standards of the Ladinos; (f) tendency toward secularization of the important fiestas (patron saint, carnaval, semana santa, etc.); (g) greater acceptance of secular events and their consideration as a form of recreation and enjoyment independent of religious duty; (h) disintegration of the group religious organization and the beginning of religious events held in the family or among friends; (i) decline of these religious organizations and preponderance of political groups; (j) absorption and control of both on the part of the state and the church.

The typology of change which has been pointed out does not necessarily imply that all communities would change in accordance with such a chronological and evolutionary scheme. Specific conditions, accidental events, and specific orientations in other aspects of the culture would transform our hypothetical levels. Certain communities—Tehuantepec and Tepoztlan, for example—have changed their political structures, but have preserved traditional functions; some (Cherán and Mitla) have modified the function of the religious officials but retain their hierarchies, while others (Dzitás or Soteapan) have changed the structure as well as the functions of their political organization. There are also communities (perhaps Chacaltianguis) which never had a single politico-religious body, in which the cofradías were not of communal character, and where the disintegration of these and the secularization of their religious festivities followed other patterns. Nevertheless, considering as a whole the communities studied, the generalizations made in this paper appear to be valid.[19]

Finally, if the process of acculturation, as it is now observed, continues, centripetal organizations would be transformed into centrifugal organizations, probably giving rise to a series of changes like those which have resulted in the present orders, albeit with new symbols, qualities, and values.

DISCUSSION

(1)

Tax: We ought to get some clarification on the major subdivisions, Centripetal and Centrifugal.

Camara: The terms by themselves don't have much importance but it is the concept that is important. The centripetal community is that in which the political and religious organizations are interrelated and tend to operate as a unit for the benefit of the community. These communities are characteristically more Indian.

I looked at the whole society from the point of view of the politico-religious organization. In the first set, the political and religious bodies form a single body; in the other set, the politico-religious organizations are separate not only in body but in function.

Tumin: You are working with an ideal type continuum of different types of communities.

Camara: No one community would fit either type exactly.

(2)

Beals: I wish to take exception to this statement. It should read . . . such Ladinos as there are *live in the cabecera.*

Tumin: By and large the Ladinos tend to live in the cabecera.

(3)

Tumin: Do you mean the Indian section of the community? Are you excluding the Ladinos?

Camara: The greater part of the population in the centripetal community is Indian. In the other type it is the opposite.

Tumin: I am thinking of San Luis Jilotepeque, where power seems to focus on certain particular Indians—when there is a place for the Indian. San Luis would be centripetal—there is a tendency for the Indians to hold offices.

Camara: But the political and religious organizations do not form a single body. They are completely separate.

Tumin: Effective power is not in the hands of the Indians.

Wisdom: If you consider the whole population of Jocotán, there are two different bodies.

Tax: In one type of community you are talking about the Indian population; in the other type you are talking about the whole population.

Whetten: If the Indians have lost most of their political authority can you call just the Indian section of it centrifugal? You do have to consider that the Ladinos have the political authority in the community.

Paul: Have the Indians lost control? In San Pedro la Laguna the political body is different from the religious body.

Camara: They are separate but they

are interrelated. This is the whole idea: that the politico-religious bodies are interrelated.

Paul: Were there any communities where there were no Ladinos?

Camara: X-Cacal in Quintana Roo is an example of this.

Tax: But in Yucatan they don't have this system.

Paul: X-Cacal is quite a different thing from what you get in places where Ladinos have taken over power.

Tumin: Then we have a difference between an all-Indian community where the politico-religious structures tend to be integrated and a situation like Yucatan. . . .

Camara: In X-Cacal it is a religious and political body at the same time.

Tax: How about Chan Kom?

Camara: I didn't consider Chan Kom Indian.

Tax: The people are all Indians in Chan Kom. You're saying that the political organization is a constitutional organization and therefore not Indian, but that's the question we're raising. Aren't there all-Indian communities in which there are separate organizations?

Camara: Chan Kom is going to a ladinoized pattern. People speak Spanish and are progressive in every sense of the word. They tend more and more to become Ladinos. Since in their politico-religious organization they tend to be separate, I classified it as a Ladino town.

Tumin: The more Indian a community is, the more likely it is that there will be juncture of the two.

Camara: We can't separate the politico-religious organization from other aspects of the culture.

Tumin: Is it generally true that as a community becomes ladinoized there tends to develop a separateness of the religious organization from the political organization?

General assent.

Tumin: This would hold true even in mixed communities. Those which were less mixed than others would show a closer relationship between the political and religious structures.

Tax: More Indian, more interdigitation; less Indian, less interdigitation.

(4)

Villa: In the political organization in the Indian communities of Chiapas, there are two organizations. In one, the Indians are the highest officials and the Ladinos tend not to have anything to do in connection with that organization; the other is the group that is in relation with the state. In the Indian political organization, it is the Indians who hold the highest offices.

Tax: Without political authority?

Villa: Among the Indians, they are the real authorities.

Beals: Where the Ladino population is very small, Ladino political power doesn't make so much difference.

Tumin: If we accept this proposition aren't we saying that there is a breakdown of the system? If you characterize Middle American political structure is it primarily centrifugal?

Tax: We agreed on that.

Camara: All the similarities differ slightly in degree, so we have to be very careful in considering these similarities.

Tumin: These are tendencies. Some of these generalizations refer to conditions that are becoming less and less true, and some refer to conditions which are becoming more and more true.

(5)

Tumin: We have several elements here: (1) the transition from Indian to Ladino; (2) the degree of separation of the political and religious organizations; and (3) the difference between centripetal and centrifugal communities, the former being community oriented and the latter individually oriented.

Camara: In the villages of the centripetal communities, every year they are compelled to take *puestos* and *cargos;* in the other type the people act of their own will, taking cargos and puestos voluntarily.

Paul: You have to have motives to take them in the second type.

Camara: Yes. They get social prestige.

Paul: In the first type they take it because they're expected to do so.

Camara: In many cases, when the people refuse to take a puesto or a cargo, they are put in jail; membership in political organization is more compulsory.

Tumin: How general is this in Mesoamerica? Is it true that in the former the community tends to be community oriented in terms of motives, while in the latter it tends to be individually oriented?

Tax: The question is: are there contradictions to this? Are there Indian communities in which you don't have this close relationship, and are there Ladino communities in which you do?

Stone: There are Ladino communities without any Indians which have some religious setup in a certain sense similar to that of the Indian communities you are talking about. It's not general, but they have them.

Tumin: Are they also community centered?

Stone: Yes. These are Ladino communities, one of which was the ancient capital of Honduras.

Camara: We have to make a distinction between the political and religious organizations operating together and the two being structurally together. There is quite a difference.

Tumin: Which is the more folk-like —the centripetal, when the same people occupy the same position?

Camara: I do not say that any community will exactly fit this classification. The point is that the politico-religious organization is breaking down. Take Tenejapa, for example; there you find that many people refuse to take the servicio.

Guiteras: But in the more Indian groups it is a duty; people will not refuse.

Paul: In the centripetal community, do people get rewarded monetarily?

Camara: On the contrary: they have to pay for the cargos.

Paul: They derive no monetary advantage as a result of the puesto?

Camara: Their relationships with other people while in office may be advantageous.

Paul: But they can't make a living?

Camara: No.

Tumin: We have a distinction then, of voluntary as against compulsory?

Camara: Exactly.

Tax: Do you think that's the main criterion?

Camara: That's one, but the main criterion is that in one case the bodies of the politico-religious organizations are together, structurally and functionally; in this case Yalalag fits well.

De la Fuente: They're not paid.

If I may point out a continuum, I would say that in most of the Sierra communities, the political and religious hierarchies are interrelated. There is a hierarchy. One would go through the offices until he reached the highest post of judge. That is the general case for most of the communities. In Yalalag you have different individuals holding different offices. In order to maintain a more complete separation of cargos an authority is paid.

Beals: I agree to your general distinction, but not to being paid as a distinction.

Paul: We have the following distinctions between centripetal and centrifugal:

(1) One is collectivistic and the other individualistic.

(2) In the first, political and ceremonial tend to be fused in both conception and organization, and tend to be disparate in the second.

(3) The socio-ceremonial system in the homogenous case tends to be a system of ascribed status by which the individual may come up by a predetermined route, whereas in the other, it is a system of achieved status.

Tumin: He's trying to show several continua—those three, plus a fourth, the Indian Ladino distinction.

(6)

Tax: We should not neglect the factor of the size of the population of a centripetal community. Everybody can't go through the political and religious organizations in a community of 25,000. Compare the Indian communities of Chichicastenango (population 25,000) and Panajachel (population 800): Panajachel has a real age-grading system; everybody is in the system somewhere; while in Chichicastenango you tend to get the formation of social classes.

Camara: I consider that as one of the forces that makes the community change. With a larger population it is impossible for everyone to go through the organization.

Beals: I think the idea of everybody's serving in a cargo is an ideal. What enters in there is an economic factor. The man who has a lot of sons and has land can take these jobs.

Tax: Then the ideal is realized in Panajachel. Everybody goes through it. The difference is that the wealthier person goes through more quickly; he gets out of the system and becomes an elder earlier.

Wisdom: Prestige is connected with it.

Camara: In Tzintzuntzan the person is more respected, but having only one cargo, he is still considered respectable and he has social prestige. In the centripetal communities you need more than one cargo.

Tumin: Are there more differences between a larger and a smaller Indian community in this regard than a small Indian community and a small Ladino community? Take an Indian community of 2,000 and an Indian community of 20,000. Is the fact of number enough to override the Ladino-Indian fact?

Tax: Chichicastenango structurally has the same system as Panajachel. In every respect it is the same, except that everybody can't go through the organization. There is an aspect of class that enters into it because of the larger community, but I don't think that in any other respect the thing is broken up or that there is any individual initiative. Within the class you have the same thing happening that happens in the whole community somewhere else.

Paul: This seems to say that the ideal is present whether it is larger or smaller, but that it's the more realized in the smaller community.

Tumin: Then the fact of number is not enough to overcome traditional ideas.

Kyte: In the community of Los Morros the situation seems to be quite different. There is a tremendous amount of disorganization in the community as a whole. It's a very small community and you find that they are not organized.

Camara: All these organizations are breaking down.

Tumin: How do things get done in this community?

Kyte: It's usually people who want to make a contribution who take the offices. Quite often the nominations are turned down.

Tumin: But there is extra-pueblo control?

Beals: That you find in places such as Cherán where they had a military governor.

(7)

Kelly: I wonder if we shouldn't make a provision for the negative situation where there is none of this organization. Quite often outside of the area of which we've been speaking there are no cofradías, no organization of religious personnel. We should think of the possibilities that don't fit this picture.

Beals: Has what you described never existed?

Kelly: There is no tradition of it. In one Totonac community there was no church; it had fallen down about thirty years earlier and not been rebuilt.

Paul: What are the areas with little organization—Totonac and Huastec?

De la Fuente: In some parts of the

Huastec region there is religious organization; in other parts there isn't.

Stone: It disappears when you get away from the Maya cultures.

Beals: You get tendencies toward the disappearance of the centripetal community, for example, the Yaqui and the Mayo. You get cases where the political organization is all in Mestizo hands.

De la Fuente: The same thing holds for the Mazatec.

(8)

Camara: The point about the *principales* is a question of degree. Principales are vanishing in the centrifugal communities.

Tumin: Does this generalization hold true?

Tax: In some communities the highest office happens to be the *alcalde,* a civil office; in others the *fiscal,* a religious one.

Camara: We have to make a distinction between those political puestos in which some duties and special qualities are related to the person.

Paul: This statement would hold in San Pedro la Laguna. When a man spends money in a religious cargo, it's considered a good thing.

Tax: That doesn't work very well in Western Guatemala. There you do your job and everybody else forgets about it. Nobody pays any attention.

Camara: In this case we have to make a distinction between political and religious ceremonies.

(9)

Beals: The question of motivation is quite important. There is really a religious motivation for the religious cargos; not a striving for status, but for emotional satisfaction.

Tax: There's another one which is almost contradictory. Where you have this system which everybody must go through, there's a motivation to get through and get it over with.

Beals: I can cite a case of emotional motivation at Ayutla, where one of the wealthier men has voluntarily kept a *mayordomía* for many years and has spent a lot of money on it.

Camara: Cherán also has family ownership of the *santo milagroso.*

Tax: There's another thing: compensatory beliefs. It is considered to be good fortune to have a santo in your house.

Camara: In the centripetal type the religious and political organization functions primarily for the benefit of the community; in the other type, the main object is the acquisition of political power.

Beals: I think this emotional need is a powerful individual motivation.

Tumin: You mean that in the minds of the people what they do redounds to the community. The primary satisfactions are those of community welfare.

Paul: The community doesn't have an emotionality; it's individual. The point is: should the individual fail to accept the post, would he feel that he's injuring the well being of the community?

Beals: It comes out in details; in Cherán, for example, ceremonies are not open to the public.

Camara: This is related to the whole question of the servicio system. In the first case one finds servicio, in the other personal choice.

Tumin: Are there exceptions, or is this generally true for everybody from this area? I take it there are no exceptions. Will you state another large point of difference?

Camara: The elaboration of ceremonies, and of structure itself, is much larger in the centripetal communities than in the centrifugal.

Tumin: Proportional to the population?

Camara: Yes, Mitla has one body, but although I classified it as centripetal, in many other aspects of the politico-religious organization it is centrifugal.

De la Fuente: San Juan la Laguna and other villages in which ceremony is highly elaborated are distinguished from many communities which can't have many fiestas because they are very poor.

Camara: It's not only the number of fiestas but the kind, how many people are involved and take part. In the centripetal communities, the whole population goes to the cabecera to attend the fiesta.

Tumin: Is there a larger number of ceremonies?

Tax: When the two organizations are really one, we can't make a distinction between them.

Tumin: You're saying that the distinction he makes doesn't hold?

Tax: I don't think it does. Twice a year everybody comes out for Holy Week and the feast of the patron saint. Otherwise, all rituals are taken care of by the members of the organization who are in office that year and you get the strong feeling that so far as the religious context is concerned, everybody has the feeling that this is being taken care of and they can go on about their business.

Tumin: Is this general?

Guiteras: That's the feeling I have about the towns in Chiapas.

Beals: You have a feeling that someone is taking care of the ceremonies but you don't take any particular part in them.

Paul: Apart from the degree of participation by the public, do we say that the fraction of the individual's time devoted to the system is greater in the centripetal or the centrifugal communities?

Tax: You could measure the percentage of man-hours devoted to ceremonial activities. All the people in the organization are busy; nobody goes to fiestas, because that's the official's job. The percentage of their time which the officials spend on the fiestas is very great.

De la Fuente: There is a relative lack of correlation between the number of fiestas and the number of people.

Tumin: We would have great difficulty in making generalizations about the elaborateness.

Camara: But we can say that there is a tendency for the centripetal communities to have a larger number of officers and festivities.

Tumin: You're saying that the economically better-off communities are the ones with the more elaborate ceremonial structure.

Tax: How about per capita wealth?

Kelly: Among Mexican Indian groups the Totonac are probably among the most prosperous, and yet they have very little politico-religious organization.

Tax: Around Lake Atitlán the two poorest towns have more fiestas than any of the rich towns. The population factor is important. In the 1918 influenza epidemic a certain town was decimated; you can see that these people could easily get poor by attempting to keep up the same ceremonies.

Guiteras: I don't think we settled the question of the people coming to the fiestas. In one group it is only those who take part who come.

Tax: That's why it's your duty to do it, because they're depending upon you to do it.

Camara: I don't agree. This is a matter of taking part both for those responsible and spectators.

Beals: We're talking about two different things here. You have the actual carrying-on of the ceremonial activity which in both cases is a family activity. You have the difference that in the centripetal community the major ceremonies of the mayordomías are attended by a larger number of people; whereas in the centrifugal communities only the friends come.

Tax: There is a regional difference. I would say that at a ceremony in a town like Chichicastenango, there are no people there except for the political and religious officials. They go through all the ceremony, the only people who participate are the 200 or so officials. There are no spectators.

Tumin: So we get considerable community involvement on the one hand

and, on the other hand, participation only by the specialists.

Camara: We are forgetting the other type of community.

Tax: In the other type of community you have the mayordomía, taken by one person who gets his friends to help him.

Camara: But it's not a community festivity.

Tumin: There are apparently a number of factors here: vacant-town settlement pattern, size of town, ladinoization, and a number of people holding cargos.

Stone: The fewer the Ladinos, the more communal participation.

General assent.

Tax: The ideal case would be that of Chamula. Nobody lives in the town; there are no Ladinos, but there is no participation except by officials. What you have here is a kind of a system of specialization, an elaborate system of hierarchical structure. When you have a system like that, the question of community participation is rather irrelevant. Over a number of years everybody participates.

Paul: What happens when you get vacant towns which are centrifugal?

Tax: You don't get them.

Kyte: Participation of other groups might be a matter of enjoyment. This would influence the number of people that would come out.

Tumin: Would you say the more secular the fiesta, the larger the number of people who would participate?

Guiteras: Carnaval attracts more of the population.

Tax: It depends upon what goes with it—markets, dances, etc.

De la Fuente: Also on whether it takes place in a village or takes place in a town.

Tumin: Then the more centrifugal, the more community participation.

Beals: We're using the word participate in two senses.

Tumin: How about ritual participation?

Camara: In the centripetal communities more people are involved in ritual participation.

Kurath: I would like to know more about these dances; in the centrifugal type would you get the European type of dance? One wonders whether in Indian communities you would not find more survival of the ancient types.

Guiteras: There are two distinct types. The animal dances are exclusively in connection with ritual.

Paul: I should imagine that wherever you have the cofradía organization you would have dances of European type.

(10)

Beals: I don't think you could apply this to centripetal communities—that religious cargos are "better" than political puestos. What makes a post better or worse is how far it is up the ladder.

Tumin: Depending upon the local definition of the prestige ladder and depending upon the amount of money involved. There are variations.

(11)

Gillin: Isn't it true that there's an ambivalent attitude? It seems to me that a cargo can be taken literally by many people. The form is to politely refuse it in some places. In San Luis Jilotepeque, many people actually don't want the cargo.

Tumin: No matter how much prestige you get, you'd rather not impoverish yourself.

Paul: Everyone would like to be a principal in the long run, but in the short run he doesn't want to do it at the moment. It's part of the Indian character that you act as if you didn't want it; then they persuade you to do it.

Wisdom: Is this general?

Tax: I think it's more characteristic of Eastern Guatemala.

Paul: It's found in San Pedro.

Camara: I think it's due to a general modesty.

Paul: It's etiquette.

Beals: They will say that it's not good for a man to seek office.

Tax: But sometimes they say, "I can't afford it," and they stick to it.

Tumin: How much does this fit in with the pattern of concealing your wealth, or do Indians get prestige by open display of wealth?

Beals: In Cherán, wealthy men live very modestly but at the time of a wedding there is a display of wealth.

Tumin: But the regular course of events doesn't call for conspicuous consumption.

Paul: If you accept an office right away it might appear that you are eager. The traditional thing is to say, "I don't have enough money."

(12)

Camara: In the centrifugal communities the old hierarchical order is almost completely broken down.

Tax: It might be interesting to consider some of the ways in which the hierarchical order is breaking down, for example, in San Pedro. The literate people are of particular value, and at the same time, know their rights; they get special consideration.

Camara: Also in Ayutla where the *secretario* didn't have to perform as mayordomo. But in Mitla the secretario did have to have a mayordomía. So there can be two ways of adjusting to the same situation.

De la Fuente: The secretario is a paid functionary. Mitla is an exception.

Camara: This is a concrete case of how a new tendency can be formed in two opposite ways.

Tax: Another way in which the thing breaks down is through Protestantism. How far does this go? In Guatemala there are a number of communities in which the missionaries have made inroads.

Wisdom: Not in Eastern Guatemala.

Tax: The Quakers are there now.

Kurath: How about linguistic missionaries?

Tax: They don't perform missionary activities.

Kelly: In Jalisco Quakers don't proselytize.

De la Fuente: In the Sierras you get a breakdown of religious organization and the breakdown of *tequio.*

Paul: I can give you some of the motives for some individuals becoming Protestants. The Protestant Ethic, for one; it's better to become a Protestant and spend your money in another way. Then there are some who have money and drink a lot at every fiesta; they're not supposed to drink, so it saves them money if they become Protestants. Preserving wealth as an individual achievement is bringing more people into the Protestant fold.

Beals: I've seen this going on in Ecuador. It's not a question of becoming a Protestant. They simply say that the cargo costs too much, and refuse it.

Tax: In Guatemala there's another way of getting out of it, and that's by joining the military. Once you have done your year of military service, you're through for life, except for parading on Sundays, etc.

Tumin: What are other accepted reasons for refusing a cargo?

Guiteras: Ladinoization of people has a lot to do with it. Boys who have gone to school away from the community, when they come back, wait until they can become *síndico* or *presidente.* They refuse the lower cargos.

Tumin: How about the more traditional communities—what reasons are given there?

Tax: Sickness and poverty.

Tumin: What about the claim that one is incapable of discharging the cargo?

Tax: If you're the only one who can do the milpa that's an equivalent of poverty.

Gillin: There's an interesting case in San Luis Jilotepeque. The old scheme still goes on that you may get to be a principal but the main qualification is wisdom and personal qualities. The position is now democratically within their reach but they still have the old tradition that you have to be qualified.

Tumin: In this case, some Indians can run for office but they say they don't want to run for office because they're not capable.

Gillin: It's a different sort of a qualification.

Tumin: Would you say these are rationalizations for escaping from duty?

Gillin: It may be.

(13)

Tax: In Western Guatemala no family heads interfere.

De la Fuente: What Tax says differs from the Mexican situation.

Tax: What do we tie this to—ladinoization?

Camara: Possibly.

Guiteras: It's always in relation to the regional government.

Villa: Camara's point is seen more in the communities of Chiapas. In Chan Kom the state of Yucatan is more important. Even small family differences are taken before the authorities.

Tax: In that last point: how do you account for Zinacantan?

Villa: Your Zinacantan data is just from the head town and you don't know the people in the parajes. You're just saying you don't know the cases that were arranged outside.

Tumin: We know more about those disputes that are brought to the authorities than those that are settled privately.

Tax: Except that you can measure from town to town the number that are settled publicly.

(14)

Beals: In some communities the pagan ideas have all but vanished. I would say that roughly, from somewhere in Oaxaca through the rest of Mexico, you have no real dependence of agriculture on ceremonial activities. There are no specific cult or ritual activities connected with agriculture.

(15)

Paul: Altáres domésticos are not found in San Pedro. They don't have altars; there is no family worship.

Tumin: Is it true that as communities become more ladinoized the religious images disappear from the house?

Tax: No. Then there are more.

Tumin: It's more a Ladino characteristic?

Tax: They become more elaborate.

(16)

Villa: In X-Cacal they do not have a priest and even so the ceremonies are more orthodox.

Whetten: Are priests comparatively scarce in these small communities?

Camara: Yes.

Wisdom: Among the Chorti in the northern municipios there are no resident priests. In Quetzaltepeque there is a resident priest who is very active and yet there is a big cofradía there.

Tax: But Quetzaltepeque is less Catholic than other places. They have a non-Catholic saint.

Beals: Parsons says there are a number of communities where you have had a priest for years and even the new priest does the ritual the local way.

Whetten: Would there be a less or a greater tendency to find a priest in the centrifugal communities? Do they tend to gravitate more to the Ladino communities?

Camara: Yes, that's quite true.

(17)

Tumin: Regarding the statement that curers and diviners are generally outside the organization. How much overlapping is there?

Gillin: There is no overlapping.

Tumin: Only one of the principales is believed to be able to make magic. It was my impression that there was overlapping but that there was only one case.

De la Fuente: Dreams and visions are absent in Oaxaca.

Tumin: Does anybody get the call?

Tax: A shaman gets the call.

Guiteras: In Chiapas he learns his power through a dream.

Villa: Also in Oxchuc and X-Cacal.

Tax: Huehuetenango is another example.

Paul: This is where the cofradía is weak.

Tax: Where you have this whole cofradía system that we've been talking about you have the shaman outside the system.

(18)

De la Fuente: Economic solvency is not necessary in all cases. One of the functions of the mayordomía tends to level fortunes, but in many cases it doesn't matter what the economic position of the individual is.

Tax: I've known cases in which a man has borrowed a lot of money in order to do it.

Tumin: What we mean is that it always costs money to discharge a cargo.

De la Fuente: In certain types of communities, money is collected as an individual task.

Camara: But even in those cases there is someone who is responsible. There is always one person who is in charge.

Tumin: We can say that money is necessary in the performance of the cargo.

Tax: Not only money but time.

(19)

Tumin: The general impression from the paper and discussion is that the similarities are greater than the differences and that there are variations of degree.

Tax: I confess that I'm exceedingly surprised that we've been able to talk so well in the same terms.

Kelly: The reason we have been in agreement is because in a large part this is an overlay—this whole organization.

Tax: That's where a comparison with Peru, for example, would be profitable.

Beals: If there were a slightly different phrasing of statements, many of these would apply in Peru.

Camara: In Cuzco—a great many of these characteristics fit the centripetal communities.

Beals: The sort of things that would throw this out in Ecuador are such as the fact that the influences of the priest is much greater and certain of these offices are filled by appointment of the priest, but otherwise the pattern fits very nicely.

Wisdom: The difference between these two is really one of degree. Aren't these centripetal communities becoming centrifugal?

Tax: We assume here that there is a movement toward the centrifugal.

Beals: I think we've gotten this crystallization better in this paper than in many of the others.

Tax: Can we summarize then, by saying that where the Spanish came into a highly organized Indian community with their well integrated organization the result was the centripetal community. Where the Spanish came into less organized Indian communities, the outgrowth was the centrifugal community.

Beals: That sounds reasonable but I think we would have to review the historical data, such as the royal instructions on the formation of Indian towns.

chapter 8

THE LIFE CYCLE

by Benjamin D. Paul and Lois Paul

THIS survey of attitudes and practices concerning the life trajectory from pregnancy and birth through adulthood and death is based on familiarity with the culture of San Pedro la Laguna,* on impressions gained from discursive reading of Middle American materials, and particularly on a systematic comparison of relevant data in a sample of ten community reports. For Mexico the sample includes the Tarascan village of Cherán (Beals, 1946), the Nahuatl-speaking village of Tepoztlán (Redfield, 1930), the Zapotec communities of Mitla (Parsons, 1936) and Yalalag (De la Fuente, 1949), the Tzeltal (Mayan) village of Oxchuc in Chiapas (Villa Rojas, 1946), and the Yucatan Mayan settlement of Tusik (Villa Rojas, 1945). For the Maya of Guatemala it includes Santa Eulalia

* A 12-month field study of this community in 1941-42 was made possible by a Social Science Research Council travel fellowship to B. D. Paul, as well as a grant to Lois Paul made by the Committee for Research in Dementia Praecox (supported by the Thirty-third Degree Scottish Rite, Northern Masonic Jurisdiction).

of the mountainous northwest (La Farge, 1947), San Pedro la Laguna of the Lake Atitlán region (Paul, MS.), and the eastern villages of San Luis Jilotepeque (Tumin, 1945) and the Chorti (Wisdom, 1940).* Some attention is paid to regional variation but the greater emphasis is on general trends which may be inferred from the particular reports.†

Having Children. From the native viewpoint children are a natural consequence of marriage. Failure to have offspring is judged a grave misfortune. A large family is a source of pride, status and economic assistance. Sons are more valued than daughters, especially as first born, and the payment to the midwife may vary with the sex of the infant she conducts into the world. But in practical fact the best combination of children is a balance between the sexes in order to lighten equally the burden of both parents in their advancing years. Contraceptive efforts are condemned.

Barrenness often produces marital conflict and disruption. The curse of sterility is variously attributed to fate, witchcraft, improper sexual indulgence, and to a "cold" condition incurred by drinking acidulous juices or by other means. Attempted remedies include herbal mixtures and appeals to appropriate saints. (It should be realized that new conditions occasioned by urbanization tend to alter attitudes in regard to birth control and optimum family size.)

Knowledge of abortifacients is widely known even though their use is denied and decried. Methods include the consumption of "cold" substances, deliberate overexertion and similar violations of pregnancy injunctions.

Children of common law marriages, as contrasted to civil marriages, may be classified as illegitimate on official government records, but they are not so regarded locally. To the natives illegitimacy applies to cases of unacknowledged paternity. In this sense, illegitimacy may be tolerated or even interpreted as a token of the woman's fertility, as in Santa Eulalia. Most generally however the mother of an illegitimate child is censured for her illicit sexual experience. But the scorn is not enduring and the stigma does not rest heavily on the fatherless child. Indeed bastard children are sometimes thought to have an extra measure of perspicacity or good luck.

* The work of assembling this material was facilitated by the Laboratory of Social Relations, Harvard University.

† The present draft profits from the comments made by the participants of the Seminar.

Conception and Pregnancy. Children are born about a year after marriage and at intervals of 18 months to 3 years thereafter. The average of 7½ births per woman in Cherán may be taken as a fair estimate for the area in general. Conception is clearly linked to intercourse although the assumption prevails that successful procreation requires a series of sexual efforts rather than a single act of intercourse. Generally reckoned by lunar cycles, the duration of normal pregnancy ranges from 8 to 11 months by native accounts. The time of gestation is thought to differ for first and subsequent births, and for male and female babies. In parts of the Mayan area at least, the relative "strength" of each parent is considered a factor influencing reproduction. A person's "strength" is governed by his or her day of birth and in turn controls the difficulty and duration of conception and pregnancy, as well as the preponderance of boys or girls born into a family.

The symptoms of pregnancy are failure to menstruate, abdominal swelling, fetal movements, and appearance of food cravings and aversions. Not infrequently women experience nausea, disturbance of appetite, lassitude and "abdominal pains." The side on which pains or twitches appear may signal the sex of the fetus.

Pregnancy Observances. Pregnancy intrudes little upon a woman's customary routine. The changes are gradual and inconspicuous. The ideal of womanly behavior calls for a show of modesty and a sense of shame. The Spanish term *vergüenza* is freely used to express these attributes which pregnancy only serves to accentuate. Pregnancy is an occasion for increasing reticence rather than proud exhibition. It is not a fit topic of conversation in the presence of children, or even before girls in their first pregnancy who are often assumed to be innocent of their condition until the time of delivery. Older women cannot pretend to ignorance but they may grow uneasy when attention is directed to their pregnant state. The lowland Maya surround the subject with less secrecy but even here the topic is removed from polite discussion.

No period of formal seclusion is enjoined but the circle of social participation is slowly narrowed. This retreat obeys the dictates of propriety but is also buttressed by such considerations as a sense of ritual uncleanliness, the danger of imparting "evil eye" to infants, a fear of incurring witchcraft, or the risk of trespassing magical interdicts. But women continue working at the loom, grinding the corn and carrying water for the household. Heavy loads or extreme exertion are avoided but constant activity is a necessity and may even be urged as beneficial.

Minor modifications in diet occur. Some foods such as lemon juice are to be avoided because they are excessively "cold"; others are banned in accordance with magical belief. Thus if the pregnant woman eats chicken hearts her child will be slow in speech or "heavy hearted." The expectant mother should indulge her food cravings lest she fall ill, bear a sickly child, or likelier still, suffer miscarriage. A pinch of salt or some other conventional substitute is available to women who cannot otherwise satisfy a specific craving. In San Pedro la Laguna, perhaps elsewhere as well, the cravings originate with the fetus but express themselves in the appetite of the mother and also of the youngest child in the family. The demands of the youngest child, like those of the mother, can be ignored only at the peril of displeasing the fetus and provoking its premature departure from the womb.

Pregnant women, and sometimes their husbands, are supposed to refrain from a variety of acts in the interest of insuring a normal delivery. To avert birth complications, for instance, the woman must take care never to leave her loom entangled and her husband must hasten to untie his burden knots on returning home. The number of these injunctions is more impressive than their effectiveness. Most of the avoidances cause little practical inconvenience and many turn out to be magical props to sustain the cultural standards of conduct and industry. Some are devices for fixing retroactive blame.

Especially prevalent is the belief that sight of an eclipse will induce miscarriage or deform the developing fetus. During an eclipse women should remain indoors or wear a protective object. This may be a kerchief or belt worn about the waist or a metal item such as a key or a pair of scissors tucked into the belt. The ancient Aztecs carried an obsidian blade for this purpose.

Restrictions on sexual intercourse are imposed as early as the third or fourth month of pregnancy or as late as the seventh. Reasons given include uncleanliness and fear of causing complications. Intercourse should not be resumed until 5 to 15 weeks after delivery. Among the Chol Maya of Dolores a man customarily slept in the house of idols from his wife's fifth month of pregnancy until the fifth day after the baby was born.

Where the fact of pregnancy is not explicitly acknowledged it nay seem strange that the newly married girl should yet follow the appropriate observances and avoidances. But the girl is not accustomed to question instructions from her mother or mother-in-law. Both sides find it convenient to engage in a conspiracy of silence on the delicate matter of being pregnant for the first time.

Professional midwives are unknown in Tusik or Oxchuc where older female relatives assist the delivery. But the general practice is to place pregnant women under the care of midwives who enjoy a respectful and sacred status. Midwives are usually summoned early in the pregnancy. They return periodically to administer abdominal massages in order to facilitate normal presentation. Midwives can determine the position of the fetus by palpation. Miscarriages occur fairly frequently and account for some of the anxiety surrounding childbirth. A midwife in San Pedro la Laguna estimated the incidence at 10%. Miscarriage is variously attributed to a fall, a fright or a physical strain; an unrequited craving; a breach of conduct, magical or moral; enemy malevolence; or the dictates of fate.

Childbirth. Delivery takes place in the privacy of the home though occasionally as in Oxchuc the woman goes into the *temascal* in the event the house is occupied by shamans performing protective rites. Only the midwife and adult members of the household attend. Others are excluded out of modesty and the wish to protect the infant from "evil-eye" and other magical harm. Presence or absence of the husband varies locally depending on which of two considerations preponderates: the principle of sexual modesty or that of impressing upon the husband the seriousness of life and duty. Thus in San Pedro la Laguna the reluctant young father is forced by the midwife to help in the delivery so that he may know "what parents must go through to bear children"; the act of childbirth is exploited to dramatize the precepts of parental responsibility and filial devotion. But in most communities, the husband is not present at the delivery. Duration of labor is quite variable, ranging from under an hour to a day, depending on the case, and on the interpretation of the somewhat ambiguous use of the term "labor."

In some cases the woman delivers while lying in a hammock or bed, or in a standing position, supported by a rope or sash, as among the Maya of Yucatan and Chiapas. But commonest throughout the area as a whole is the "Nahua position," that of kneeling or squatting. Women exert pressure by pushing against the floor or an object such as the *metate*. Where the man is present as in San Pedro la Laguna or at times in Cherán, he is seated behind the woman pressing his knees against her back while holding her under the arms. The most widely used aids for facilitating delivery are massages with warm ointments and "hot" drinks such as camomile tea, liquor or coffee.

When delivery of the baby or the placenta is prolonged the woman may be told to blow into a shell or bottle, or the husband instructed to wear his trousers inside out. The mother or midwife may walk the girl back and forth or stimulate effort by scolding or even slapping her. Protracted cases call for a variety of magical expedients such as pouring rum over the woman's lips or having her drink the warm urine of her husband.

Babies born in unusual positions complicate labor and may result in death to the infant or mother. Abnormal or unduly difficult deliveries often presage a special destiny for the child: shaman, midwife, sorcer or witch. Twins are explained by the fact that they were conceived when Gemini was ascendant, that two fathers were involved or, more commonly, by the fact that the mother ate twin fruits. Twins may be considered *santos* as in San Pedro la Laguna and should not be denied food or other request.

The cord is cut at a length of several fingers or a span. In most of the area a knife or scissors has replaced the cane blade still used for this purpose in the vicinity of Tusik where metal objects are thought to be injuriously "cold." The end of the cord is singed with a candle or heated blade. Warmed oil or tallow or a little salt may be applied at once.

The afterbirth is sometimes burned but more commonly wrapped and buried, often near the hearth, to avert the death or sickness of the child. The ancient Aztec buried it in a corner of the house. Markings on the cord at birth may prognosticate, as in Cherán and San Pedro la Laguna, the number of future children in the family and the spacing between them. In San Pedro la Laguna a child that loses its cord in a few days will be generous, one that holds on for over a week will be stingy. The cord that falls away is invariably disposed of in a special manner to promote the proper development of the child. A common pattern is to bury the cord of a girl under the fireplace or suspend it near the hearth to keep the girl from wandering away from home, and to hang the cord of a boy on a tree or corn crib in the fields to make him a diligent worker. Widespread is the belief that careless disposal of the cord (or afterbirth) may bring blindness to the child. Conversely the dried cord has remedial properties especially useful in curing cases of sore eyes.

Length of post-natal seclusion varies but the modal period is one week. In the highlands, sweat baths are prescribed for post-partum mothers. Bed rest permits the mother to regain her strength, recover her figure and avoid being chilled since she, as well as her infant, is peculiarly susceptible at this time to the noxious effect of "cold" (and of *aire* in the lowland Maya region). Her diet is commonly confined to "hot" foods and drinks designed to maintain her health and insure a good flow of milk. The midwife looks after mother and child during confinement, often massaging and pressing down on the woman's abdomen and, in the highlands, supervising her sweat baths. An abdominal band is worn by the mother and by the infant in some but not all localities.

Visiting patterns during the lying-in period vary widely. In Tusik no one may enter the room for a week except the husband and women in attendance; they might bring sickness in the form of evil winds or "evil eye." On the other hand, hosts of friends and relatives may visit during the first few days among the Chorti, or in Tepoztlán and San Pedro la Laguna, where they bring gifts of food and drink. Visitors are circumspect in their admiration of the baby in order not to antagonize the fates.

Naming. Children receive Spanish first names, although some communities still base names on the native sacred calendar. Commonly the child is given the name of a saint appearing opposite the child's date of birth in the Catholic almanac. It is also common practice to name the child after a living or dead relative. In northwestern Guatemala and parts of the Tarascan region the first name of the father becomes the last name of the children. In San Pedro la Laguna, where children carry the surnames of the two parents in Spanish fashion, the first boy and the first girl in a family are named after their paternal grandparents while succeeding children are named for siblings of the father. Any system of naming however has its individual exceptions to satisfy caprice or to improve the child's luck by identifying it with the good destiny of a shaman, a godparent or some other special person. Spanish given names are generally shortened and altered, sometimes beyond immediate recognition, in accordance with local speech patterns. In many places a sex classifier is prefixed to the Indian version of the given name.

Nicknames are very common and may be based on individual peculiarities or even on the peculiarities of other people by analogy of name, descent, occupation or residence. They serve the variable purposes of ridicule, identification and affection. They are generally used in addition to the regular name but in some places such as San Antonio Palapó and Oxchuc nicknames replace the formal names within the intimacy of the family circle.

Infancy Rites. The end of confinement is customarily marked by ritual bathing of mother and infant by the midwife. The procedure in San Pedro la Laguna will serve as an example. Female relatives and friends of the post-parturient mother prepare a substantial quantity of ritual foods including meat and *tamales* which are sent to the home of the midwife early on the morning of the eighth day. Later that morning the midwife washes the mother's hair in the patio, bathes the infant inside the house, and wafts incense into the four corners of the room while thanking the spiritual guardians of the childbed. She then whips the hammock which is to be the infant's day-time cradle, threatening and cajoling its supernatural guardians to protect the child from falls and magical dangers. At the end of these ceremonies the midwife is served chocolate and bread and paid a fee ranging from 25 cents to a dollar depending on the means of the family. Her formal responsibility for the welfare of mother and child is now explicitly ended. Nevertheless she continues to return during the ensuing month or two.

Children are made members of the Christian community by baptism. It is generally believed that baptism should be accomplished as early in infancy as possible to avert the danger of dying without being baptized. This is not only dangerous to the child, which would be consigned to limbo, but to the living community as well, since it is frequently thought that unbaptized spirits return in some guise to cause sickness and death, whereas children who die after baptism become angels and may promote rather than damage the interests of their relatives. There are however various factors causing the delay of baptism: the infrequent visits of the priest, the difficulty of paying the baptismal fee, and the fear of "evil eye" or witchcraft. Depending on the balance of influences, communities differ widely as to the usual time of baptism, the age of the child ranging from several days to many months or even several years.

Children are brought to the baptismal font by their godparents who give the child an item of clothing and usually pay the fee. In return the sponsors are the beneficiaries of a little feast at the home of the parents. Godparenthood inaugurates a set of enduring mutual obligations, those of the godparent including the responsibility of contributing to the physical and spiritual well-being of the godchild and looking after it in time of crisis. When old enough the child is taught to show deference to its godparents who occupy, in some respects, the status of auxiliary parents.

Baptism and godparents are lightly regarded in some places but in others the sponsorship pattern is elaborated to include a series of formal petitions, confirmations, thanks-giving, and other ritualized events preceding and following the actual baptism, arrangements sometimes beginning before the child is born. Persons preferred for godparents may be older relatives as in Yucatan, friends and respected individuals, Ladinos, or members of a professional group as in Chichicastenango or among the Chorti. Successive children in a family may have identical godparents, different godparents, one set of sponsors for girls and another for boys, or the godparents may be changed after three children as in Mitla. The child may acquire godparents only at baptism or it may acquire secondary ceremonial relatives in connection with confirmation, communion and other occasions including marriage. But always the baptismal godparents remain the principal godparents.

In some localities as in Tepoztlán and Mitla where baptism is accomplished very soon after birth a second ceremony called the *sacamisa* may occur when the baby is a month or two old, the child attending its first mass and minor festivities taking place at the home.

In Yucatan the *hetzmek* ceremony is performed at the time the infant is first carried astride the hip, ideally at the age of three months for a girl and four months for a boy. The act symbolizes the faculties and skills desired. Amidst prayers and offerings, a grandparent puts the child astride the hip and successively places a miniature *machete,* a hoe and an axe in the hands of a baby boy; a *mano,* a needle and a scissors in the hands of a baby girl. Similar in its symbolic implications is the occasional practice in San Pedro la Laguna, and possibly elsewhere in the Maya region, of placing a small machete and metate on the back of a week-old boy so that he will become a good worker, or setting a basket containing a tiny spindle over the bed of a baby girl.

Infancy. The belief is widely held that the fate and character of the child are controlled by its day of birth, but only in some of the communities is it a regular practice to ascertain its destiny by consulting a shaman or soothsayer. More often the ritual practitioner is consulted only in cases of unusual births.

A belief recurring especially through southern Mexico and northwest Guatemala is that the child's spirit is associated or identified with the spirit of a certain animal which may or may not be connected with the child's day sign. Some peoples strew ashes in or near the house after the baby is born in order to identify the animal companion from its spoor. In places such as Mitla and San Pedro la Laguna the soul of a child may be linked to a flash of lightning or a streaking meteor. One is not to call out or clap his hands on seeing such a flash lest it bring death to a mother in labor or to the child.

Early infancy is regarded as a very critical period. Infant mortality is indeed high, owing to diarrhea, enteritis, intestinal parasites and other ailments. In terms of native conceptions of disease, "evil eye" is the most prevalent danger, causing diarrhea, listlessness and death. It can be imparted by the look of a menstruating or pregnant woman, a man returning from the field in perspiration, an emotionally disturbed person, or by the mere presence of too many people. To guard against "evil eye" the infant may wear charms and amulets, be fed cooking oil, or protected by burning incense. But the safest measure is thought to be seclusion of the infant and keeping it covered when carrying it about the streets. Eggs are used in various ways to diagnose and draw off "evil eye." Other general causes of infancy sickness in native conceptions are "fright," "soul loss," and "aire." Young children commonly wear a kerchief or cap as protection against "aire." It is thought that divine punishment or witchcraft meant for the parent may strike the more vulnerable child instead.

Throughout the nursing period the baby receives affection and attention from all members of the household. Given the emotional restraint characteristic of the Indian cultures of the area, babies tend to be the only socially approved objects of affectionate display. Mothers keep their infants near them, carrying them in a shawl when they travel. In some communities infants are swaddled for the first few months, particularly when put to sleep. They may sleep through the night with the mother's nipple in the mouth. The baby is nursed whenever it cries; nursing is a pacifying gesture as well as a feeding. The baby is not deliberately allowed to cry since a fit of hard crying might subject the child to injury or illness.

The newborn infant is ordinarily not immediately nursed by its mother; lactation may be insufficient or the first milk may be considered harmful. The infant may be nursed by another woman until the mother's milk begins to flow on the second or third day. The mother's milk is stimulated by a special dietary regimen and if necessary by breast massage. If milk fails an attempt is made to place the baby with a wet nurse. Bottle feeding is unknown except in urbanized areas.

Infants are usually nursed for at least 15 or 18 months though the period may run to three years or longer in the absence of a new baby. Terminal children especially may continue partial nursing until the age of 5 or 6. Among Mayan groups last children are designated by a special term; it is sometimes said that they continue to be more assertive and self centered than other individuals. In some communities children are allowed occasional breast feedings even after a succeeding child is born. Thus in Yalalag it was formerly not rare for mothers to nurse children until the age of six, frequently nursing two children at the same time. In contrast, other communities provide time limits within which infants may properly nurse. Thus the Chorti believe that a child should not nurse longer than two years lest it bleed at the nose and die. Mothers in San Pedro la Laguna remove children from the breast when they are in about the fifth month of pregnancy, for the milk at that time is said to become unfit for consumption. In this village the temper tantrums of a two- or three-year-old is attributed to the mother's pregnancy. To hasten weaning, women in some communities apply disagreeable substances to the nipple, in addition to offering alternative foods.

Early Childhood. Nursing babies customarily receive unspiced *atole* as their first food supplementation. Around the age of eight months, as teeth appear, they are given bread, *tortilla* and meat. By the age of two they eat almost everything. Toddlers are indulged with special treats such as fruits or sweets or between-meal snacks to appease their emotional outbursts.

Children who walk and talk early are generally regarded as *mas listos* while those that take two years or more may be considered backward. Early mastery of motor skills is welcomed in a culture which values and depends on physical fitness but children are seldom prodded beyond their natural pace. Children of crawling age are not permitted to cruise about extensively unless attended, for they may get into the fire, break pottery or pick up diseases from the dirt floor. Customarily children at this age are still carried about in a shawl by an older sister or another member of the household. Children usually begin walking between the ages of 10 and 18 months. In Cherán and San Pedro la Laguna, bars and other walking aids may be provided. When walking is considerably retarded resort may be made to *secretos* such as placing a crab on the soles of the child's feet or rubbing its legs with rabbit grease. When the child begins to babble it is encouraged to speak by prompting and commendation.

Toilet training is not rigorous and begins only after the child has learned to walk and understand instructions. Full control is not established until the age of two or three years. In cases where children of older age continue to wet the bed, parents resort to public shaming devices, apply pinewood sap to the navel or expose the child's genitals to smoke.

Childhood. Children begin to assist their parents by the age of 6 or 7. From an earlier attitude of leniency and indulgence parents now shift to an expectation that the child apply himself seriously to the task of learning his *oficios*. In their apprenticeship children contribute to the family welfare even while preparing themselves for adulthood. Boys go to the fields with their fathers as soon as they are strong enough to endure the walk. They stand guard against birds when the *milpa* is sown, begin to wield the hoe and machete, carry home small bundles of firewood by the tumpline, and accompany their fathers on short trading trips. Girls grind coffee beans on small metates, carry miniature water jars on their heads, and act as nursemaids for babies.

Even before they are physically capable of performing certain tasks, children get psychological preparation through play patterned on adult activities. Parents fashion or purchase dolls and toy animals and the like but for the most part children improvise play items from materials about the yard. Thus a discarded match box may be used to mold little adobe bricks for building play houses; fragments of pottery serve as money in going to market. Boys and girls play together until they are five or six at which time they begin to separate. Not only do their interest and activities grow increasingly divergent, but girls begin to have vergüenza and even to feel threatened in the presence of boys, while the latter adopt the attitude that it is beneath their dignity to traffic with girls except to tease them.

Organized competitive games of native origin are virtually unknown throughout the area. Some modern competitive games have been introduced through the schools.

The government requires that children attend at least two or three grades of formal schooling. Although some progressive parents want their children to learn Spanish and receive an education, many fail to see the benefit, particularly for girls. Indian parents ask, "Will it help the girl make better tortillas?" They also begrudge the time lost by a boy who might more usefully be helping his father. Boys tend to retain their knowledge of Spanish, at least in the spoken form, since they have occasion to practice it in trade and other contacts, but girls in all-Indian communities like San Pedro la Laguna quickly relapse into monolingual status, a process which is hastened by the ridicule of other women who consider Spanish speech an affectation.

Respect, industry and emotional control are the chief character traits parents expect their children to acquire. These qualities are inculcated with little conscious direction, the countless examples of daily life serving as cues to correct behavior. But the learning process is also reinforced by scolding and by whipping, especially for disobedience, as well as by threats of witches and *espantos* of various sorts. In contrast with the frequent North American Indian pattern, the right and duty to chastise children tends to rest more exclusively with the parents rather than to be allocated to uncles, aunts or other kinsmen.

Puberty. No ceremonies mark the attainment of puberty and with few exceptions no formal restrictions are required of menstruating girls. Among the Chorti, girls fast for a week following their first menses, eating only maize and performing light work, but more generally throughout the area menstruation, which is attributed to the influence of the moon, is treated with shame and secrecy. Girls are not prepared or forewarned except insofar as they acquire surreptitious information from friends and they may be frightened at the first appearance of blood. Only then do their mothers inform them that it is a recurrent experience of women, cautioning them to keep the matter confidential. Girls are usually watched with especial care from the time of puberty until they are married for fear that something might "happen" to them. Adolescent girls are expected to be shy and demure and to ignore overtures from young men. In effect the onset of puberty in girls is stressed in the negative.

While puberty in boys is not attended by any formal observances, it nevertheless heralds an important turn in their social activities in some Middle American communities. To take San Pedro la Laguna as an example, adolescent boys tend to cluster into cliques or boys' "gangs" which are not accorded formal recognition by the culture but which receive the implicit approval of the parents. These groups include members ranging from about 13 to 22 in age who submit to the authority of a "natural" leader and conform to the expectations of the group by virtue of informal but effective sanctions which include ridicule and occasional physical punishment. Rivalries between various groups within the village enhance the bonds of solidarity within the group. Members continue to eat their meals at home but characteristically they no longer sleep under the parental roof. There is no formal men's house such as served the natives of Yucatan, Tabasco and the Mexican highlands in ancient times, but the practice by some parents of setting aside a spare house to which an adolescent son brings his companions at night serves a like purpose. The groups assemble around a fire on the lake front after dark to tell stories, exchange experiences, and talk about women. If a boy is reluctant to sleep with the group or expresses fears that his parents will object he is derisively informed, "Go home and embrace your mother." Strong pressures are exerted to push callow youths into courting girls. If the boy is too shy to go alone several friends go along to give him instructions and encouragement. Among other functions, these groups in San Pedro la Laguna serve the purpose of helping to wean youths from parental dependence and prepare them for marriage by imparting "know-how" and initiative. As members marry they gradually lessen their participation in the group.

Unmarried boys in Cherán likewise spend little of their leisure time around their own homes, congregating in the streets and making arrangements to "steal" their sweethearts preliminary to formal marriage. Youthful cliques are apparently absent in decentralized villages such as Chichicastenango, but entrance into public service between the ages of 14 and 18 gives the boy a measure of freedom from parental control.

Marriage. Occasionally girls marry at the age of 12 or 13 but more commonly between the ages of 15 and 18. On the average boys are several years older when they marry. Choice of partner is usually confined to the same ethnic group and to the same village or group of related villages. With some exceptions, marriage to cousins, especially on the father's side, is prohibited or disapproved, nor should a person marry into the family of his godparent. Within the limits of family exogamy and village endogamy a fairly wide choice of mates is available unless the total community is quite small.

Marriage frequently seals a bond of social and economic solidarity between the respective family groups, and in weighing the merits of a girl the parents of the boy take into consideration the industry and morality of the prospective daughter-in-law, as well as the standing of her family. Parents need not consult the wishes of their children but in point of fact they usually do. This is increasingly the case today in contrast to former times when group interests took greater precedence over individual interests. In many localities the partners make their own choices, the boys informing their parents, who then proceed to make the proper arrangements, often engaging the services of matrimonial agents to facilitate agreement and dignify the occasion. Negotiations consist of a series of meetings conducted discreetly under cover of darkness to avert embarrassment and interference by meddlesome outsiders. The petitioners may bring ceremonial gifts including drinks and may ultimately convey a sum of money as a sign of good intention, to help pay for the bridal outfit, or in compensation for the girl.

Since adolescent girls are usually chaperoned and restricted, contacts and courtship are typically clandestine and mediated by companions. Formal courtship patterns prevail however in many of the Maya villages. Taking San Pedro la Laguna again as an example, courting occurs on the paths leading up from the lake in the late afternoon when the boys return from the fields and the girls go for water. As the girl begins her ascent balancing the water jar on her head the boy steps out of a bypath to grasp her wrist from behind, pleading his case while she remains motionless. This is repeated for weeks or months until the girl indicates consent by her failure to return a packet of old coins *(prenda)* which he drops into her blouse. The girl has the deciding voice in electing the form in which the marriage is to be accomplished, whether by formal petition or informal elopement.

Elopement is not sanctioned as a means of acquiring a wife but it is not uncommon in the area as an expedient to circumvent a refusal on the part of the girl's family to accept the suitor. Stealing the bride with her connivance is the dominant, if deprecated, practice in Cherán and San Pedro la Laguna (but it is not dominant in most other communities). The girl's parents attempt pursuit but usually in vain. In Cherán elopements are subsequently validated by a marriage ceremony.

Church weddings may be standard practice or virtually unknown depending on the village. Civil marriage is required by federal law but it is lightly regarded locally and often overlooked. But in any event it is customary to celebrate the marriage at the home of the boy's parents. This ceremony is variously marked by feasting, dancing, drinking, and street processions. As a rule marriage godparents take an active hand and contribute to the expense. At Cherán the wedding is an occasion for ostentatious display of wealth and exchanging of gifts; arrangements are so complex as to make necessary a marriage party manager. In contrast, traditional marriages in San Pedro la Laguna are concluded with modest ceremonies involving food for the marriage witness and his wife, the immediate relatives on the male side, and the dispatch of food to the parents of the girl.

Marriage is prevailingly patrilocal. Transfer of the bride is anticipated by gifts from the side of the bridegroom, by token payments and sometimes as in Northwestern Guatemala by appreciable monetary considerations. During the interval between betrothal and marriage, the boy may demonstrate obedience and good intention by bringing loads of firewood to the home of his future parents-in-law. This is a traditional Maya practice. In addition to gifts or "bride price" the newly married man may give his wife's family labor service by living with them for a limited period, before settling down with his own parents. In particular cases where the bride belongs to a wealthy family or where she has no brothers to work and inherit her father's lands, her husband finds it advantageous to settle permanently with his parents-in-law.

Monogamy is the rule but marriage is fairly brittle in early years. Separation imposes little stigma and most people remarry in short order. In the absence of intimate courtship it is only within the framework of marriage that young people can learn to adjust to each other and to explore their mutual compatibility. Pressures from parents, godparents and marriage witnesses, particularly when bride gifts are at stake, act to reduce the incidence of precipitous ruptures during the first trying months of married life, but the most effective stabilizing factor is the arrival of children. Even so it is not unusual to separate after the advent of children, whose disposition depends on their age and sex. Widows may remarry or not depending on age and opportunity. The levirate and sororate are absent as established practices.

Among Ladinos the pattern of extramarital relationships is supported by the romantic tradition as well as pressures arising from the inability to dissolve an unhappy marriage once sanctified by the church. The Indians of Middle America also have clandestine affairs but these are neither frequent nor well-patterned owing to the absence of romantic values and to the relatively low incidence of church marriages.

Adulthood. Whether the young couple share the house of the boy's parents or live in an adjoining house, they generally remain under the jurisdiction and supervision of the husband's parents for several years or even until the father dies. Officially or unofficially they tend to assume control of their own land and household management after several children are born.

Adult status is attained in stages. An appreciable degree of adult responsibility is achieved at marriage and by entering the system of community service but complete adulthood does not ordinarily come until children are born and the couple assumes control of its own affairs. In the life of the individual, responsibility comes early and authority late; it takes a full measure of both to qualify the man or woman as socially mature.

Even after the domination of the mother-in-law is removed, women remain subordinate to their husbands. Their social participation is more limited than the man's and their daily routine is often more onerous and repetitious. Despite these apparent disabilities, married women are characteristically jovial and convey the impression of enjoying at least as much self-assurance as the men. As they marry and have children women assume management of the household and eventually of their daughters-in-law; they participate in fiestas and religious events; and they become increasingly freer in their social contacts, gossiping with other women and joking with men under the protection of public view. The menopause, as elsewhere in the world, is not accorded social recognition.

Men and women continue at their task into old age as health and energies allow. The comfort in which the aged live depends upon their success in building up the family fortune and, in some localities, upon the disposition of their inheritance, for they may find themselves faced with difficult alternatives. If the old man postpones division of his property he may earn the resentment of his married children and gain the reputation of a miser. If he yields to the expectations of his children he may run the risk of becoming a poor relation when senility makes him burdensome.

By ascending the ladder of public and religious offices, men assume more dignity and earn increasing status, the wives sharing their prestige. In reward for serving the community and upholding the religious tradition, which consists of fulfilling offices rather than personal piety alone, men graduate around the age of 60 or 65 to the position of *principales* or village elders. They are exempted from further services, formally consulted on important village policies, and accorded deference in greeting. They occupy honored positions in religious processions and wear ceremonial kerchiefs or equivalent badges of their status. They may be more respected than loved and in part their status as elders may be an honorific compensation for declining age, but their psychological integrity is preserved. However, as Indian communities are drawn more into the national current, practical skills such as ability to speak and write Spanish tend to override traditional qualifications for attaining positions of eminence, with the result that a man may become a principal at an earlier age than was formerly the case.

Death. Death in old age is usually accepted with resignation but death may be attributed to sorcery or seen as punishment for wrong doing. Prayers may be said at the bedside of the dying to relieve the last agony. In Todos Santos if the shaman or pulse-taker predicts death the patient accepts the verdict; he ceases to eat and his family stops offering him food.

The wake follows a Catholic form and commonly includes night watch, prayer and lighted candles. Relatives, especially the women, weep and often drown their grief in alcoholic drinks which are freely distributed to attending friends and relatives. Observances for a dead child tend to have a formally cheerful character consistent with the idea of baptized infant blessedness.

The corpse, which is usually dressed in fresh clothes, is buried within a day after death, wrapped in a mantle or enclosed in a wooden coffin, a cross marking the grave. Since the spirit is assumed to survive the body, intimate articles appropriate to the sex and station of the deceased are frequently buried with the corpse, a bundle of pitch-pine to light the way and drinking water to ease the journey. The dead are usually removed from the house feet first and often interred with the head to the west. Bodies of persons who met death through accident or violence may be carried to the cemetery on special litters and buried face downward but, except for such cases of unnatural death, there is little dread of corpses. There is however a mild uneasiness over the possibility that the spirit will linger uncomfortably long in the vicinity.

Upon the anniversary and at other intervals, relatives may hold commemorative services for a deceased adult to insure the welfare of the departed spirit, lest it return to plague the living. In San Pedro la Laguna it is explained that the "spirit" of the pennies offered for prayers on behalf of dead relatives ascends to pay their "fine," releasing them from "jail" and hard labor; the grateful souls repay the favor by interceding with the higher powers to confer health and good fortune upon the solicitous descendants.

chapter 9

ETHOS AND CULTURAL ASPECTS OF PERSONALITY

by John Gillin

ALMOST any short statement regarding ethos and cultural aspects of personality structure in modern Middle America made by an individual worker in this field is certain to be greeted at the present time by a certain amount of disagreement, or at least, demands for further clarification, for several reasons. In the first place, I am aware of no comprehensive scientific studies of these aspects of culture and its effects in Middle America that have been published to date. The existing material is mainly oriented in terms of the ethnographic, philosophical, historical, and acculturational points of view. In the second place, the general concepts involved with ethos and cultural personality have not been thoroughly analyzed on a theoretical level and subjected to empirical test. Thus, at the present time there is no general agreement on terminology, concepts, or methodology in these matters. A third reason for possible disagreement or confusion is, of course, the fact that the culture, and therefore the ethos and cultural personalities, of all Middle Americans are not precisely alike, are not homogeneous throughout the area. The most important distinction is that between Indian cultures and those of Ladinos, Mestizos, or however one wishes to label the carriers and practitioners of Modern Latin American culture or civilization.[1] Nor is either one of these two major cultural manifestations uniform throughout Middle America. The Indian cultures vary along a scale of acculturation from the less Europeanized to the more Europeanized or modernized. Also, the aboriginal bases of the original Indian cultures were by no means identical in content, organization, or cultural status. On the Ladino side of the line several factors of variation must be recognized. Some Ladino exhibits are more acculturated by the aboriginal cultures than others. These are apparently the more isolated and "folk-like" communities. Also the Ladino culture is exhibited in a variety of community situations. To mention two of the most important, the rural and the urban situations, I believe that Redfield and his co-workers have demonstrated that, other things being equal, the rural situation produces a more homogeneous or more closely integrated culture than the urban environment. Thus, even if it can be shown that there is a general Indian ethos and personality distinguishable in pure form from those of Ladinos, each would show several subforms. Likewise we may expect to encounter many mixed forms—cases, for example, in which the ethos is midway between the ideal types.

If one focuses on all of these variations among the life modes of Central America he may either be overcome by confusion, or be inclined to insist that we must carefully study a whole series of separate cultures in Middle America rather than venturing generalizations about all of them, or about Indian and Ladino, respectively. This may turn out to be the only valid operational position, and nothing said here is to be taken as didactically negative to it. In fact, I believe that from one point of view it is proper and necessary to recognize a series of cultures or subcultures in Middle America and to study them as such.

However, for this symposium I am going to begin by taking the position that throughout the many Indian and Ladino cultural exhibits, respectively, there are to be found certain common denominators[2] and I assume that my colleagues in the discussion wish to focus their attention upon them with a view to discovering whether or not we can arrive at a reliable notion of an Indian ethos and a

Ladino ethos, an Indian personality type and a Ladino personality type. Cases which are exceptional to the generalization should be brought forward with all candor, as well as interpretations that do not agree with those suggested by myself. As I see it, we are embarking upon a strictly exploratory venture, and we need to keep open minds.

If this much is granted, then, let us define in general terms the fields of interest. Ethos is taken to mean the constellation of acquired drives or motivations which are characteristic of a culture, plus the goals, both explicit and implicit, toward which cultural activities are directed or upon which high value is placed. The concept can and should be more thoroughly analyzed, but I shall not attempt to do so here. Considered as a whole, such a configuration of drives and goals imparts to a culture a characteristic quality which can be compared with those of other cultures.

The aspects of personality with which we are most concerned here are those which are produced or influenced by the operation of the culture and which are in some measure common to "typical" members of a community, society, or region who practice a common culture. I am aware of practically no work which has been done on depth psychology or psychoanalysis with a cultural orientation in the Middle American area, and only one series of Rorschach tests has been published which makes possible a systematic comparison of Indians and Ladinos. Thus we are not equipped at present to discuss on the basis of data the deeper levels of personality organization and formation, although I believe that it is within the province of this symposium to make suggestions for research along these lines.

I shall take as my point of departure the community of San Luis Jilotepeque in the Department of Jalapa, Guatemala. It is the Middle American community which I personally know best, having spent three field seasons there in the last seven years. San Luis also happens to be a community which contains both Indians and Ladinos, each still preserving separate and distinguishable cultures, so that one is in a position to observe and test the differences in a situation the other components of which remain constant. Starting with this situation, then, I propose to set out certain propositions which, on the basis of reports from other Middle American studies, seem to be generally typical throughout the area, for Indians or Ladinos as the case may be. At least the propositions are intended to be amenable to research and open to investigation. It is taken for granted that it is not our function to judge the cultures and personalities in terms of our own cultural preconceptions. Our job is to understand them. No remarks herewith imply either approval or disapproval.

1. The principal and fundamental goal of Indian cultures is to effect a peaceful adjustment or adaptation of men to the universe. In contrast, the main goal of Ladino culture is to effect control of the universe by man. The Indian wishes to come to terms with the universe, the Ladino wishes to dominate it.[3] Connected with these goals and motivations are two different sets of underlying premises. The Indian attitude is not one of abject submission to natural and supernatural forces.[4] The basic assumptions in Indian cultures, however, do hold that man is in a world which operates according to certain laws or rules ultimately controlled by that part of the universe which we would call the supernatural or the unseen, that this general plan of things is ongoing and immutable,[5] that man must learn certain patterns of action and attitude to bring himself into conformity with this scheme of things, and that if he does so he will receive the minimum amount of punishment or misfortune and the maximum rewards of which such a scheme is capable.[6] Some suffering or misfortune is inevitable, but the culture also provides patterns for mitigating it once it has befallen, as well as for avoiding it. These assumptions are implicit to most common men, and even uncommonly gifted men among the Indians of these days seldom raise them to the status of philosophical principles. The Ladino, on the other hand, assumes that the universe, including its supernatural department, can be manipulated by man; that control and power can be established not only over things and other animals but also over other men; that man has a will of his own and that the supernatural realm is also inhabited by beings with individual wills or personalities; that God and the saints can be dealt with on a personality basis, even though at times this necessarily must be done through the mediation of constituted priests; that in manipulating the universe human ideas or beliefs are more important tools than are material artifacts; and that destructive force, even to death, is the legitimate and ultimate technique for the removal of barriers to the individual's control.[7] It is recognized that many persons must because of circumstances submit to frustration in this life, but the philosophy holds that this is no reason

that they should not keep on trying to avoid it or remove it. Ladinos are usually much more glib, although not necessarily more explicit from a logical point of view, about the assumptions of their culture than are Indians.

In the Indian scheme of things, the individual as such counts less than the group.[8] To put it another way, the individual exists as a member of the group which is adjusting to nature; by following its patterns he survives and prospers; but man, not any individual man, is the higher value among the Indians. In contrast, among the Ladinos the individual personality in the abstract has the higher value. This value does not attach to all specific Ladino individuals equally. But the individual soul, ego, personality or what-have-you confronting the universe is of high value in Ladino thinking. The group, or certain groups such as the family, the clique, or the faction, exist to promote the individual, rather than the reverse. Another pair of corollaries is as follows. For Indians uninterrupted routine practice of the traditional patterns of adjustment has high value. For the Ladino such routine is intensely boring and dissatisfying. Periodic change of power locus together with constant struggle which such involves breaks the routine for the Ladino, adds zest to life. Struggle and the oscillation of power are definitely patterned in Ladino mental culture. They are part of the system.

2. The universe in any way of thinking, of course, takes in a lot of territory. However, in Middle America it is always much more restricted from the point of view of Indian culture than for Ladinos. The Indian universe is spatially limited and its horizon typically does not extend beyond the limits of the local community or region This is not because Indians—especially Indian men—have never seen or visited other localities. In San Luis, for instance, practically all men have served in the army in Guatemala City or elsewhere, and throughout their lives they make periodic trips to El Salvador to sell pots or to the United Fruit plantations to earn money. The average man in one sample could name 14 other localities with which he was familiar. Yet these other places are not part of his universe, except in a most casual sense. The nearest analogy of which I can think is that of dream scenes for normal persons among ourselves. The Indians pass through other places, remember odds and ends about them, but do not think of them as part of their structured life experience. The result is, of course, that concepts of nationalism, of regionalism, tribal unity, One World, and the like,

are beyond their ken. Tax has reported the same local focus among the Indians of Western Guatemala.[9]

Likewise the Indians of these days live in a restricted time space. The universe of the Indian does not extend backward to a remembered past, glorious or otherwise.[10] Even the Indians who live on the sites of the great ruins of antiquity do not connect these with their own ancestors. Nor do they project changes for the future. According to the Indian scheme of things life goes on in a timeless present, it has been this way as long as any one knows, and one will be content to see the pattern continue indefinitely. The object of life is to keep the scheme going according to expectations.

The typical Ladino, on the other hand, lives in a universe considerably more expanded both in space and time. His notions about the great world beyond the limits of his own community may be uninformed and naive from the point of view of modern science, but he does not believe that the world ends at the limits of his township or local region. Ladinos have kinship, political, and economic connections with the capital and other towns. They cultivate a concept of nationality, which may differ considerably from that held in the United States, but which enables them to see themselves as part of the Republic. The goal of control with its underlying assumptions may lead the Ladino into frequent revolutions and feuds in order to impose his will or that of men with whom he is associated in the nation, but the nation always figures in his thinking. Furthermore, the Ladinos hold the view that their ancestors came from Europe, that they are the descendants of civilized men with a long and glorious past. Historical details are usually unknown to the average Ladino, yet Ladino culture in its more intellectual circles fosters a strong interest in history, which is the only social science which, until recently, has been well-developed in Latin America. Thus the Ladino's universe takes in at least his own country, and usually he is also aware of the world as a whole, although in a comparatively ignorant way. The Ladino's strivings or drives are seldom entirely restricted to his local community, but are also oriented toward goals whose locus is in the larger outside world. In fact, the major rewards of life, from the Ladino point of view, are to be found in the provincial capital, the national capital, or even in the United States or Europe.[11] What one achieves in his home town is merely a stepping stone to further achievements outside.

Not only is the universe large, but it can be made over and manipulated for the achievement of human desires.

3. The differences between the goal of adjustment and the goal of control are seen in many details of the cultures.

a. Throughout the area consuming interest of both Ladinos and Indians is land. The Indian identifies with the land; there is a reciprocal relationship between milpa and man; a man's fulfillment in one sense comes from his opportunity to work out this adjustment between himself and a milpa. Thus, in San Luis, an Indian speaks of "my milpa," even though he and his father before him have worked it for decades on shares from a Ladino owner. Indians are interested in owning land so that they personally can work on it. Even those who own so much that they must pay other men to help them, invariably also work themselves. A man has not achieved his life goals unless he personally, with his own hands, can work milpa. If an Indian is successful in some specialized non-agricultural occupation, such as tile-making or adobe making, his notion is to give up such a business as soon as he has been able to acquire enough land to satisfy his needs. No Indian ever tries to acquire wealth or skill so that he can retire from the land, but rather the reverse. The Ladino, in contrast, personally works the land only when all other means of livelihood are unavailable. The Ladino wishes to control land—the more the better. He wishes to own it, to have other people work it for him under his orders. Control of land is a subgoal in itself for a Ladino; even if it is not financially profitable, it enables the owner to master the lives of his tenants and workmen, to exert influence in the town hall, and to bask in a certain prestige. If it is financially profitable, the return on the land places in the Ladino's hands the instrument for acquiring control in other fields.[12]

b. The approach to things is typically more direct in Indian culture than in Ladino culture, which patterns the use of instrumentalities as a general rule. The Indian tills his milpa, cuts wood, gathers grass for house thatch, makes pottery, and so on, with his or her own hands, aided by a simple array of tools, and he transports himself and his burdens with his own feet planted directly on the ground. The weariness that comes from physical toil is one of the facts of life, not a resented punishment to be avoided at all costs, and one receives the approval of his fellows, rather than their derogation, for doing these things. Quite the opposite is true of

Ladinos. Labor in the field or in the household is, from the Ladino point of view, properly performed through the instrumentality of other men or women under one's control. Toil is not only unbearably wearisome, but also disgraceful. A Ladino does not walk, if he can help it, but always rides an animal or a machine. He never carries a burden.[13]

c. In relations with other men, the Indian pattern is adjustive and permissive, the Ladino pattern ordering, dominating.[14] Ranking or stratification into classes is not characteristic of Indian society, is always present among Ladinos if their numbers exceed a handful. Statuses of leadership among Indians, such as *mayordomos, principales,* and the like, are thought of as obligations, rather than something to be striven for competitively. Every man who follows the pathways of the culture and who gains the respect of his fellows may expect to assume some such position of prominence during his lifetime; these statuses are not thought of as a restricted group of prizes for which many must compete and few attain. Envy and competitiveness are regarded as an anomaly or a crime. One of the categories of magical illness among Indians is *envidia* (envy) which is believed to be caused by witchcraft perpetrated by an envious person. The victim has the perfect right, with the approval of the community, to kill his magical attacker if the latter can be discovered. Open expression of envy or competitiveness is unthinkable. An Indian in a position of prominence never gives orders to his fellows. He may point out the proper pattern to be followed in a ritual or suggest practical modes of action, as in building a house. But this is in the manner of dispensing superior knowledge, not of dominating others either by force of personality or by authority of position. Age gives knowledge and wisdom and is respected *sui generis.* Group decisions are taken by consensus rather than by majority rule or dictatorial fiat. Perhaps one can say that almost all patterns of social activity in Indian culture lead toward mergence with the society, rather than toward individual distinctiveness. The approved way of doing things is to live and let live, to adjust to other human beings, to avoid conflict. This does not mean highly organized cooperation—in Middle American Indian society one does not find large work gangs among Indians (unless they have been dragooned into them by Ladinos), one does not find elaborately planned projects in which every individual or group has a clear-cut place in an explicit scheme of cooperation, one does not find communism in property. Rather one finds a picture of individuals, families, and relatively small groups each going about its business and not interfering with others. As regards Ladinos and others outside the Indian circle of society, the pattern normally calls for avoidance or submission within limits, rather than protest or conflict. Overt expression of resentment or disagreement is avoided. Political controls are regarded simply as means of keeping the system operating smoothly.

Ladino patterns of social interaction reflect the basic goals and attitudes. Ceremonial politeness with a great tenderness toward the other person's social position and ego is characteristic of Ladino behavior toward strange members of the same caste. Restriction of social contacts with members of lower groups, domineering or ordering behavior toward persons of lower status, and development of factions within the same class are common. Feuds between families and cliques occur with regularity, and in some communities the feud lines are of sufficient antiquity to be regarded as institutionalized. Gossip, character assassination, oaths, and insults are common on the overt level. Strong verbal protest against actions or attitudes disapproved by the individual is expected. The individual strives for prominence, a feat in which he is often assisted by his family. Competition or conflict is typically encountered along the road to power, and the average male must learn techniques of open or covert aggression. High status means the right to plan and order subordinates, but also demands a certain deference to their desires if one's subordinates are not to desert to a rival. The *caudillo* pattern, whether in military affairs, or otherwise, is well established in Ladino culture. But a given caudillo seldom stays in power very long because of the variant drives of his followers. Political advancement is regarded as a legitimate means of advancing one's own interests, if necessary at the expense of other members or factions of the community, including other Ladinos.

As democratic forms move into this area the goals and drives may well be changed for both Indians and Ladinos as the greater rewards of the new dispensation are demonstrated, but the foregoing features seem to be characteristic of the respective ethos at present.

d. Attitudes toward women and family on the whole are consistent with the basic orientations in the two cultures. Although the husband is officially dominant in Indian families, in actual practice the patterns require a reciprocal division of labor and of authority within the family. When a man takes a post of public responsibility, his wife shares the honors and the responsibilities. Man and woman form a cooperative partnership in the general pattern of adjustment to the universe, and to this team are added the children at about the age of seven or eight. Exploitation of one sex by the other in the family is atypical, nor are children dominated by physical or other heavy punishments imposed by the parents. Bickering and fighting between mates is not characteristic. In case of continued incompatibility one or the other mate, usually the woman, retires from the menage rather than continue in opposition to the other spouse. Again the implicit notion seems to be that adjustment without friction is the goal, and that if this proves to be impossible, withdrawal rather than domination is the answer. Several authors have mentioned their impression that sex is of no interest to Indians. My own material does not confirm this. Not only men but also women say that they enjoy the sex act. In one series of 21 women interviewed by my wife, only three, or about 9 percent, could be called cold or indifferent, but even they did not regard sex as repugnant or strongly distasteful. If I interpret the ethos correctly sex is regarded as necessary, but also as natural. It is readily available before marriage and between spouses, and dissatisfied spouses do not hesitate to fill their needs by adultery. Jealousy does occur, but I am certain that from the Indian point of view the use of sex for exploitative purposes is inconsistent with the ethos, just as are all other forms of exploitation of human beings. Sexual prowess does not add to the lustre of an individual.

Among Ladinos marriage is always a contract between families as well as individuals, and tends to be calculated with heavy attention to the social status of the prospective spouses, a feature which does not occur among Indians.[15] The husband's authority is definitely superior in the family, according to the ideal patterns. Women's influence is exerted by devious or indirect means. The man does not expect his wife to share with him his public life in politics, business, and the like, and attempts of the woman to exert authority in these spheres are rejected. The woman participates in social life only with families whose relations with her own household are the most intimate. Double sex standard prevails. Sex is regarded as necessary for men, not necessarily so for women. It is much less easy to come by than among Indians, and prostitutes, Indian women and déclassé women provide a degree of satisfaction to men for gain. This does not mean that there are not many happy marriages among Ladinos. The Ladinos, however, as civilized Christians feel greater guilt about transgressions of the Christian sexual code than do Indians. Although the attitude of fathers toward children is not notably oppressive, children are more dependent upon the father's standing and his goodwill and advice than are Indian children. Fathers project more upon their children, because the latter are reflections of their own egos, and consequently are more insistent that children follow certain lines of conduct specified by the parent. In San Luis, at least, physical punishment is by actual count about three times as frequent for children of Ladino families than for Indians. These authoritarian patterns of family life are gradually being replaced by more equalitarian practices, but the dominance of the father and husband is still the ideal pattern, and it is of course reinforced by church doctrine.

e. The point has often been made that religion among Middle American Indians is not a departmentalized aspect of culture, but that it tends to permeate all of life, whereas Ladino culture appears much more secular. Here again I believe that the differences can be interpreted in terms of the respective ethos. Just as there is no notion of compartmentalizing society among the Indians, so likewise is the idea of compartmentalizing the universe foreign to them. What modern Western Man calls the supernatural is not so distinguished in the Indian culture; the universe is viewed in these terms as a more or less integrated whole. In the less acculturated Indian communities remnants of the old gods still govern the various empirical aspects of the world—gods of the winds, of the sky, of the caves, of the game, of the maize, and so on. Among nominally Catholic Indians who still have not been converted to Ladino culture, the same basic notion persists, although in attenuated form and often the old gods or spirits have been replaced in name by Christian saints. But the planting ceremonies, the rain-making ceremonies, the divinations and magical cures operate without any distinction between empirical and spiritual worlds.

Among nominally Christian Indians, a readily distinguishable difference in attitude and basic assumptions is apparent when compared with their official brethren in the church, the Ladinos. Of course, certain differences in participation in worship are symbols of social distance and cultural difference enforced by the Ladinos—for example, the pattern found in many churches of the Indians worshipping on the floor at the rear of the church and the

Ladinos on chairs or prayer benches toward the front, the Indian women without head covering and the Ladino women obeying St. Paul's injunction with a veil over the head. But apart from these slight differences I believe that a major distinction in culturally generated attitude can be discerned. Very few Indians are accustomed to approach God or the saints alone; few Indians confess to the priest, except under Ladino coercion; prayers and masses for the individual souls of the dead are uncommon, not only because of the cost, for quite expensive rituals are undertaken by Indians, but because of comparative lack of interest in the individual soul, as conceived by Catholic doctrine. The Indian approach to the supernatural is the group approach. In San Luis, at least, the Indians always confer with the priest in a delegation, practically never as individuals. The saints are venerated in *cofradías,* a form of organization and activity in which Ladinos show little interest. Holy water for the planting is brought from Esquipulas by a delegation; a commission carries out the rain-making and thanksgiving ceremonies. The priest is really an outsider; the real repositories of Indian religion, in a sense the effective priests, are the principales, who are also the holders of political power within Indian society and the judges of disputes and controversies which do not reach the civil authority. They symbolize in their multiple functions the intertwining of religion throughout life experience. When an Indian prays in earnest, it is necessary to have a principal, an agent of the society as a whole, do it for him. In prayers I have recorded it is interesting to note that even when a request is made of a particular saint, the saint is addressed as a member of a group. As many as forty-five saints' names may be involved in an invocation. Thus one group—the earthly society—approaches another group—that of heaven. Individuals have souls, yes; but for an Indian the soul is necessary for life in this world. Real anxiety occurs when the soul escapes from the body, as in *espanto,* or magical fright; but little anxiety is generated by contemplating the fate of the soul in the next world. Even in the recovery of the soul in espanto, the procedures require the presence of a group, and most of the therapeutic measures involve restoration of the patient to full social functioning. In short the Indians are not worried about their souls in the hereafter; but they are concerned about them here and now. The person who has lost his soul is incapable of carrying on his routine interaction with his fellows—and that is much worse than hell-fire or damnation.

For the Ladino, on the other hand, religion has somewhat different meanings. In contrast to Indian women Ladino women show more devotion than men, a fact that can probably be correlated with their more restricted roles in the home and the world of affairs. However, on the whole, organized support of the church is striking by its absence in Ladino communities. One of the prevailing complaints of the hierarchy in Mexico and Guatemala, at least, is the unwillingness of Ladinos to support the cult either by money or deeds. Cofradías do not flourish among Ladinos. Fiestas are attended for their commercial and merry-making features. Political and economic affairs tend to be separated from the religion. However, Ladinos are quite concerned about their immortal souls. Although men do not confess regularly, all men (and women likewise) are strongly impressed by the necessity of confessing before death, either to a priest or by act of perfect contrition. Masses for the dead, novenas, and anniversaries of death are religiously celebrated. When a Ladino does pray it is usually as an individual. The usual approach is toward a saint or the Virgin as a supernatural personality who takes a personal interest in the supplicant. Vows are made by the supplicant, presents are made by him as an individual to the image, pilgrimages are made alone or only incidentally in company with other individual pilgrims. Priests are regarded as officials who have special powers to perform certain offices, such as the sacraments, for the benefit of the individual or for his children, land, or animals. Otherwise, in matters which do not directly involve the individual soul, the average Ladino is inclined to ignore the church, except as it may affect his social standing. It is customary to assure everyone that one is a good Catholic, very devoted, who has contributed so-and-so much to the temple, for such a show of conformity may enhance one's prestige. But the typical Ladino is not interested in the dogma of the church insofar as it does not affect him as an individual, and he is bored by most of the routine ritual. His everyday affairs are not believed to be governed by God or the saints except in a far-removed fashion, and he is skeptical of assertions by priests and old women to the contrary. In short, the Ladino cultural attitude is secular.

In the present state of our investigations any remarks about personality type for the Middle American area as a whole must be taken as strictly hypothetical or suggestive, to be validated or rejected on the basis of more detailed and intensive investigation in the future.

In San Luis Jilotepeque the Rorschach material and observational material alike show what appear to be some fundamental differences, at least, in the public, social, or cultural personalities of Indians and Ladinos, respectively. For both castes the range of the culture is distinctly limited and, as might be expected, this is reflected in a relatively restricted personality type in both castes. Neither Indians nor Ladinos show on the adult level much original intellectual ability, freedom in solving problems outside the patterns of the culture, or imagination.

On the Indian side of the line the personality of the typical individual, provided his cultural routine is not interfered with by outside individuals or forces, is relatively more secure and perhaps better integrated than that of the Ladino.[16] In some respects the Indian personality might be considered compulsive. At any rate there is evident what would be called in other countries the compulsive following of the approved patterns of the culture without any strong motivation toward special rewards, distinctions, prominence, or the like. This is especially evident in the work patterns, and the Indians, male and female alike, follow with the utmost diligence the standard routines, such as milpa work, pottery making, corn-grinding, palm-braiding for straw hats, and other activity patterns. The same careful following of pattern is likewise evidenced in ceremonial activities, such as fiestas, cofradía ceremonies, magical cures, and so on. For a great many reasons it seems obvious that the Indian maintains a feeling of personal security so long as he stays within the framework of his culture and is enabled to follow the pathways without deviation which it lays down for him. The adult personality is, on the surface at least, characterized by calmness and comparatively little affect, or show of emotion, in comparison with the Ladinos. However, the typical Indian personality does not show a neurotic constriction of emotion or the flat schizoid reaction. The *abrazo* is given, although not with a great show of enthusiasm; patting of the back and the arm, and handshaking are indulged in without any noticeable stiffness. Also, joking is characteristic although always in a restrained manner when the individual is sober. The belly laugh and hearty laughter of any type is not characteristic. Likewise there is normally little show of aggressiveness on the part of Indians. That Indians are capable of aggressive actions is shown by a good many incidents, however. Several cases are on record of Indians attacking each other with sticks or machetes; these cases are always precipitated by some rank breach of the code, such as a man catching a lover with his wife, gross interference on the part of a father-in-law, or something of the sort. Overt aggression usually appears only when the individuals are under the influence of alcohol. That there are aggressive feelings against Ladinos for the restrictions and punishments which the caste system has laid upon the Indians is evidenced by such things as violent attacks made by Indians on certain Ladinos at the time of the 1944 revolution in Guatemala and by the fact that several of the "devils" who are supposed to snatch souls in espanto are called by Ladino names.

Although one would expect that a constricted character structure of this sort, somewhat compulsive and not given to overt expression of emotions, would be the product of an authoritarian type of child-rearing, the fact is that the first five or six years at least of the Indian's life seem to be quite permissive. Children are nursed whenever they cry and they are not expected to develop sphincter control until able to understand language. Babies are not wrapped in constraining clothes or cradles and, in fact, do not even wear diapers as a general rule. Small children are hardly ever physically punished and are given the utmost freedom to explore their own bodies, the furnishings of the house, and their surroundings. However, they are always under supervision either of one of the parents or of an older sibling in order to protect them from accident. However, this protection is not given through punishment but simply through removing the child from the source of danger and directing its attention upon some other object. For example, if the child crawls toward the fire, he will be lifted up and placed on another part of the floor and given some object to play with, but he will not be spanked or switched. There is no weaning trauma nor, in fact, any other startling experience through which the normal child goes as he emerges from infancy into childhood.

Our Rorschach and observational material indicate that children up to about the age of 18 have a much more out-going type of personality than they develop as adults. They show more imagination than their elders and a much greater readiness to experiment with adjustive techniques not in the pattern. It has been our opinion that part of the constrictive and relatively rigid character structure of the adult is the result of inhibitions inculcated by the caste system rather than the training of early childhood.[17] Boys and girls are inducted into adult patterns gradually and begin to be useful workers in their respective spheres about the age of eight. Motivation based upon respect from others instigates the child to imitate the work patterns of adults, and the adult attitude is that children should not be "forced" but that they should be given responsibilities and allowed to perform activities which are commensurate with their physical and mental development.

It is, I think, noteworthy that what might be considered neuroses within the Indian framework are of two general types which can be interpreted consistently with this view of Indian personality. The principal neurotic manifestation is phrased as espanto or susto (magical fright). It is of importance that from the native point of view this personality upset is believed to be caused by a sudden fright or startle. In other words, the personality can be thrown off balance by any incident which interferes with the smooth performance of the routine patterns. In analyzing a number of cases and cures it also is evident that the person in this condition suffers from heavy anxiety regarding his social relationships, that is, the person with espanto is always out of touch in some way with his fellows and feels that he has lost integration in the social group. The other principal neurotic manifestation is envidia. This literally means envy and is believed to be caused by witchcraft whereby the victim is magically and secretly attacked by someone who is envious of him or otherwise aggressive toward him. In view of the fact that overt aggression is either repressed or constricted in the culture pattern, it is not surprising that anxiety concerning aggression should take the form of fears concerning sub rosa magical attacks. It is also of interest that whereas elaborate patterns are available for warding off, curing, and carrying out magical attacks, there are no clear-cut patterns of overt aggression in the culture. When an individual attacks another physically, he uses whatever weapon may be at hand and the attack exhibits a sort of random trial and error flailing about of the arms. This is in contrast to the very careful procedures used in witchcraft.

In summary it seems to be clear that adult Indians at the present time are little adaptable to changes in the situation. By the time they have reached maturity their habit patterns, both overt and non-overt, have been so firmly established that any deviation from the routine tends to upset the personality integration and to create an insecurity feeling in the individual. However, the young individuals are quite plastic. The fact that this is so seems to account for the comparative ease with which Indians pass into the Ladino status if they are removed from their Indian cultural environment while young and given an opportunity to learn Ladino patterns.

The Ladino personality structure in San Luis, at least, is also constrictive. This, however, seems to be the result of isolation and of the comparative poverty of local Ladino culture in areas outside its home grounds. In contrast to the manifested personality characteristics of Indians, the Ladinos show much more emotionalism. Not only are likes and dislikes more demonstratively expressed, but the average Ladino is characterized by mood swings which range from depression and helplessness to feelings of high euphoria. Consistent with this is the impression that the typical Ladino is basically much less secure than the typical Indian. He has no feeling of certainty that any of his available culture patterns will produce satisfactions which he expects and he is uncertain about their effectiveness when practiced outside the community. The result is that many Ladinos tend to withdraw from or be hesitant about interaction in the larger world outside, but, since they wish to adjust to the larger world, this produces feelings of frustration and inadequacy. Ladinos are much more aggressive, at least on the overt level, both toward themselves and toward members of the other caste. This aggressiveness can be interpreted in the light of the frustrations which Ladinos face. Furthermore, the Ladinos show a higher percentage of hypochondriasis, psychosomatic ailments, neurotic twitches, and the like. That Ladinos habitually get more drunk more often than do Indians, seems to indicate that they find release from anxiety and frustration in alcohol as well as in hypochondriasis and aggressive outbreaks. Many Ladinos resort to cures for relief from magical fright and witchcraft, but do so with an ambivalent attitude. In other words, Ladinos only half believe in these conditions and the measures taken to alleviate them, but this tendency among Ladinos indicates again their willingness to try anything for relief from anxiety of frustration feelings.

Child care among Ladinos is fairly permissive as compared with middle class patterns in Europe or America of 25 years ago, but it is probably more authoritarian than the Indian system. Within the last few years some upper class Ladino families have instituted formula feeding on schedule, rigid cleanliness training, and so on—patterns which have been acquired from the great world outside—but these are not characteristic of the Ladino pattern as a whole up to the present. However, the Ladino child is usually dressed in diapers and underpants, earlier attempts at cleanliness training are instituted by parents than among the Indians, and the authority of the father in particular is more strict. Although small babies are given the breast whenever it is desired, the typical Ladino mother tries to wean her child by the end of the first year and does not permit the child to soil the house once it is able to crawl about. Also the higher one goes in the Ladino class system, the greater is the rigidity of child training.

Ladino children are sent to school at the age of six and subjected to fairly rigid schoolmaster's discipline which emphasizes the values of Ladino life. Proportionately fewer Indian children go to school, but for those that do so the transition from the Indian home to the school room is more of a trauma for the Indian child than for the Ladino, because the teachers have traditionally taken a negative attitude toward their Indian pupils who are frequently unable to understand or speak Spanish by the time they arrive in school. If the Indian child suffers a greater shock in going to school, he usually escapes from it within a relatively short time. Thus the school discipline has had up to now a relatively insignificant influence on the development of Indian personality patterns, because few Indian children enter school and most of those who do drop out after the first year or two. With the Ladino, on the other hand, the child goes through the three or four years of elementary school offered locally, and it is the ideal pattern then to send children away to other communities where they can at least get through the sixth year. Thus the typical Ladino is subjected to at least six years of the compulsive type of discipline which has been characteristic of Guatemalan and Mexican elementary schools up until very recently. At the end of this time most of the Ladinos come back to their home town. Indian children of this age have already worked into the adult patterns which they expect to follow throughout their lives. The boys are helping their fathers in the fields and on pottery-peddling trips. The girls have mastered the techniques of the woman's world. The young Ladino, however, emerging from school is provided with none of the patterns which he will expect to use as an adult, except literacy. The result is that there is a period of adolescent adjustment for Ladinos which does not have a counterpart among the Indians. During this time the girl receives some instruction as to how to manage a house and waits hopefully for marriage. The boy seeks to find a place for himself in the Ladino adult world. Since there are a wider variety of patterns open to the Ladino men than there are to Indians, a certain element of choice is involved here rather than merely the safe road of following one's father's footsteps. Since manual work is not regarded as desirable for Ladino males, but rather manipulative activities are valued either in managing agricultural or business enterprises, the adolescent Ladino male is often at loose ends. He is not mature enough to assume the managerial role nor are the patterns whereby he may do so clear to him, except if he belongs to an established family or is able to develop personal contacts. The rather vague and often unobtainable goals of Ladino culture have been implanted in his thinking by the school and by his fellows. Just as is the case with the Indian youngsters, Ladino youngsters also show more malleability and plasticity than do their elders. By the time a Ladino boy has reached maturity he has either found a place in the local system which usually does not appear to be entirely satisfactory to him, or he has moved away from the community to seek his rewards in the outside world. At any rate those who remain suffer from feelings of anxiety, frustration, and insecurity which we have already mentioned. The high degree of verbosity which many observers have mentioned in connection with Ladino personality traits can, I think, be interpreted as partly related to the comparative insecurity of the real world. Even in a small isolated community like San Luis, Ladinos are given to living, as one might say, on a partly fanciful level in which argumentation and discussion about ideals and ideas takes up a good deal of time. In rural communities the ideas themselves may be comparatively naive but they are usually discussed with great affect. As a North American would say, they are taken more seriously than would seem to be justified. Since the culture of the Ladinos does not offer many and sure rewards when their attention is directed primarily toward things, it is perhaps to be expected that fantasy reward on the level of verbalization may serve as a compensation to some extent. If one cannot manipulate things to his own satisfaction, he can at least manipulate ideas or emotions. Thus the Ladino is often a violent partisan when it comes to any matter of opinion or policy.

These suggestions taken from studies in San Luis Jilotepeque may or may not be generalizable to the Middle American area as a whole. Certainly they would probably have to be modified when applied to other localities.

Nothing has been said about dream interpretation, both because of diffidence and because of lack of material. I have a collection of dreams from San Luis, but I am convinced that it is neither extensive nor deep enough to permit generalizations. Interpretations seem to be consistent with what has gone before. However, systematic dream collection will be necessary before final interpretations of the deeper personality levels can be attempted.

DISCUSSION

(1)

Villa: I should like to point out the presence of peculiar traits that belong to a certain type of culture—the folk. Are you discussing the ethos of the Indian or the ethos of the folk society? And is this not a part of the content of a culture?

Gillin: The theoretical position, as I understand it, is that ethos is not the content of culture. The ethos that I attribute to the Indians here is put forward as something characteristic of Indian culture in Middle America.

Paul: These are sort of basic premises, usually implicit, by which many specific things can be better understood. It's something which can be reduced to a limited number of things.

Redfield: The chief difficulty I see arises from the fact that Gillin is attempting to distinguish Indian ethos and Ladino ethos apparently in much of Latin America. As a result the respects in which the Indian views of life in Middle America differ from the Indian view of life elsewhere in America is not considered. Gillin is interested in the Ladino-Indian contrast almost everywhere.

The question will arise as to how much of these characteristics of Indian ethos is true of Indians outside of Middle America. For the comparison which would answer this question, you can think of Elsie C. Parson's discussion of the subject in Mitla, of Bunzel's account of the Zuni view of life in the B.A.E., and of the interesting account of Navaho ethos by Kluckhohn in Northrop's volume on "Ideological Differences and World Order."

Incidentally aren't we getting too many words for really the same idea—ethos, ideology, basic configuration, supreme values, normative social theory and so on?

(2)

There followed a discussion of depth psychology studies which have been made in Middle America. Gillin and Davidson have administered Rorschachs and Goodenough Draw-a-Man tests; Lewis has given TAT's in Tepoztlan; Paul has obtained psychiatric material in terms of deviants; Ruiz de Galvez has tested Caribs in Honduras; Kyte has obtained many varieties of personality data; Tax, and others, have taken life histories. It was agreed that much needs to be done in this field.

(3)

Tax: It's worthwhile to recall Gordon Childe's main distinction of what happened with the Neolithic revolution. Agricultural people—people who make pottery, etc., are different from food-gatherers: they're interested in changing the world. A similar distinction might be made at a higher level, between the Indians and Ladinos. And the Ladinos, in comparison with the atomic scientists, accept the world.

Gillin: I'd say it's a matter of attitude, rather than technology of the culture.

Tax: That's what Childe would say too.

Goubaud: There is a very important matter to be brought up here. Would you attribute historical circumstances to change in ethos. When you consider the wars that used to be prevalent among these very same Indians in pre-Conquest times, it would seem to be a matter of nonadjustment to the environment.

Gillin: That's just the sort of point I'd like to have brought out.

Goubaud: I was wondering whether it could be postulated that historical situations could change the ethos?

Watkins: Don't you need to say how that happened?

Goubaud: It was an adaptation of man to the universe, and the human beings are a part of the universe. Nowadays the Indians try to avoid conflict whenever they can.

Paul: It seems to me that this can be accepted in a spirit which wouldn't be contradicted by the presence of war. The Indian's attitude is that of an individual working within a frame of reference rather than against it. The constant idea of western culture is "We're conquering nature." Folk people the world over are cooperating with nature.

Mrs. Paul: The difference is in where the locus of power lies. In the Indian attitude, the ultimate locus of power lies outside of man and in the universe. These are powers which ultimately determine man's fate. The Indians also use various methods to effect a change but ultimately their fate is in the hands of powers which lie outside their own control.

Goubaud: If the locus of power is in the universe, they are certainly trying to change it.

Mrs. Paul: Was there in Aztec times also the feeling that supernatural powers might ultimately give favor to one side or the other?

Goubaud: That's too broad. Everybody had powers to invoke. Bows and arrows are not a peaceful adjustment.

Tax: The original question was whether ethos can change with historical circumstances.

Gillin: Ethos is closely connected with the total configuration of the culture. If there is change in the cultural whole, there would be a change in the ethos. One point I'd like to raise: neither the Aztecs or the Maya were ever imperialistic, in the modern sense of the term.

Stone: The Aztec were.

Goubaud: The Quiché had obtained a certain sovereignty over neighboring groups.

Gillin: The Aztec trait of taking prisoners, not to dominate men, but to get sacrifices, is quite different from that of seeking a dominating power.

(4)

Watkins: The Indian attitude is not one of abject submission. How much of this is applicable to tribal peoples, whether they're in Middle America or anywhere else; to industrialized peoples; or to any other kind of people? Suppose you discuss this with reference to any place where you have Europeans and natives in contact?

MacNeish: There's a feeling among the people that they have to take an active part in keeping the universe running; they have to keep up their ceremonies. The urban man doesn't care about keeping the universe running.

Goubaud: How about the Auracanian Indians who were as much subjected to conquest forces as the communities of the Andes, and still presented a terrific resistance?

Paul: The mere fact of resistance wouldn't deny the ultimate validity of this proposition—the disposition to regard themselves as working within a much larger frame of reference.

Gillin: Among the Inca, for example, the emperor was a brother of God. He did things that he wanted to do, in his own name and through his status. Now to be sure, it was a matter of social planning—roads, terraces, the conquering of nuisance peoples. He didn't wait to see what God was going to do. That's quite different from that which pertains to Middle America at the present time. The Inca had an ethos different from that of Middle American Indians, but it was not the European ethos.

Paul: He's objecting to the statement that this is European. I would say this is wider than Middle America. If we can make a generalization for Middle America that will apply widely, so much the better.

Tax: How about commercialism? The individual who is trading isn't accepting nature; he's inventing new ways of making a living.

Paul: He has the inclination to say, "This is the will of the universe," if he doesn't succeed as a *comerciante*.

(5)

Jimenez Moreno: I agree with most of the points in Dr. Gillin's paper and I have a few disagreements, especially on this point that we are discussing now, where he says that in the Indian culture, the general plan of things is ongoing and immutable. The Aztec ideas were against that because they had four or five periods in which the idea was that historical events more or less happened in such a way that there were closed cycles; each cycle closed by a catastrophe. Regarding the main god of the Aztec, you find a very personalized concept of a deity, one who does as he wills. So apparently there is not a common ethos for all of Middle America. We have at least to distinguish between that plateau region which was dominated by the Aztecs, and the Maya area. Among the latter specialization had a chance to develop in more or less stable ways. The heart of the Maya area was not touched, whereas the Central Mexican plateau had people coming in and going and there was always a disturbance. This would materially affect the ethos of a people.

Tax: That's a beginning of what we ought to be getting at in a comparison of the old and the new.

Paul: Even though it might be true that there was great domination, you have to distinguish between the political elite and the people who were dominated. The ethos of the leaders might differ from that of the people.

Tax: The dominant group was in the same position as that of the Ladinos now; the masses of the Indians are the same now as in the past.

Jimenez Moreno: The dominant people came from the plateau.

Goubaud: Some qualifications should be made here. Did the ethos of the social classes vary from class to class? It would be very important to discover if attitudes of dominance are found in the ethos of the Indian elite at the present.

Paul: There is no Indian elite.

Gillin: I make the point that the Indians within their own circle do not take a dominant attitude toward other Indians. This needs to be looked into more thoroughly.

Tax: Perhaps we could look into some of these conditions now. How about some of the groups that have felt the white domination less since the conquest, e.g., the Tzeltal or the Lacandon? Do we notice any difference in their basic attitudes toward the universe?

Beals: I think you could contribute quite a bit. Among the Yaqui, for example, I don't feel that there's this attitude of not accepting the universe, and they're certainly not submissive.

(6)

Jimenez Moreno: As regards the attitude of the Indians toward the universe, it is worth remembering that apparently the Indians felt that they had to feed the universe. In Middle America the emphasis was on feeding supernatural powers so that they could continue their job of giving food to the world.

Paul: It was a matter of ingratiating a higher power.

Watkins: How much control is there when you pray to the saint to help somebody to get well?

Paul: Do Ladinos do it?

Tax: The associated Catholic ethos reinforces the Indian's type of ethos. In Catholic theology, the tendency is to accept the will of God much more than in Protestant theology.

Gillin: With respect to the Ladinos. I don't know everything about Middle American Ladinos. But what I say about Ladinos here seems to be true of Colombia, Peru, Ecuador, as well as to those I know in Middle America. I think the Ladino tries to make a deal with the saint and tries to get on a personal basis with the saint. Ladinos have personal saints that are almost guardian spirits. The Indians do it in a group fashion.

Watkins: But if you get on a personal basis with a saint, you're still not dominating the universe.

Gillin: But you're manipulating him to do something for you.

Goubaud: If we compare certain aspects of Catholicism with Indian religion, there are so many parallels—where are you going to stop? The Catholic has a belief in a guardian angel and the Indian has a belief in a *nagual*. Then you have the case of the Indian going up to the mountain; he has to take so many pounds of incense, the price of what he will ask for. There's a definite personal relationship of the shaman with the divinity. Indians pray in the church, asking for special favors, so it is difficult to distinguish between the Catholic and Indian beliefs. If you make broad enough generalizations they are almost aspects of the same pattern.

Mrs. Paul: In some cases it sounds even as though the Indian approach to the supernatural is even more personal. They will approach the saint with arguments, and even cajolery, almost as if they were speaking to a person of higher authority.

(7)

Paul: This fits into the statement that for Ladinos "it is believed that man has a will of his own." I think the Indians likewise so believe. The Indian supernaturals certainly have individual wills. They're not beings who judge in terms of wrong or right, but they have a lot of power and one can get in good with them.

Gillin: San Luis Jilotepeque might be anomalous in that respect. They approach the group of saints.

Tax: That's true in Midwestern Guatemala. There you get the same thing; the Indian refers to *all* the saints.

Gillin: That's why I say the Indians approach the saints as a group.

Wisdom: I have the feeling that all this saint worship is man to man, as opposed to the relationship between man and deity.

Camara: The people go to the image and talk to it.

Wisdom: The saint is much more personalized.

Tax: Because you've got an image.

Guiteras: I think it's more personal among the Ladinos. A Ladino can ask personally for forgiveness; an Indian won't do that. He can ask a favor, but if he's done wrong, he has to make things right with his fellow men.

Camara: We have agreed that Ladino houses have more domestic altars.

Stone: I think this is one of the times when the Indian mentality comes out.

Gillin: Is there any place where the

Indians will talk to a saint by themselves and to only one saint?

Beals: In most of the plateau places I know, they go to a particular saint and talk to it.

Gillin: In San Luis, an Indian will never pray to a saint by himself. If he's really praying he has somebody else do it for him.

Guiteras: When a shaman is making a cure, the amount of incense burned will always be the same. If the cure is not effected, it's because he has made some mistake. My point is that it's not the same as the Ladinos do; they make offerings and vows. The shaman will always have to perform the same magical rites.

Jimenez Moreno: I think that Miss Guiteras meant that the Indians are more formalistic, more prone to formulas and to act within them. I think the Indians are much more prone to make deals with the saint, as you mentioned. For instance, if it rains too much they may take the saint to the lake and punish it.

Guiteras: It's less personal.

Jimenez Moreno: There's another very important point that Goubaud made: that it is difficult to distinguish between the Christian religion, especially Catholic, and the Indian. I think it's just because there are so many similarities between the previous Indian religion and the Catholic, that acculturation succeeded so well in countries like Mexico. The Indians had a kind of baptism, a kind of communion and confession. There is a common ground for both religions, and since the core of this culture was religion, I think that explains acculturation.

Goubaud: Miss Guiteras was actually speaking about rites. In that sense all religions have definite ways of performing a rite. The Catholic mass, for instance, can't be changed. If we are speaking about rites, there seems to be a formalized way of performing them. I thought we were speaking about the more nonformalized ways.

Gillin: There's nothing in the Catholic doctrine which prescribes that you have to set up candles before all fourteen saints. The fact that you find it where it's not imposed is important. The other answer is on the informal level where you're trying to get in touch with the saints but you have to get an intermediary.

Beals: Now you're generalizing from the particular of Guatemala. I want to go back to the possibility of fundamental differences between the native religion and the Catholic religion. The Mixe who has a sick relative goes to a specialist to find out what he should do. The specialist may prescribe that he make a sacrifice at a certain spot; he may hire the specialist to do it for him. Or if the specialist says to burn a candle the man does it himself. In the one case it's his own personal relationship with the saint; in the other case he will get someone else to perform it for him. I'm suggesting this might indicate that there are two fundamental attitudes which are related to the two religions.

Stone: One thing you said about the question of the Indian and the punishing of the saints—that it was Indian and not Ladino. You have this all over—even in the U.S. I wonder just how much of that is Ladino.

Beals: Medieval literature is full of it.

Watkins: The main point in the paper is that the Indian adjusts himself to a world that he can't very well manipulate, and the Ladino manipulates it. Could we say that the Ladino tends toward one pole and the Indian toward the other one?

Beals: I have the feeling that this expresses something which we've not yet learned to state correctly. I agree with the general proposition but I find myself in opposition to all the examples.

Gillin: The technical position on this hasn't advanced to an exact science yet but from what's gone on before in our discussion it appears quite clear that there are several culture areas among the Indians of Middle America. There would, therefore, be several ethos.

Tax: Can we delimit several ethos? Do we see any substantial difference between them? Do you think the Mixe accept nature more or less than the people of San Luis Jilotepeque?

Gillin: The other side of the point is that this may be a general folk ethos. It's not world wide but what's Middle American about it?

(8)

Kyte: You have to consider the community more in the Indian culture.

Paul: That's part of the Old World romantic conception present in the Ladino, to a degree that it's less present in the Indian.

MacNeish: The Indian community simply spends so much more time doing things for the community. Certainly the Ladinos I know did nothing of community concern.

Watkins: They have public works for the community.

MacNeish: I mean ceremonial.

Gillin: The question is: what's the motivation of the individual? If he's getting paid, I'd say he's a Ladino. The Indian doesn't operate on that basis.

Goubaud: I would say that the statement that the individual counts less in the Indian groups is true because the Ladino is more individualized. This statement seems to hold true.

Watkins: A corollary to that is that Indians go to the gods as a group and the Ladinos go as individuals.

Wisdom: We've already discussed the point that there is a great deal of individual praying to the saints.

Watkins: If the Ladino goes to the gods in the organized church, that isn't individual is it? The prayers are already written aren't they?

Paul: If this point means anything, it should mean that the Indian works in an ascribed status system. He exploits people but that exploitation is in terms of offices, in terms of relatively fixed ascribed statuses. If this is true, for the Ladino there should be a method of achieving status through manipulation.

Gillin: What does exploitation mean?

Paul: He'll exert authority in office.

Gillin: Is it done at the expense of someone else? I'd say such is not typical of Indian culture.

Camara: As I see it, we're still within the concept of folk culture vs. urban culture.

Watkins: It could be Mesoamerican if the Indians are more folklike.

Tax: If you're going to say something about the ethos of Middle American Indians as opposed to some other people, you can say that they're different from Ladinos.

Beals: This problem hasn't been worked out and rationalized.

Gillin: There is a good deal of content here that doesn't apply to folk cultures all over the world. Mixed Catholicism or the cofradía system, for example.

Tax: But that doesn't give you their ethos. Certainly among the more commercial peoples that I know, in the cofradía system and in the centripetal communities where you have this whole hierarchical system and everything is organized, I think you have a kind of impersonality much more than you do in much of the folk. Therefore, this system of ascribed status, etc., might actually be an indication in contradiction of what you're saying, because it permits people to forget about the universe, so to speak. Furthermore, in these communities where social control is on a local level, you get a kind of impersonal institutional behavior which is not characteristic of the folk. Maybe this is one kind of folk.

Paul: You have a machinery to take care of the universe. The Protestants claimed that the Catholics had intermediaries; the Protestants didn't and went directly to the gods. In that respect you can say that the Catholic structure, originally at any rate, was more folklike than the Protestantism that later arose.

Gillin: If we still go along with our

original assumptions as to the nature of ethos and what it is, then we want to get specific, or find out what the specific goals and specific traits are in Middle America.

Beals: Regarding the question of the motivation of the Ladinos in performance of ceremony. The Ladino is in part taking an active participation in his religious ceremonials for the purpose of the salvation of his own eternal soul. The Indian isn't; he is taking part in religious ceremonies to assure the continuance of the group, etc. He's not worried about his soul. I would say that the Catholic ideology plays a minor role.

Watkins: The next point made is that the universe of the Indian is more limited in time and space than that of the Ladino. What have we on that?

Gillin: Geoffrey and Monica Wilson, in their book on social change in Africa, used the concept of cultural range. We might say that the cultural range of the Indian is more limited.

Goubaud: I would like to ask Mr. Gillin if he didn't reach a conclusion as to the restricted universe of the Ladinos in San Luis Jilotepeque.

Gillin: I would say all the Ladinos in San Luis had their eyes on the provincial capital.

Tax: What is the community? What is society? All that you can say is that the societies have a wider range.

Gillin: It works both ways. You can't have a wider society without a wider cultural range.

Tax: What we ought to do is find some significant correlations.

Gillin: One might be that if the Indians of Panajachel were to be united in a society with other Indians around the lake, then the culture would expand.

Jimenez Moreno: I think what Dr. Gillin says is corroborated when you say that the Indians don't have the concept of a general history, but only local histories. It's rather difficult to have a general history of the region. You have to go back and establish the history of each town. I think some of the things that he says are worth examining. It's a question of a rural society vs. an urban society. How much of that is due to the fact that it is a rural culture or how much is due to the fact that it is an Indian culture? The other point is about the Indians who these days are living in a restricted time-space. This is true, but it has not always been so.

(9)

Tax: There is evidence that no matter how far these Indians travel, when they return their horizons aren't extended by personal experience.

Kaplan: They're travelling to the U.S. They're becoming ladinoized when they return.

Camara: How are we going to explain the ladinoization?

Goubaud: The question of ladinoization is important, because we have instances of Indians who have come to the U.S. selling their wares. When they return to Guatemala they go to Guatemala City and open up a store.

Beals: In Cherán my impression is that those who come back slough off whatever influences have come from outside; those deeply affected don't come back; they stay in the U.S.

Camara: You could find a range of variation.

Guiteras: Doesn't the fact that they leave mean that they're more ladinoized?

Tax: Not necessarily. You find this local view of the world even among those who go on commercial trips and come back.

Camara: But in that case we could predict that the Indian culture is going to last forever.

Gillin: The explanation offered is that ladinoization takes place among younger individuals—before the age of 25.

Jimenez Moreno: That's not the only way in which ladinoization takes place, but one of the more important ways. *Criadas* should be studied more carefully. The criada goes to the city and marries a Mestizo; her children are Ladinos. This problem is being worked on at the present by a sociologist, Dr. Carroll.

Paul: These children are out of their original community.

Tax: There are obviously two ways: (1) People leave the town, and (2) the whole town becomes ladinoized.

Jimenez Moreno: We might also consider what happens within the community itself; many people come and have sexual relations with the women —that's one of the ways you get your Mestizos. When the Spanish came in the sixteenth century a similar situation prevailed, and the criadas with whom sexual relations are sought are abandoned in the same way today as were the Indians by the Spanish.

(10)

Watkins: How about the point regarding the difference between European and tribal peoples?

De la Fuente: I want to qualify this statement as to the universe not extending backward through the remembered past. The Zapotec have no remembrance of previous conditions.

Goubaud: I think the whole subject matter has been well taken with regard to the fact that a restricted culture will create a restricted universe. In Rabinal however, where a French priest wrote a drama dating back to probably 1400 A.D. which it presented to the people at various times, the Indians will point out to you, "There is where the Quiché king lived."

(11)

De la Fuente: Is there a contradiction between the last two sentences? The object of life is to keep the scheme going. Is it the scheme as a whole or just part of the scheme? Or is it just keeping one part of the scheme going indefinitely?

Gillin: In the mechanisms of acculturation the very ethos can change. For example, in the U.S. we started out with a certain view about democracy, which has since been changed.

You get acculturation in spite of ethos. Actually there's another type of ethos: to try out everything new.

Paul: In the U.S. you have a future orientation—"We are making Progress." In the Indian community it is: "Maintain what we used to have." But the advance of technology in the latter robs the elders of the locus of power; there is always a rebelliousness among the younger generation. When the elders start losing their power, then revolutionary things begin to happen; youth begins to assert itself. Then you get sudden spurts of acculturation.

Beals: I think we talk so much about cultures as integrated wholes that we tend to forget that Indians don't think this way. Quite often they will accept change in one part of the culture without realizing that this will change the whole pattern in the future.

(12)

Watkins: The point to be discussed is that the Indian is related more intimately to the land than is the Ladino, although the land is important to both.

Tax: Obviously here you get a class sort of thing. You have a class of workers and a class of landowners; it varies from place to place, for in some cases the Ladinos are as much peasants as are the Indians. You could distinguish the Ladino population, generally speaking, by two or three economic classes. In Guatemala there are places where the Ladinos work the soil with the hoe and generally live "like Indians"; you get a class difference here. So with respect to this business about land we must be sure that we are dealing with people of the same economic position.

Tumin: There is an actual investment by the Indian in the land, whereas there is no such investment by the Ladino. The focussing of the Indian's personality is tied up with the concept of being closely related to the land.

Goubaud: I would like to express the proposition that Ladino culture is urban oriented and that the Indian culture is country or land oriented. The Ladino culture comes from the Mediterranean basin, where it was the Roman policy to urbanize. There is a supervaluation or urban values in the Ladino culture. If you consider that the whole outlook in Ladino culture is to consider the peasant as definitely less desirable in status than the urban man, this would tend to corroborate what Tumin has said.

Stone: I think what you say is absolutely true for most of Latin America but it doesn't hold true for Costa Rica. The people who went there went to farm.

Goubaud: That's a wonderful example of a case outside of Mesoamerica.

Stone: The people who went to Costa Rica were peasant farmers to begin with.

Tax: There's another reason why the Ladinos should have that orientation. The Spanish were townspeople; the Indians originally became Ladinos as they became attached to towns, so that Ladinos traditionally are the townspeople. Even though there were some who have become farmers, I suppose the urban tradition of the Ladino still holds.

Gillin: Are there any other places in Latin America like Costa Rica?

Beals: In Argentina.

Camara: Also in parts of Colombia.

Goubaud: If you took the younger generation in Costa Rica and asked them whether they wanted to go to the city, that could be important in its implications. The Indian doesn't want to go to the city.

(13)

De la Fuente: There is a sweeping statement that "A Ladino never carries a burden." This is more true in Peru than it is in Middle America. I was impressed in Cuzco because the Ladinos there do not carry anything at all.

Camara: I wouldn't agree with that.

Paul: Within the area, if the Ladino doesn't walk, in part it's because the Indian does walk. And if the Ladino doesn't carry things, it's because the Indian does.

Goubaud: In Jocotán, my wife became acquainted with a woman who used to carry a basket with forty dozen eggs in it at a time—and she was a Ladino! I am sure that the wealthy Indian would also have a servant.

Tax: You would argue that if the Ladino had money, he wouldn't carry burdens.

(14)

Watkins: How about the statement that "In his relations with other persons, the Indian is ready to adjust himself, while the non-Indian is domineering, etc."?

Beals: Is this an Indian-Ladino distinction, or a class distinction?

Paul: I think it's a class position if the ethos is drawn strongly from the class position. The Indian is actually in a social situation where he has to be submissive.

Goubaud: The question of permissiveness is not correlated with social position or ethnic position, but is definitely a pattern within a culture. You have brought up the fact of the permissiveness with regard to the children in the Indian culture, and less permissiveness in other cultures. Would you say the terms adjustive and permissive are comparable to submissiveness and dominance?

Jimenez Moreno: I want to go back to a previous point. I think there is a need to state how conditions were in Spain before the Conquest, in order to understand the whole thing. This reluctance to do manual work is something that already existed in Spain before the Spanish came to America. There were many statements to that effect. We have to take into consideration that the Spanish before coming to America were at war for many centuries against the Moors; the whole pattern of domineering was already evolved in Spain, where the Moors were concerned with working in the fields.

Paul: Isn't this a reference to a class in Spain?

Beals: They came to the New World to get out of that.

Goubaud: The proposition by Jimenez Moreno is that the Spanish, when they came to Spanish America, belonged to a feudal system in which the values were in a warrior class.

Tax: They came here to get out of the peasant class.

Gillin: I wouldn't go along with calling this a class difference.

Paul: I use class in a generic sense, to distinguish it from a homogeneous society.

Wagley: I'd like to point out some doubt in point of contact in point (c). From my experience I would say that Indian society is ranked. The degree of dichotomy between the lowest and the highest man is not as great as in Ladino society. There are different ways of ranking, but in my experience, Indian society is highly ranked. On the other points of this paper I find myself much in agreement.

Wisdom: I thought we said before that there was not this competition—that these positions are looked upon as obligations. Won't Mr. Wagley tell us where there is this competition?

Wagley: Let's begin with ranking and status: certainly all farmers have the lowest rank. I could rank each individual in the culture in terms of status. In Chimaltenango, if you don't have much land, you just can't be considered for a *mayordomía* or any of the positions as you move higher up; if you don't have land you leave the community. In a survey of 250 men, there were only five without land. I believe this a ranking system almost as strict as that of the Ladinos.

Paul: I would agree except I would not say these are class differences. It hasn't congealed into a class system.

Wagley: I am talking about ranking or stratification into classes. Now certainly ranking is quite mobile in the Ladino classes.

Paul: There's ranking but no classes.

Wagley: Ladino society is potentially a much wealthier society.

Paul: We've decided against classes but not against ranking.

Tax: In a series of communities in Chiapas, it means death to show the slightest sign of wealth. On a less extreme level in the Midwest Highlands of Guatemala, you don't try to show your wealth.

Wagley: Is wealth the only criteria?

Tax: You don't strive for office when it costs you money.

Mrs. Paul: In San Pedro the important men are those who do have money.

(15)

Watkins: How about the statement that "Among Ladinos marriage is always a contract between families as well as individuals."

MacNeish: Among the Mestizos, it's strictly an individual contract; the families have nothing to do with it.

Kyte: I'd like to ask whether sex is readily available before marriage.

Beals: No.

[There was little agreement with Dr. Beals.]

Tax: San Luis Jilotepeque is probably at one extreme in sexual behavior, while many parts of Middle America are at another extreme.

Paul: Indian men are interested in sex.

Guiteras: It's important.

Paul: The double standard prevails in Ladino culture as well as Indian.

Mrs. Paul: Ladinos feel greater guilt.

Guiteras: I think it's the opposite.

Paul: There's some feeling that there's some accomplishment in sex among the Ladinos but not among the Indians.

Gillin: In the cases I have seen in San Luis, the Ladinos always felt guilty.

Tumin: I got the impression that it was standard practice among Ladino males to have extramarital affairs. Among the few cases of the Indians I knew, I thought they were more disturbed by it.

Goubaud: It seems to me that the Indian places less emphasis on morality and sex than the Ladino does. The Ladinos belong to a culture in which sex was always considered a sin. The Indian doesn't have that sense of sin, so it's less of a morality problem.

Jimenez Moreno: I agree with Dr. Gillin about the sense of guilt being more widespread among Ladinos. We have found that in spite of that there are many instances of these sexual sins without a sense of guilt. I think it has something to do with the difference between the Catholic and Protestant attitude. In the Catholic attitude you never think of changing the rules, but you break them.

Paul: On this question of guilt, I'm not sure who has more guilt. To the extent that the Ladino transgresses, to the extent that he has misgivings, it's because of his own salvation; to the extent that the Indian has misgivings, it's because he's worried about doing harm to the community.

(16)

Watkins: Do we agree that Indian personality is more highly integrated on the whole than is non-Indian personality.

Jimenez Moreno: One thing that has always been noticed among Mestizos is that they lack cultural stability. The Mestizo doesn't know where he stands; whether he's Indian or Spanish. I am speaking of the *criollo*.

Paul: You're making a trichotomy.

Jimenez Moreno: I feel the need of discussing the criollo, the Mestizo, and the Indian.

Tax: From the point of view of the Ladinos in the area as a whole, do we now consider that they are an intermediate group? Is it a two-class or caste system, or a three-class or caste system? There's no consciousness of the upper class.

Gillin: I agree.

Jimenez Moreno: The trouble is that we're talking about only a section of Middle America.

(17)

Watkins: With respect to the statement that the restricted element in Indian personality is more a product of the social system than it is the experience of the child in his individual development, Mr. Goubaud wrote a paper about the freedom of the Indian in early childhood, with controls imposed later in life.

Mrs. Paul: I would agree more or less with Goubaud's point on this. In material dealing with people, who have emotional and temporary breakdowns, the locus of their anxieties very frequently relates to this conflict with authority—with parents, etc. You get anxieties surrounding food or guilt over sex in other areas. In our material at least a great deal of the stress material comes out in connection with conflict with authority in which the parent or parent surrogate figures. There is this constant feeling of repressed hostility on the part of the child.

Paul: There is this permissiveness in the Indian culture but it is limited at a certain age.

PART III. CONCLUSIONS: THE OLD AND THE NEW

chapter 10

NOTES ON ACCULTURATION

by Ralph Beals

THIS chapter must be regarded as a series of somewhat random observations, hunches, and suggestions for investigation rather than any definitive statement in the field.

The first topic I wish to discuss is the question of the origin of traits. It is, of course, a truism that all Indian cultures in Middle America today are of mixed origin. Nevertheless I have the feeling that the analysis of this mixture and the understanding of its significance in long range interpretations of culture change and acculturation is rather underdeveloped.

In the first place, I suggest that culture traits—and I use this term in its broadest sense—can be classified in preliminary fashion in ways that have some significance. On a broad basis the mixed cultures of Middle America can be classified on the basis of content, structure or organization, and ethos, as defined by Gillin in his illuminating paper. Additional subdivisions may be possible or desirable for detailed analysis, but for general purposes these three suffice.

These three major divisions can be subject to further classification and analysis. A great many traits of content can be arranged somewhat as follows:

a. Indian elements which are unique to the area or to a group. The point of interest here is not so much whether the element is or is not found in other areas, however, as is the point that it is not shared with white or Mestizo culture.

b. Elements of Indian provenience which are shared with Mestizo or white culture. The obvious examples here are such things as agricultural techniques, maize foods and their preparation, etc., which are quite as characteristic of Mestizo culture as they are of Indian cultures.

c. Elements of European origin which are today found entirely or principally among the Indians. In the main these elements are medieval in character and were once apparently common in the Mestizo or white culture of the sixteenth or seventeenth century. To some extent they may still exist in rural Mestizo cultures but the insufficient studies of such communities makes it impossible to assess their distribution. At least they are absent in urban Mestizo cultures. Another obvious example here are the religious ceremonies and dances related to the medieval mystery play.

d. Elements of European origin which are present among Indian cultures and Mestizo cultures alike. I suggest that these are mainly elements of modern origin and are related to the introduction of parts of industrial technology—for example, the sewing machine, steel plow, factory-made textiles, etc.

Classification of these elements is often difficult because of the lack of historical information but I submit that it is becoming easier as time goes on. However, there are certain additional complications. One is the presence in Indian cultures of specialized post-Conquest modifications or inventions, often unique to a particular group. Other difficulties arise out of structuring of the elements and of the societies and the particular ethos in which they exist. Nevertheless, I believe we are now in a position, with further research, to achieve a fairly complete classification of the origins and of the unique modifications and inventions in the field of content. At the same time I think it must be seriously considered how far it is profitable to go in such a classification. My own feeling is that we should go somewhat further than we have gone but that a complete analysis would be unnecessary and wasteful.

If we can go rather far in the analysis of culture content, it is my impression that we can only go a short distance in the analysis of structure and ethos, and that in these fields we need very much more research. Although the research data simply do not exist, I have a strong suspicion that the differences between Indian cultures and rural Mestizo cultures are relatively small in the field of content or culture traits. In some cases also the Indian culture content is very largely of direct or indirect European origin, supplemented perhaps by post-Conquest invention (for example, Tarascan). In many cases, then, the major distinction between Indian and Mestizo (at least in Mexico) as well as between different Indian cultures lies in structure (and for shorthand purposes I include here such things as function), and in the differing value systems or ethos.

Turning from the problem of the origin of culture traits to the problem of acculturation, I suggest that the sort of analysis and research indicated above has important bearings on the historical processes of acculturation.

A number of years ago, Oliver La Farge presented a scheme in *The Maya and Their Neighbors* which it seems to me has not received sufficient attention. While La Farge offered his scheme for the Mayan area, with little modification it can be applied to Mexico. Indeed, my initial reaction on reading La Farge's paper was one of slight chagrin that he had beaten me to the punch. I would like to review the highlights of this paper with reference to Mexico and with some further observations on its significance even for contemporary acculturation.

In the first place, one must take into account the variable character of the Conquest in Mexico. Much has been said of the shock upon native cultures caused by the Conquest. That shock existed everywhere, at least on the psychological level, is, I think, beyond question. However, the actual effect upon given cultures was quite different among, for example, the Aztec of Tenochtitlan, and the Tarascan, who sat out the war and then accepted Spanish sovereignty years before the entry of Spanish armed forces in their territory.

More important, perhaps, is the fact that the conquest of Tenochtitlan was less a conquest than it was a revolt of dominated peoples. Spanish leadership merely touched off the spark which in a few years might have swept away the domination of Tenochtitlan and its allies without any outside stimulus. Furthermore, the majority of the societies in the central area of Mexico were highly class structured. It was the dominant classes which suffered most in the Conquest and in large measure the small number of Spanish succeeded in controlling the situation in the early post-Conquest period by virtue of the fact that they simply replaced the dominant classes. I doubt very much if the average *macehual* on the central plateau was any worse off under the Spanish or that his way of life was materially changed. For the average man I suggest the major difference for many years was simply a change of masters plus the replacement of a discredited official or public religion by another with the prestige of success.

In the Early Colonial period in Mexico a number of things occurred. One was the continuation of the class society with a great deal of intermarriage with the Indian population at the upper levels. The Spanish interest in mining together with the shortage of population caused by the devastating epidemics meant that the Indian in many cases prospered. As late as the latter seventeenth century and in some cases early eighteenth century there is good documentary evidence that the Mexican Indians were more prosperous than they had been at any time since. There is also good evidence that in the early post-Conquest period there was rapid and often eager acculturation. For many Indians the period was one of hope and progress rather than the traditional picture of enslavement and degradation. The facts upon which the traditional picture was created undoubtedly existed, but it makes a great difference whether one looks at these facts from the standpoint of modern free democratic society or from the standpoint of a pre-Conquest macehual or a subject people to the Aztec.

Another point which may have had some effect upon the acceptance of acculturation in this period by the Indian is the fact that the culture of the early Colonial Spanish underwent almost as much acculturation as did the Indian cultures. Into the Spanish and the later Mestizo cultures were absorbed at this time most of the elements which today may be described as universals—maize foods, and the absorption or merging with native technologies, etc.

The Early Colonial period, then, is the period in which most of the medieval characteristics of the content of contemporary Indian cultures was absorbed. We may suspect, but still lack data, that some modifications of structure and ethos also took place at this time.

The Second Colonial period, corresponding roughly with the

disestablishment of the missions, coincided with a radical change in both Spanish colonial society and a reflex change in the Indian cultures. The Spanish economy turned more and more to the development of plantation economies, whether in the production of sugar or the development of cattle raising. The economic position of the Indian (and incidentally of the increasing Mestizo class) took a sharp turn for the worse. Moreover, Spanish society changed from a class society to a caste society; intermarriage with Indians was prohibited. The Indian was definitely and officially relegated to a position of inferiority. Moreover, except in the regions of the *encomienda*, the disestablishment of the missions brought about a virtual cessation of intercommunication as a result of the church policy of preventing the Indians from learning Spanish wherever the church had complete control. The lay clergy was not obligated to learn the native tongue and in general did not do so. As a result the Indian was almost completely isolated linguistically.

A function of this deteriorating economic situation, the development of a caste society, and the increasing isolation, resulted, as La Farge points out, in severe disillusion, a sharp rejection of European culture, and a more or less conscious effort to revive the native cultures, an effort doomed to failure after the lapse of several generations. Perhaps the most important aspect of these observations at this point is the explanation for the origin of the strong rejection patterns which in many cases persist to the present, at least in some aspects of culture. Connected with these events was a strong resurgence of the native ethos, even though often much modified from its original form.

The remainder of the Second Colonial period and the two Republican periods can here be passed over lightly as periods of integration of the mixed cultures and of reinforcement of the rejection patterns. Much material can be adduced from the social and economic history of Mexico during these periods to explain why this should be so but I will omit detail here.

A major addition which must be made to La Farge's scheme for Mexico is the addition of a third or Modern Republican period dating from the revolution of 1910. In large measure this period is unique to Mexico and absent throughout Latin America. It involves, on the ideological level at least, the recognition by the Mestizo of his kinship with the Indian, the domination of the urban version of the Mestizo culture in national politics and economics, and perhaps above all, a pronounced weakening of the whole caste structure. Perhaps the most significant one-sentence statement one could make of this period of Mexican history is that the medieval character of society was profoundly modified and in some cases destroyed.

This final period is significant in that it is accompanied by a considerable weakening of the rejection patterns of the Indian cultures. As a result it is also the period which has seen the introduction of most of the relatively modern culture traits shared with the Mestizo culture.

The weakening of rejection patterns has not, however, affected all parts of the Indian cultures equally. It is in this fact that we can observe the reason for the sharp difference of opinion between Mexican administrators and anthropologists. The administrator is often discouraged with the possibilities of modifying the Indian cultures: the anthropologist, on the other hand, sees more change in the past 30 years than in the previous 300. The crucial point is that the rejection patterns still function in areas which the administrator—I think mistakenly—tends to regard as most important.

In all Mexican cultures with which I am familiar there is a section which is readily identified by the Indians themselves as *los costumbres,* perhaps similar to the *creencias* of the Guatemalan Indian. I prefer the term los costumbres, however, because within this category often are included many secular activities, such as kinship relations, essentially secular ceremonials such as wedding customs, etc.

Other elements or traits not classed as costumbres are regarded quite differently by the Indian and as a consequence one finds marked differences in the strength of rejection patterns and in the rate of acculturation at the present time. In other words, we find today a great deal of differential acculturation.

Such differential acculturation will undoubtedly in time affect the culture as a whole. Nevertheless, I think this factor has been underestimated even by anthropologists. In our emphasis upon cultures as interrelated wholes we are perhaps dominated by our own abstractions or constructs. While we may be aware that an Indian culture is an integrated or interrelated whole, the Indian is not and his reactions may be sharply different toward change in different sections of the culture.

While we cannot generalize about the area which is excluded

from the costumbres with exactness, in Mexico it is mainly the area of productive economy which is excluded. In this, there may be a sharp differentiation from Guatemala where it would appear that production, particularly in agriculture, is far more closely connected with religion than it is in the parts of Mexico I know. But even in Guatemala, as Tax has pointed out, the Indian is not averse to change which will improve his economic situation.

In the main the Mexican Indian then does not have sharp rejection patterns to those things which have "practical" value. This may be challenged by some who have encountered the Indian's unwillingness to interest himself in securing a steel plow. However, in a number of cases, I have tried to follow up the negative reaction toward steel plows, radios, etc., and invariably I found that the Indian gave his initial reaction, not because he did not want these things, but because he did not wish to admit that he either could not afford them or did not know how to go about getting them.

Perhaps the strongest argument in Mexico is the almost universal presence of the sewing machine and mechanical corn grinders, including power driven machines. In the case of the sewing machine, its wide distribution is related to a credit and sales policy which has been adapted to the Indian economy and has made it possible for him to get it. In the case of the manual corn grinder the cost is not excessive, while the power corn grinder, made with an improvised charcoal burner and a discarded automobile engine, does not involve excessive capital even for an Indian village.

The wide dispersal of these elements in Indian Mexico (and Mestizo Mexico as well) should give pause to some of our glib assertions about the greater resistance of women to acculturation or their lower social status. These, the most widely dispersed elements of industrial civilization in Mexico, are all directed toward lessening the work of women and are often employed over the active opposition of the men.

The point of greatest fundamental interest here is perhaps that it is in the area of resistance to change; that is, in los costumbres, that the ethos of a culture is apparently most sharply defined and most active and where rejection patterns are most developed. Even in such a group as the Yaqui, although not technically Mesoamerican, where the rejection patterns are strongest and most conscious, we find the acceptance not only of sewing machines but tractors, automobiles, and typewriters, to mention a few.

These changes outside the area of los costumbres obviously will in time have their effects elsewhere in the culture. In general, they seem to stimulate change toward a money economy, toward secularization—after all, a gasoline motor cannot be taken into the realm of the supernatural at once—increasing outside contacts and a general impersonalization of interrelationships.

To close on perhaps a somewhat frivolous note, it is my unscientific and superficial observation that most of the administrators who have sought to accelerate acculturation in Latin America generally almost unerringly pick out los costumbres as the place of attack. As a result they not only encounter the highest degree of rejection but often stimulate the extension of rejection patterns to areas of the culture in which it did not previously exist. Consequently I am tempted to suggest that so far the greatest obstacle to accelerated acculturation has been the untrained administrator. If I were to rate the acculturative forces I have seen at work in various communities I think I would suggest that one road is worth about three schools and about fifty administrators.

chapter 11

DANCE ACCULTURATION*

by Gertrude Prokosch Kurath

EUROPEAN and Catholic domination created an upheaval in the economic and ceremonial life of the New World; yet in Middle America even after 400 years the transformation is not complete. The cultural and choreographic native core remains functional in untouched survivals and in a great mass of complex and enigmatic blends, whereas foreign dances play a superficial role. Each form

* Because of the author's field of study, the discussion deals mostly with Mexico. The following works deal with the Mexican dance:

Barlow, Roberto H. and McAfee, Byron, "Un Cuaderno de Marquesas," in *El México Antiguo*, vol. 6, no. 9-12. Borja, Francisco Amezquita, *Música y Danza de la Sierra Norte de Puebla*, Puebla, 1943. Campobello, Nellie y Gloria, *Ritmos Indígenas de México*, Mexico, 1940. Christensen, Bodil, "The Acatlaxqui Dance of Mexico," *Ethnos*, no. 4, 1937. Fernandez, Justino and Mendoza, Vicente T., *Danzas de Los Concheros en San Miguel de Allende*, Mexico, 1941. Gillmor, Frances, "Spanish Texts of Three Dance Dramas from Mexican Villages," *University of Arizona Bulletin*, XIII, no. 4. Kurath, Gertrude Prokosch, "Los Concheros," *Journal of American Folklore*, vol. 59, no. 4, 1946; "Los Arrieros," *Western Folklore*, vol. VI, no. 3, 1947; "Mexican Moriscas," *Journal of American Folklore*, vol. 69, no. 2, 1949. (Contains further bibliography.) Larsen, Helga, "Mexican is the product of local tradition and character and of interaction between communities, tribes, and races. Picturesque as isolated dances may be, they are truly significant as parts of a great intertribal, interclass, and historical network.

A. *Dance Functions and Forms*

1. The true fiesta is a religious celebration, held on a Catholic holiday or saint's day, ostensibly for the Virgin Mary, Christ, or the local patron saint. The dances performed on these occasions (mostly by men)—*danzas ceremoniales*—serve the patron with devout intentness, for communal welfare, for cure, as penance, or in obedience to a vow as *danza de promesa*. Catholic and pagan images and symbols have been fused, in the Virgen-Tonantzin concept and cross-cardinal directions formula. At times the original purpose is remembered; more often it must be reconstructed by choreographic analysis.

2. Secular couple dances—*bailes regionales* or regional dances—sharply contrast with the ceremonials by their intent to amuse, their many foreign traits, their recency, and the coupling of the sexes. Though Spanish *zapateado* steps are most in evidence, the Austrian waltz and Polish polka and mazurka steps extend from Michoacán to Chiapas. As a rule they are relegated to separate *charro* festivals and to great traditional spectacles as the *Guelaguetza* of Oaxaca; but they feature in urban carnivals, baptisms, weddings, and may intrude their steps into ritual dramas such as the Oaxaca *Plumas*. Some ancient rituals have become secularized and hispanicized, especially in Michoacán—*Los Viejitos* and *Las Sembradoras*.

Thus the division is not as hard and fast as is commonly believed.

Indian Flying Pole Dance," *National Geographic*, vol. LXXI, March 1937, pp. 387-400. Mérida, Carlos, "Pre-Hispanic Dance and Theatre," *Theatre Arts Monthly*, vol. 22, no. 8, 1938, pp. 561-568; Danzas de México (colored lithographs), Mexico; Carnaval en México (colored lithographs), Mexico, 1939. *México-Leyendas y Costumbres, Trajes y Danzas*, ed. Atoyac, Mexico, 1945. Pimentel, Fernando H., "Piezas Tetrales en Lengua Nahuatl," *Boletín Bibliográfico de Antropología Americana*, vol. XI, Mexico, 1949. Sahagún, Fr. Bernardino de, *Historia General de las Cosas de Nueva España*, Mexico, ed. Robredo, 1938. Santa Ana, Higinio Vazquez, *Calendario de Fiestas*, I, Mexico, 1931; *El Carnaval*, Mexico, 1931; *Fiestas y Costumbres Mexicanas*, Mexico 1940. Toor, Frances, ed. *Mexican Folkways*, 1925-1937 (contains further bibliography); *Treasury of Mexican Folkways*, New York, 1947. Wilder, Carleton Stafford, *The Yaqui Deer Dance*, Master's Thesis, University of Arizona, 1940.

B. *Geographical Distribution*

With few exceptions, the ritual dances transcend tribal boundaries, whereas the *bailes* typify regional and tribal units.

I. Large ethnic and choreographic areas appear to coincide to an extent. *Ceremonial distribution* definitely is dependent on the date and completeness of the Conquest, which reached Sonora a century later than the Valley of Mexico and with less intensity, and which still has not penetrated the highland fastnesses of the Lacandon in Chiapas.

The richest ceremonialism centers in the Valley of Mexico. Native forms are scarce, but blends abound in every degree of admixture and a wealth of post-Columbian creations. This is the area of great *Carnavales* and pilgrimage centers, of *Moros y Cristianos** and *Santiagos*. These extend into the Sierra Madre Oriental, where they share festivals with the ancient Otomí and Totonac *Voladores* or *Tocotines* and *Quetzales* or *Huahuas*. In the Sierras of Puebla and in Guerrero they appear together with native animal maskers (*Tecuanes* or tigers) and Mystery Plays of medieval flavor. Masks and dance dramas stretch from this entire region south into Oaxaca and northwest into Michoacán. The *Concheros* societies reach from Mexico City Aztec through the Matlacinco of western Mexico to the Otomí and Chichimeca of Querétaro and Guanajuato.

A spur reaches up into the western Sierras and the Sonoran desert in the form of the *Matachini*, cousins of the *Moros*. In this area one can speak of tribal dances—the Tarahumara *Dutuburi*, Huichol *Híkuli*, and Yaqui *Pascolas*.

In the extreme north and south the New Mexico Pueblos and Guatemalan Maya-Quiché highlanders celebrate their seasonal agricultural rites, and the Pueblos and Yaqui their Deer and other animal hunting dances. In San Miguel Acatán, Guatemala, and among the Arizona Yaqui the Deer dances are approaching secularization.

As an exception, a small community may have its specialty: Tepeyanco, Tlaxcala its *Paraguas;* Santa Inez Chiautempan, Tlascala, its *Catrines;* Tepoztlan, Morelos its *Chinelos* (now a favorite in other towns of Morelos); San Marcos, Oaxaca its *Jardineros con Arcos;* Zapotlán and Tuxpan, Jalisco their *Sonajeros*.

On the other hand, certain personages are apt to appear with

* These exist also in the Andes and in Trinidad.

any dance company throughout Mexico: the *viejo-buffón, diablo, muerte,* man-woman *Malinche.*

II. On the eastern and western outskirts, as coastal Veracruz and Mazatlán, popular and ballroom dances monopolize the fiestas and even carnavales take on a secular, ostentatious character. Bailes are not, however, confined to the coastal areas. Many states and tribes have a *Jarabe* (Yalateco, Mixteco, Tlaxcalteco, Michoacano, Tapatío or Jaliscan), Chiapas has its *Chiapanecas,* Tehuantepec its *Zandunga, Llorona* and *Tortuga,* Yucatan its *Jarana.*

C. *Provenience*

I. *Native survivals* exist in their pure form only in remote highland locations. Occasionally they persist side by side with "Catholic" rituals, such as the Yaqui *Pascolas* during the Easter ceremony. Guerrero *Tecuanes* appear at the same fiestas as Mystery Plays. Modern red trousers and properties have been adopted by dancers in the eastern Sierras, including the *Quetzales, Voladores,* and *Acatlaxqui.*

II. *Blends* of native and European elements include:

1. European imports superimposed on ancient forms.

a. With the native core merely veneered *(Chinelos).*

b. With native qualities submerged *(Moros).*

2. Post-Columbian creations:

a. Religious—largely rural.

b. Secular—largely urban.

III. *Foreign adoptions,* though largely a metropolitan phenomenon, may crop up in rural, isolated communities, namely, (1), (2), and (5).

1. Mystery Plays of medieval Catholic origin *(El Cuerpo y el Alma, Las Tres Potencias).*

2. Liturgical dramas such as *Los Posadas* and *Pastores* at Christmas, and *Pasiones* at Easter.

3. Traditional Spanish secular dances, such as the *Paso doble,* belong to the Spanish upper class.

4. These and ballroom dances from Cuba *(rumba, son, danzón)* feature in night clubs.

5. Recent crazes (*La raspa,* jazz) spasmodically affect all groups —Indian, Mestizo, Spaniards, and foreigners.

IV. *Negro infiltration* is directly in evidence only on the east coast; that is, in the states of Veracruz and Tamaulipas in their popular *Bamba* and other *Huapangos*. Indirectly it has crept from the coast to Plateau cities in the ballroom forms from the United States and Cuba. The influence is neither widespread nor profound.

D. *Social Distribution*

In general, ceremonial dances predominate in rural sections, and popular secular dances of recent origin in the cities; native rites in the Sierras, Mestizo dances in the towns of plateau and coast. But *Conchero* groups are active in Mexico City, and the Sierra de Puebla Otomí dance *Huapangos* all night during religious gatherings.

The Indian tends to follow ritual traditions and the Mestizo to dance for pleasure. But again the *Concheros* include Mestizos as well as a handful of foreigners in their ranks.

Thus social acculturation is paralleled in dance: ceremonial vs. secular corresponds to native vs. Mestizo and foreign, and to rural vs. urban; but widespread dance groups and societies cross-cut geographical boundaries and social strata.

E. *Organization*

The ceremonial dances may be spectacular, but that is secondary to the ritualistic group effort. The Yaqui *Matachini* may dance in a practically empty church. This is in contrast with the bailes, which may become individual or couple exhibitions with *olés*—shouts of audience approval. Not only do Indians perform their votive dances in groups, but they obey an often elaborate military organization. The Yaqui *Matachini* are led by a *monarca* and each of the two files by a *monarca segundo;* the rank and file are called *soldados,* soldiers of the Virgin. An old monarca becomes the head of the hierarchy of Yaqui religious officials and dance societies. The Concheros have an intertribal hierarchy, headed by the Capitán General de la Conquista de Tenochtitlan; secondly officials of each group or *mesa*—first and second captains, sergeants, standard bearers, each with specific duties; then the soldados, soldiers of the Conquest ranked according to ability; then the attendant characters, Malinche, devil, sorcerers, mythological figures.

Simpler versions of hierarchies govern the majority of group dances in two lines, as the *Toreadores* of Puebla with the leading *capitán* and the *caporal* and *mayoral* heading the right and left lines; the *Santiagos* of Puebla with Santiago de Caballero leading the *capitán primero* and *capitán segundo* at the head of their lines and *Pilatos* and a *viejo-buffón* on the outskirts.

At present it is impossible to equate dance organization with specific political organization, because of the magnitude of such a survey and because of the compound nature of the usual fiesta. Only local fiestas can be said to typify the town of their setting. The great fiesta is a confluence of groups from near and distant points. Each group and its dance type would have to be identified with its home village.

F. *Historical Perspective*

Missionary chronicles give the sole remaining picture of the splendid dances before the temples of Aztec gods, and throw light on the scope and meaning of faded but extant dances of northern Mexico.

I. The continuous round of *Aztec agricultural rites* can be reconstructed only from these descriptions. The following are of particular interest, because of analogies with present-day forms:

1. The festival for the agrarian deity Xipe Totec, during the second month of Tlacaxipehualiztli, February 22-March 13, corresponding to carnaval. Men and women, linked by flowered garlands, sang and danced in serpentine lines.

2. The festival for Cintéotl, god of maize, during Huey Tozoztli, April 3-22, corresponding to Easter. Virgin votaries enacted skirmishes.

3. The harvest festival for Xilónen of young corn and beans, and Cintéotl, during the eighth month, June 21-July 9, corresponding to San Juan. Serpentines.

4. Teotleco, the arrival of the gods, twelfth month, September 10-29. Boys with masks or blackened faces impersonated monstrous animals and birds.

5. Festival for Huitzilopochtli, god of war, during Panquetzaliztli, fifteenth month, November 16-29. Skirmishes in two lines, with pine branches, by slave victims, and again by masked boy votaries of the Capulco and Calmecac. Also serpentines.

Festivals for Xochipilli, god of music, dance, and flowers featured huge concentric circles of feathered male dancers, masked animals and birds, buffoons as aged or lame personages, and curative rites.

II. Many *surviving native Indian dances* have preserved their original purpose, however attenuated, and their choreography, however modified. For instance:

1. Animal and demon impersonations, purely mimetic without a geometric floor plan: Yaqui *Maso* and *Pascola,* Aztec of Guerrero *Tecuanes,* Guerrero-Morelos-Mexico *Visionudos* (various animals).

2. Ceremonial clowns, also residual mimetic demonology: Cáhita *Chapayekas, Viejos* (or ancestors) from the Cora to the Mixtecs and Zapotecs of Oaxaca.

3. The therapeutic, circular Huichol-Tarahumara *Híkuli,* associated also with crops and deer.

4. Agricultural dances in circular, counterclockwise form: Aztec-Tepehuan-Cora *Mitote,* Tarahumara *Rutuburi,* Aztec-Otomí-Maya *Volador* (flyers).

5. Agricultural dances in longways formations: Guerrero *Tlacololeros* (planters), Eastern Sierra *Acatlaxqui* (reed throwers), and *Quetzales* (sunbirds).

6. Crises of life: baptismal *Xochitl-Coahuitl* (flower pole) of Puebla mountain Aztecs, wedding *Xochpitzahua* (flower rain) of Puebla, *Canacuas* of Michoacán Tarascans. These use longways formations (two lines). As a rule, regional *jarabes* are danced at such celebrations; and local ceremonials, such as the *Pascol* and *Rutuburi,* at death feasts.

III. *European Counterparts* show many symbolic and formal analogies. Medieval carnivals expelled death, winter, and harmful demons, by rowdy processions, mad running serpentines of masked animals, grotesques, clowns, *diablos* and *muertes,* symbolic sacrifice, death and resurrection mime, battles of the seasons, reinterpreted as Moors and Christians or other *Morisca* names. May Days and Corpus Christi featured flowered arches and maypoles, swords formed into arches or into links in a human chain. These pagan customs have been absorbed into Christianity much as the Mexican ritual dramas of today.

G. *Acculturation*

Comparison of these phenomena and of observed choreographic styles will help disentangle elements in ceremonial blends, will point up native qualities and importations, and will help explain the novel recent creations, the masks and dramatic texts. The study of blends yields comparative observations such as the following:

1. *Analogies.* Fundamental forms and functions on both sides of the ocean tally so consistently as to need comment only on two diverging points. The serpentine course, which is so important in native rites of both continents and still in Europe, survives in Mexico only as incidental longways figure, but not as a round. Skirmishes of the ancient Aztec do not survive in any indigenous dances, but only in European adoptions, thus suggesting amalgamation.

2. *Contrasts.* European influences can be recognized in:

a. Spanish texts, particularly of Catholic liturgical dramas.

b. Medieval costumes of these dramas and battle dances, modern costumes of *Matachini,* creole costumes of many regional dances.

c. Mask types: human features, European bearded faces and negroes being recent; animals, bulls, goats, horses, supplementing tigers, coyotes.

d. Music for strings, harps, *guitarras, jaranas;* for *marimbas* and brass winds. Rattles are native, as also certain drums like the *teponaztli.* Flute and tabor could be either.

e. More elaborate longways formations, such as "heys."

f. Certain steps—*zapateados, "pas de basque"* leaps, polka, mazurka, waltz—common to both ritual and secular dances; high kicks and leg swings, which occur only in Mestizo dances and which contrast with Indian shuffles and back pulls. Ambiguous steps are stamps, toe-heel accents, heel twists, grapevine, crouch, etc.

g. Couple dances of pan-European diffusion, in contrast with the typically Indian segregation of sexes, or intermingling without courtship pattern.

3. *Special Problems* remain, for instance, in the following:

a. Representations of death, which are common to Aztec and Europeans.

b. Transvestites, who everywhere symbolize phallic potency. Innumerable rituals feature a man-woman named after Cortes' mistress, *Malinche,* or, in Puebla, *Maranguilla* (little Mary?).

c. Social satire, mostly of post-Columbian origin, featuring men dressed as modern women (*Catrines* of Tlaxcala, *Jardineiros* of Oaxaca).

d. The role of women, aside from transvestite and couple dances.

Their virtual exclusion from ceremonial dances contrasts with Aztec custom and corresponds to the male prerogative of European traditions. The *Concheros* alone among blends admit women on an equal footing. Among native vestiges, tribes of the Western Sierras include women, but the Cáhita and the Eastern Sierras do not, except in non-choreographic functions.

Acceptance was facilitated, despite native conservatism, by the coincidence of dates and forms, with the substitution of *dramatis personae*. The favorable attitude towards the sixteenth century missionaries (Ralph Beals, "Notes on Acculturation"), and the novel spectacles of introduced liturgies hastened the integration of central Mexican ritual into Catholic festivals; whereas in northern Mexico greater antipathy has kept the "religion of the woods" segregated from the introduced rituals.

The blends cannot be termed truly hispanic. For the same ceremonial types spread from England to Dalmatia though they have come to Middle America mostly by way of Spain. The *Arcos* of Tlaxcala recall Basque namesakes; the *Listones* of Puebla and Yucatan have antecedents in English as well as in Catalan maypoles. The growing antipathy towards the masters, from the seventeenth century on, did not extend to other foreigners, and promoted the popularity of Slavic and Austrian steps and tunes, notably during the brief reign of Maximilian, and is now introducing jazz to the remote hinterland. Even secular couple dances show little of the Spanish provocative fire and pride, except in the few pure-blood Castilian families, and in theatre and nightclub presentations.

H. *The Study of the Fiesta Pattern*

The interest in native customs has fluctuated with changes of government, rising to its apogee in the early Twenties and late Thirties, producing a renaissance of native arts, indigenous performances at the Palacio de Bellas Artes, a shortlived School of Indigenous Dance, research sponsored by the Secretaría de Educación Pública. After the fluctuating suppressions and general disorganization, research is again under way, with Luis Felipe Obregón in the lead; and the school has been revived under Ana Mérida, daughter of the original director, the artist Carlos Mérida. The studies and publications are far from cohesive; only the Campobellos sisters have ventured into a comparative study of tribal styles of movement *(Ritmos Indígenas de Mexico);* yet these authors have now turned their attention to ballet. Higinio Vazquez Santana's projected *Calendario* was cut short by his untimely death.

In view of the complex historical situation and the integration of the fiesta into modern life, an organized study should be concerned not only with isolated routines, but with the problems of provenience suggested in this paper, with the patterns of daily life so intimately associated with the dance forms, particularly the perplexing religious patterns. The fiesta must be regarded in the sum total of its social significance, as homage to supernaturals, as a release from monotony, as a social integrator and centralizing agent for fairs, as a preserver of traditions and a medium for modernization as an outlet and incentive for the native lively imagination and artistic creativeness.

chapter 12

FOUR HUNDRED YEARS AFTER: General Discussion of Acculturation, Social Change, and the Historical Provenience of Culture Elements

Tax: This is the first of our two summary sessions. We have read Dr. Beals' comments on the general problem as well as Miss Kurath's careful treatment of one special topic. I suggest we begin with the discussion of Dr. Beals' summary, which he has discussed with Mr. Villa.

Beals: This is primarily something to shoot at, rather than representing firm convictions on my part. Villa is in general agreement with it. What I have tried to do was to express what, in general, we might accept without trying to illustrate or document it. We have agreed that there is a high degree of homogeneity in the Mesoamerican area and that the area might be sharply limited. Cultures may differ in detail but the the overall patterns are similar, for the derivations of the cultures reveal Spanish influence.

The most significant divergences seem to flow from two main causes: (1) a regional differentiation, which thus far may be only partly analyzed; nevertheless two or three main kinds of regional differences appear: (a) lowland vs. highland; (b) Maya orbit vs. Nahua orbit; (c) a division between the Gulf Coast, the Guatemala and Chiapas highlands, and the Mexican plateau. One could get finer subdivisions within these. (2) a distinction among cultures based on degree of acculturation, possibly extending far back into time.

These are some general ideas offered to see in what measure we can reach an agreement.

Villa: Regarding the first point, the existence of culture areas. How can we delimit the culture areas in the light of what has been brought out during the sessions? I think that the division of the lowlands around the Gulf of Mexico is not too convenient. I would prefer a division between the lowland Maya culture and the highland Maya culture. There are two traditions, the Maya and the Nahua, both of which can be divided into highland and lowland. I object to Beals' third division because there is a great difference in the cultural content between the northern part of Veracruz and the southern part. The Popoluca have more similarities with the Maya than with the Totonac. So we have two possibilities: one is that which Dr. Beals has proposed, to divide the area into three cultural areas; the other is that which I have proposed, a division into two Indian traditions, the Nahua and the Maya, with each in turn divided into lowlands and highlands.

Stone: Where do you place Chiapas in this classification?

Villa: I would place it with the highlands of Guatemala and also the northern part of what was Oaxaca.

Tax: What there seem to be here are four polar cultures around which would cluster, presumably, all the cultures of Mesoamerica, leaving out the northern and southern tribes. You have lowland vs. highland crossing with Nahua and Maya, giving four polar groups. When you put Oaxaca in with the highland Maya it doesn't make much sense.

Beals: In speaking of the lowland and highland division, I have in mind our discussion on the subject of markets and so on being distinctive, perhaps due to environmental causes, but these other things would cut across. In some areas there are different kinds of distinctions. Tax's suggestion takes care of part of that difficulty. You would get something like this:

	LOWLAND	HIGHLAND
MAYA		
NAHUA		

Paul: You could also have North and South.

Camara: In that case we would be stressing just geographic material.

Beals: When you say Nahua and Maya, what you're particularly expressing is a generalizing influence but it wouldn't hold true over a long historical period.

Tax: You might say that a particular geographic area is typified by a kind of culture. Oaxaca fits into the southern.

Beals: Villa didn't say all of Oaxaca; he just said parts of it.

I don't think we've got this documented. I'm trying to summarize a general impression of the area. We might spend a good deal of time arguing about details, but I believe the overall picture will fall into a pattern something like this.

Watkins: Are these subdivisions based on content and the organization of traits or on content alone?

Beals: I think they would fall in both.

Tax: As we discuss these things we always have to make distinctions along these lines. Lots of things are true everywhere, but when distinctions are made we seem to group Guatemala and Chiapas together, and frequently Oaxaca too, as opposed to the Tarascan or Yucatan area.

Kirchhoff: Could somebody give a list of name groups for each division? Villa said he felt that the Gulf Coast might not be a valid grouping because of the contrast between Totonac and Popoluca. When we have full information on the Huastec, perhaps we would find the strong contrast between the two groups in the South wouldn't be as strong.

I believe that one of the greatest difficulties in setting up culture areas in Middle America is that there are cultural islands. It may well be that such groups are the tail end of a group somewhere else.

It's obvious wherever we have large groups like the highlands of Guatemala and Chiapas that they make more sense as culture areas than where we have secondary little groups here and there. Somehow the Nahuatl and also the Otomí are not at all represented here.

Beals: The Nahuatl are the most neglected group.

Toor: Some work has been done, but it hasn't been published.

Tax: Do I understand you to say that three criteria might be applicable: a cultural criterion, Nahuatl and Maya; an areal criterion, North and South; and at a more generic level, Highland vs. Lowland? There might be an area in the middle of the highlands which, because of being virtually lowland, would have different characteristics simply because of its location. Do I understand you to say that we have to take those three things into account, aside from the more general acculturation process?

Beals: I thought they were things that needed discussion. I doubt if we'll ever get an agreement on a hard and fast line drawn on a map; you get overflows which blur the boundaries.

Kirchhoff: We have to recognize the fragmentation of Indian groups; this is not a situation which lends itself to the establishment of culture areas. Where, for example, is the cultural focal area for the Tarascans? Such a question cannot be answered.

Beals: If you were looking at Mexico and Central America as a whole, you would see that the Tarascans represent a tradition that's different in many respects from Nahuatl, but they have shared the Nahuatl tradition for a long time, so they would fit in with that picture, rather than the Maya. People on the plateau have been subjected to somewhat similar forces so that the Tarascans would fall closer to peoples in the general plateau area than they would with the highlands of Guatemala.

Tax: If you have only the dual division, you would throw the Tarascans in with the Nahuatl. How about the tripartite division?

Beals: It depends upon into how many slices you want to cut the cake. If you want to make a broad division, you can put them with the plateau group; if you want to make finer distinctions you can do so.

Villa: The reason that I put aside the Totonac is that Miss Kelly felt that the Totonac were too much apart from the cultural traits which were discussed during the previous sessions. On the basis of these traits I would consider the Totonac as different from other peoples living in Veracruz.

Tax: There are two problems here: the relations between distributions at the time of the Conquest and those of the present time.

Kirchhoff: In Colonial Times I think the Totonac had a high highland ingredient in their culture. I would be prepared to accept the Totonac in the Gulf Coast area, but if you add the Huastec to it you will get a different picture.

Beals: This sort of schema does recognize that you have two cross-cutting forces, and although both are at work in a particular group, you can't recognize their operation. There may be a variation in the degree to which it is the Lowland aspect or the Northern aspect which predominates.

Kirchhoff: It is possible that in Columbian times some groups would have to be divided.

Beals: I'm not even sure about the division of contemporary cultures. We need a study of the highland Totonac as thorough as Miss Kelly's study of the lowland Totonac.

Villa: Perhaps Mr. Jimenez Moreno will comment on our agreement reached last night that there were two ethos: the Nahuatl and the Maya.

Jimenez Moreno: There is a discernible difference between the coastal cultures and those of the plateau; this is noticeable in attitudes. You find more gaiety among peoples of the coast in pre-Columbian cultures; for instance, one sees those laughing faces. Such a thing as laughing is almost unknown to the plateau region. We might say that the plateau peoples had a tendency toward self-control whereas the coastal peoples are more extroverted.

Villa: We referred to the ethos of the Maya and Nahuatl groups.

Jimenez Moreno: I was really referring to the Maya area in general plus the coastal area of the Gulf of Mexico, as against Central Mexico.

Tax: Where would the Tarascan fit?

Jimenez Moreno: In Central Mexico.

Tax: Is there something more to be said on these general points?

Kirchhoff: I am still in doubt as to the meaning of the threefold division. Is that in conflict with the fourfold division?

Beals: No, I don't think so. My tripartite division was: (1) Gulf Coast; (2) Guatemala highlands; (3) Mexican plateau.

Kirchhoff: Would the term Gulf Coast include everything as far as Yucatan?

Beals: Yes.

Wisdom: What would you do with Eastern Guatemala?

Tax: That still fits into the Maya highlands doesn't it? It is somehow not quite like the highlands of western Guatemala and Chiapas, yet even less like the Maya lowlands.

Paul: The Chorti seem to fit more closely between these two. San Luis may come more into the Highlands.

Beals: Here are four types with all sorts of intergradings.

Kurath: Would you equate the coastal area with the lowlands and the highlands with the interior?

Tax: It doesn't make much difference.

Tumin: Assuming that these are four perfectly good analytical categories, would this classification be any more relevant than any other?

Tax: I think it's worth-while having a classification that seems to fit a real situation.

Tumin: But the classification raises problems, doesn't it?

Tax: It's aimed at a variety of problems. We have to know what are the areal distributions in order to see how we can account for them. As Beals said, we saw first that there is a Mesoamerican area as distinguished from tribes to the North and South. Within this area there appear to be some subareas.

Beals: We can make certain generalizations, but they don't make a perfect fit to the area, for there are cultural variations within the area. Not all the interest in this group is in conventional social anthropology.

Jimenez Moreno: I would like to indicate my view of the situation, both from a cultural and an historical standpoint. With regard to Dr. Kirchhoff's limits of Mesoamerica, I feel that there is a fundamental difference between the two—arid America, and Mesoamerica—from the historical standpoint. You had a sedentary population in the South and a nomadic population in the North; there was interaction between the two.

Consider this historically as referring to Mesoamerica only. There is a major difference between coastal cultures and plateau cultures. The coastal cultures predominate up to about 900 A.D., when the Toltec came, apparently from the Northwest; from then on you have the plateau cultures dominating. The Gulf Coast region, as opposed to the Pacific Coast area, is apparently more open to the coming of new peoples, whereas the latter region is where the oldest cultures survived and is a kind of marginal area.

Another point of view is gained by considering the difference between the Maya areas as a whole and central Mexico. On any map the Maya linguistic stocks form a kind of a block in this area, except for Huastec. This region is off the corridor of migrations, which didn't come in here and only touched the borders—Chichen Itza, for example—but the core of the Maya area was the country that was conquered last, and was the one which was least disturbed by foreign influences. This area, as a result of remaining relatively undisturbed, had its own culture and a lasting stability of cultural development. The central Mexican area, on the other hand, was in a corridor of migration. Its culture was always being disturbed, but at the same time, it was always invigorated by new peoples.

Tax: That tends to support the general view that you have been taking here, doesn't it?

Kirchhoff: I would like to know why Chiapas and Guatemala are so different as far as acculturation goes?

Tax: There are at least two reasons: (1) They started out differently; and, (2) different things happened to them.

Kirchhoff: I can't find any old cultural boundary.

Stone: The viceroyalty of Guatemala only went down to Granada in Nicaragua; it didn't go beyond that.

Jimenez Moreno: But where did it begin?

Stone: I think they started off with a division from Chiapas to Panama, but it didn't last very long; they made another arrangement.

Jimenez Moreno: But then again they rechanged the whole thing.

Stone: But the political lines never went further South. I bring that out because of what Kirchhoff said about acculturation. It had a completely different historical background from then on.

Tax: This is only relevant to conditions that may have existed North and South of Guatemala.

Kirchhoff: I would include the Xinca and the Lenca. It is difficult to find out because there are so few left and they are so isolated.

Beals: I think our suggestion on the Pacific lowlands is unimportant in Mexico down to the Isthmus. South of there we have so few groups and know so little about them that in terms of modern conditions we can't do anything with them.

Tax: Shall we now turn to Beals' paper? Villa has some comments he wants to make, and then we have the paper on dance acculturation by Mrs. Kurath.

Villa: The point that Dr. Beals makes is that the scheme of cultural development in Mesoamerica originated by La Farge can be extended to the Central Plateau of Mexico. As you know, La Farge worked in the Cuchumatan region of Guatemala, and has presented the outline of what happened in that area. I saw that his scheme was applicable to the Chiapas highlands, as did Mr. Camara. Now Dr. Beals says that it is possible to apply this scheme to the highlands of Mexico. The importance of this scheme is that it shows the processes of acculturation.

According to La Farge, there are five periods, which are:

1. The Period of Conquest, 1524-1600, one of violent changes in the Indian cultures. It is convenient, as La Farge says, not to pay too much attention to the dates, but to the happenings, to the different rhythm of acculturation.

2. The long period from the sixteenth century to 1720, during which the *encomiendas* and forced labor were developed, and most of the Indian traits were suppressed or entirely changed. Indian traits were disappearing and Spanish traits were absorbed.

3. From 1720-1800 was a period of relaxation of Spanish authority. The encomiendas were abolished, Indian traits emerged, and the Indians tried to revive some aboriginal ways.

4. From 1800-1880 is a beautiful period of readjustment. In 1880 the communal lands were abolished, since a new type of economy had evolved with the development of the coffee plantations. The Ladinos began to spread out into the more isolated areas where only Indians had lived till this time.

5. Then follows a period of increasingly sharp conflict between the Ladinos and Indians, and a new type of life begins.

Now Dr. Beals adds a new period: from 1910 (in Mexico) to the present time, a period in which the rhythm of acculturation has had a faster development. It seems to me, however, that there are but five periods, after which you find a declining of Indian cultures. It seems also that the rhythm of acculturation will be faster—and the decline of Indian cultures also faster—because the Mexican government is trying to change the cultural traits of the Mexican Indians. As an example of the rapid change that now may occur: the government is building roads and a dam, the biggest dam in Latin America, in the Mazatec region. Now one can travel by car in an hour from Mexico City to the Mazatec region.

De la Fuente: I would like to add a few things to the scheme Dr.

Beals has presented to us. I would consider the picture incomplete if we didn't include acculturation—cases of interaction between Indians and Negroes, and Indians and non-Indians. There is also a type of acculturation which took place mainly on the upper levels of society. The last period that Dr. Beals brings in is one of a change of focus or influence from the so-called European orbit to the North American orbit. This differs a little bit, and perhaps adds to the picture we have now.

Beals: At least in Mexico there are certain other things that could be brought in. The time of the disestablishment of the missions is a case in point. Up to that time the policy was to isolate the Indians from the Spanish; the missionary was obliged to teach only in Indian languages in various areas, and not to teach the Indians Spanish. There was a sharp break in communication between the European and Indian traditions for the mission Indians. At this time you get not only the beginning of integration of the two cultures, but you get the development of the rejection pattern, which had not existed in many places up to this time. The rejection pattern was associated not only with the disestablishment of the missions but also with intermarriage between Spanish and Indian. About this time you get a prohibition of intermarriage, which approached a caste situation.

The Republican period actually worsened the situation of the Indian, because the Crown laws protecting the Indian were abolished and he was bound to be exploited. You then get the reinforcement of the rejection pattern.

This point, about the 1880's, is spoken of by some as the beginning of industrialization. You didn't get industrialization, however, you merely started getting all the modern gadgets. But to get them you had to increase colonial agriculture. All of these events reinforced the rejection pattern.

At this point in Mexico (1910) you get a change of attitude toward the Indian; there comes the rise of the Mestizo culture and the rise of the Mestizo class to power and dominance. So that you get here the beginning of the rejection pattern. The Indian begins to accept things particularly at the industrial level of culture. It was the Mestizo recognition of the Indian background and that something had to be done about it.

Tax: Jimenez Moreno, do you see this as a general tendency?

Jimenez Moreno: Most of what Dr. Beals has said is true. I notice a kind of delay in the process in Chiapas and Guatemala that should be brought out. He mentioned that the abolishing of the communal lands came in Guatemala around 1877; it came a little earlier in Mexico, around 1859, with the laws of reformation, but was not much enforced until 1867. The dissolution of the missions, which came in Guatemala in 1720, was about 60 years earlier in Mexico, around 1660.

Considering the first period—roughly in the sixteenth century—in which the Indians first received the impact of Spanish civilization: it is true, as Dr. Beals said, that the Indians were much undisturbed. In answering a student of mine who asked me why he found nothing about the Conquest in the Indian chronicles, but did find references to priests in later writings, I told him it was because, to the Indians, the coming of the Spaniards was merely another source of domination, no different from that of the Aztec. The Conquest was not considered as important by the Indians as we think it should have been! The first attempts at Christianization resulted in the Indians accepting the Christian religion superficially, but still carrying on pagan rituals. It is in the records of 1540 that the Indians had not yet accepted Christianity, but by 1570 or 1580 the Indians were interested in Christianity to the extent of founding their own *cofradías*. The picture has changed.

The Spanish culture also has different aspects. The Spaniards had to take a defensive attitude; this can be seen in their building of churches which were fortresses, not against attack from the Indians, but to defend the acculturated Indian as well as the Spaniard from the attack of barbarians. With the end of the war of the Chichimecs around 1590, the whole style of architecture changes, as they no longer worried about that defensive type of building.

I protest against the idea that the Indians were prohibited from learning Spanish. On the contrary, I find that in the 1550's a bishop was enforcing the learning of Spanish by the Indians. The early friars took great pains to teach the Indians in their own language, it is true. After the secularization of the missions in the 1660's, the lay clergy had no interest in preaching to the Indians in the native tongues, although a few continued to do so.

Another important thing that has not been mentioned is the change in the basic economy of the New World. It was at first a mining economy, especially in the sixteenth century, when you had cities which grew up about mines and became mining centers.

There was then a shift to an agricultural economy, after a transitional period when agriculture, cattle-raising, and mining were of equal importance, perhaps. The *encomienda* system became replaced by the *repartimiento* system of forced labor about 1600. The encomienda was not abolished in Guatemala until much later. All these differences account for the different situations in Mexico and Guatemala.

Tax: Jimenez Moreno has suggested that there is a time gap in Guatemala, as compared with Mexico. This may extend from the very beginning to the *indigenista* revolution. You might argue that there has been a retardation all along the line, but there must be other factors as well.

Paul: How about the factor of the differences between the orders of the missions?

Tax: How much do we know about where they were and what differences it made? Does it make any substantial difference?

Beals: I would suspect that it does, but I don't think we have much information. Some of the differences are quite clearly due to differences between the Dominicans and Jesuits. We have documentary evidence, for example, of the Jesuits having invited Indians to perform Indian dances in the church in certain areas. This would make a considerable difference.

Paul: One might have stressed the role of the cofradía more than others.

Tax: In the Chiapas and Guatemala highlands, there were all the different orders.

Paul: The difference between the Dominicans and the Franciscans partly explains the situation in Western Guatemala and Southwestern Guatemala. My general impression is that the humanist movement in the church centered primarily in the Franciscans, and not in the Dominicans or Augustinians.

Tax: Another possibility is, of course, that of differential acculturation according to greater or lesser degrees of isolation.

Kirchhoff: I want to come back to the terms acculturation and rejection pattern; I believe you used that as a contrast. You can look at it from the point of view of how much of the Spanish culture is taken over, or how much is rejected, or how much of your own culture you retain and how much you lose. I have always had the feeling that workers in present-day Middle America, even when well informed on the pre-Columbian native cultures, had no idea of the tremendous chunk that was taken out of native culture. It is impossible to estimate it in terms of percentages, but I would say it was between 90 and 99 per cent.

Tax: You think there might be as little as only one per cent left?

Kirchhoff: Yes. It seems to me that the fundamental characteristic of Mesoamerica was that it was a stratified society, one like ours or that of China, based on the axis of city and countryside. There was a native ruling class, with a class ideology and organization, which disappeared entirely; there were great cultural centers which, just as in our life, are so essential that if you described the U.S. without New York, Chicago, etc., it would be absurd. The same thing happens when you don't describe these centers in ancient Mexico.

Tax: This depends also on how you define a culture. In one sense—like a language—every individual is a carrier of the whole culture, or most of the culture, insofar as he is a sample. Most of the culture would be left, even if you destroyed the class structure, etc., because the basic system of values must still be there. But if you're talking about culture with a capital "C," most of that went. We wouldn't agree on our percentages.

Kirchhoff: I think we would after discussing it. It's not only the arts, crafts, and sciences which constitute the great changes, but the basic form of the culture changing from a city structure to the most isolated form, which is, in my opinion, the most total and radical change anywhere in history. It's not a question of losing temples, etc., although this would be a formidable change, but the most important thing to me is this structural aspect of the city vs. country. When the city is cut off what is left over is attached as a subordinate to the new city-centered culture.

I think a study of Colonial history is the only thing that can close the gaps in our knowledge. At the beginning of this downward curve, the Indians find themselves without cities, and without cultural leaders. Who were, at that time, the leaders of the Indians, and under whose leadership did the following readaptation take place? That is a fascinating question and will give us a key to all the things that have happened since.

Tax: Leadership rather than a social process.

Kirchhoff: I want to know what the answer is.

Beals: I'm rather impressed with this idea of Kirchhoff's. If you were to cut off the United States and left the Ozark mountains, would the ethos of that area give any representation of the culture of the U.S. as it is today?

Wisdom: Even if you only had a small town of 5000 in New York State, you would have American culture.

Tumin: I would like to ask two questions: (1) Are there any data on the comparative populations of the city and rural Indians? (2) To what extent was the culture pattern of ancient rural Mexico a reflection of the urban centers?

Kirchhoff: I have no information on this. In spite of this negative answer, I would still be firmly convinced that from what we know generally about Mesoamerica, and from the general pattern the world over, wherever humanity has reached a cultural level of having city vs. country, the leadership has always been in the city.

I want to mention a very interesting case of something similar happening in pre-Columbian days. When I first started working in Mexico I thought Mexico was far advanced, and that all of Mesoamerica had attained that level; then I realized that there were sections that didn't fit into the picture. The Otomí seemed to be still on a tribal basis; while there were some Spanish cities in their area, and some beginnings of internal stratification, lately I have become aware of a tremendous historical break in Otomí history. At some time they had what others reached afterwards—a great city and an advanced type of society. In a complete catastrophe, a large part of them were forced to move and the rest were pushed back into the mountains. They were the first who became situated with relation to the ruling cultures in the manner of the present day Indians in Middle America.

Beals: There is also the question of areal isolation. I would put the Mixe as remaining in this Colonial period today. It's the sort of condition that we assume was set up in many places in this post-Conquest Republican period. It still exists there, particularly in the conservative type of Mixe village. The conservative village is still right back in this Colonial period. In addition, extreme isolation plus some cultural factors which lead the Mixe not to go out of his own territory if he can help it, lend to the conservatism.

Kirchhoff: Following up Dr. Beals' remarks, we all agree that the Spanish moved into the most advanced sections, geographically speaking. Therefore they touched least the least advanced groups as a whole. I have always thought of the Mixe as an earlier type of a people. The Spanish touched the culture in and around the great city centers and not the people in the economically least favorable regions.

Beals: The Aztec did the same thing.

Kirchhoff: Yes. But it's very interesting that what was left was somehow more isolated, more backward.

Tumin: This would mean that the most Indian type of culture was the one that was least disturbed for a long period of time.

Jimenez Moreno: What Dr. Kirchhoff has said about the tremendous impact of Spanish civilization and what it meant for Indian culture to lose their leaders as a result, is entirely true. But I think that the culture in many Indian areas, as regards what you call the ethos, is still more Indian oriented than what we might admit. In spite of the fact that technologically the Indians are entirely or almost entirely Europeanized, yet there is much of that Indian orientation that remains today, even in Mestizo peoples, as a part of their inheritance from Indian culture.

I think we have to consider what parts of Middle America were more or less influenced by Spanish culture—which were more disturbed? I believe that the Spanish influences more or less followed the pattern that had been established by the dominant Tarascan and Aztec in the past. The Spanish domination and culture were more effective in areas which had been subordinate to the Tarascans and the Aztec, for example, among regions like this the impact of civilization would be greater than in the regions to the east. This region of Mexico depended, of course, on the leadership of certain cities like Tenochtitlan. When Tenochtitlan disappeared the impact on the Indian world must have been tremendous. But among the Mixe, or in the regions of the Tzeltal, I think conditions were different; I think in this case they had no important city centers.

Tax: How about Yucatan? That was a city-dominated place.

Jimenez Moreno: There was a fundamental historical difference. The Maya civilization was already disintegrating when the Spanish arrived. Politically, as you know, this peninsula was divided into many small centers, and I think they had not the same cultural strength as this other region, so they were already disintegrating. There is a great difference between the peninsula of Yucatan and the region of Chiapas and Guatemala. I think that also accounts for differences. This, of course, was the last flourishing section of the Maya area, whereas in the area of Chiapas and some sections of Guatemala, they had already begun to lose their political importance previously; ever since the decline of the "Old Empire," this southern region had lost a great deal of its importance. There were still some centers like the Cakchiquel, but most of this region was already politically and culturally disintegrating. Yet I think they were not so much disturbed by Spanish domination.

Kirchhoff: I think there is an obvious correlation between conditions in certain areas with the fact of there having been or not having been a great politically unified area. I think that where the Spanish met the most compact unified political units, they had to do the hardest fighting, not only in the sense of battles, but working on the ruling class, etc., where they moved into the heart of the cities. That is the big difference between Central Mexico and Yucatan. There could be no great opposition in the Maya area. Important segments of the ruling group were disturbed throughout the Aztec empire and also through the smaller Tarascan empire. The greater strength of the Indians lead to greater destruction. It provoked, in turn, a more systematic attack on the part of the Spaniards.

Beals: Once the headship of Tenochtitlan was destroyed in a large part of this area you had relative acceptance of the Spaniards. The Tarascans accepted missionaries before there were any military men in the Tarascan area. In the Jalisco area the acceptance went all the way to the coast and was completely peaceful. In this region, one of small city-states, you got a peaceful relationship and an acceptance of Spanish domination after the fall of Tenochtitlan.

Tax: It certainly seems to fit part of the areal picture that we were drawing this morning. It would appear that there wouldn't be so much room left for such minor factors, which may still be important, nonetheless, as a little more or less isolation or Franciscans vs. Dominicans.

Jimenez Moreno: I think it's worth-while, since Dr. Beals mentioned the situation in Jalisco—prior to the Conquest there existed many petty kingdoms which only allied themselves as a confederation when there was danger of Tarascan domination. These confederacies did not exist all the time. It was a temporary confederation of small groups against the power of the Tarascans. As Dr. Beals said, the first contact of the Indians and the Spanish in that area was rather peaceful, but in 1531-2, we have a different situation. Then you had a conquest of that area which was very bloody and the conquest of New Galicia was conducted by the Atzec themselves. It's not exactly a Spanish conquest. It's important to consider what happened in New Spain up to 1531-2 and later, because up to that time the Spanish were following the same system that had already existed. Later on they began to change. In Jalisco we have to take into consideration the fact that there were many small kingdoms in existence when the Spanish came to that region. The influence of the Aztec who came to that region as auxiliary troops was very important in the Mexicanization of the region. Also the friars enforced the teaching of Nahuatl to all of these communities. These factors combined to lend to the disappearance of a good deal of native Indian culture, especially language.

I want to add a few words regarding that region that formerly was part of the Aztec area, and its development. Regarding the political situation, we find that the Spanish first kept the rulers of the dominant houses in Tenochtitlan and other places. Later on when there is no need to call them kings, they become governors. This happened about the middle of the sixteenth century. About 1560-70 they ceased to be governors, and were called judges. Gradually they lost all importance.

I also want to mention the importance of the breakup between generations that took place, not only in the Valley of Mexico, but also in Puebla and other places. You find this with regard to the preaching of the Gospels, as the friars realized the importance of working with the younger generation rather than with the older, whom they merely subjected to mass baptism. As a result of this concentration on the younger generation, there arose conflict between the two generations, in which the older generation stuck to the old religious practices and the younger generation mocked them.

Mason: I think Dr. Jimenez Moreno has given us the wrong impression by referring to all the peoples north of Mesoamerica as being nomadic. There were sedentary agriculturists in that region also.

Jimenez Moreno: These peoples living here in the Northwest were different culturally from those here. Both of these areas belonged to arid America or the greater Southwest, and for that reason I was speaking of both of them. There were small islands of agricultural peoples.

Tax: I think we ought to find time to speak about modern trends in acculturation.

Jimenez Moreno: I think it would be a definite achievement if we could try to map out the degrees of fusion of cultures in Middle America. Certain regions are the most hispanicized, others are basically Indian. I would like to propose that a committee of perhaps five persons be appointed.

(Following committee appointed: Ralph Beals, Julio de la Fuente, Wigberto Jimenez Moreno, Sol Tax, Alfonso Villa Rojas.)

Tax: Shall we look at the problem of dance acculturation as a case of what could be done with a number of items of culture? Mrs. Kurath, do you have any impressions of what has been said today as applied to the problems of the dance?

Kurath: It makes a difference in the type of dance that you find in different areas whether it belongs to the period of 1520-1600, or whether the type of dance was introduced later. I think the general impression has always been that the Indian had an antipathy toward the Spanish, but if you had an acceptance at an early period, that would account for the acceptance of dance forms from Europe. I think it's very important to find out what types of dances were introduced at a particular time.

Beals: Los Morros and *la Conquista* were early introductions.

Kurath: I think that accounts for the acceptance and popularity of them. Then there is the matter of the completely European type of Mystery Plays. Were they introduced about that time? They are the only completely European type of dance that you have.

Beals: The dramatization as employed in the old *Moro* dance is European.

Kurath: I think you find a great deal of native underlying the Moros and *Cristiano* type. A great many of these texts are in the native tongue. The Mystery Plays are in Spanish, but the Moros-Cristiano type is usually spoken in the native tongue.

Jimenez Moreno: We have a definite date for the beginning of these dances. They were introduced in Tlascala in 1519. Tlascara was the first most successful meeting place of Indian and Spanish culture. The Tlascalans played a very important role in the spread of dances and other traits everywhere in New Spain. When you remember that the Tlascalans went to the North and even as far South as Peru, one begins to realize how important it was that in Tlascala they first initiated these dances.

Stone: Do you mean that you don't agree that these dances are Spanish?

Jimenez Moreno: Of course they were of Spanish origin but they began to be enacted in Mexico in Tlascala. The Indians didn't know how the Moors dressed and they invented dresses for the Moorish people, etc.

Kurath: The hybrid costume. The steps throughout are native; perhaps the friars weren't able to teach the steps. Sometimes the Moors did have a medieval type of costume.

Jimenez Moreno: Even in the *Codices* you see Spaniards dressed with turbans, so we shouldn't be surprised that the Indians were familiar with the Moorish type of dress in the sixteenth century. Moorish costumes and customs were important in New Spain at that time.

Gillin: Is there any tendency to express aggression through the dance? In Peru, in practically all the dances in which the Spanish are portrayed there's at least one person made the butt of jokes, as ritual clowns. This is one time that the Indians have a chance to take a crack at their conquerors.

Kurath: I don't remember seeing the Spanish portrayed as buffoons.

Gillin: What theme did the Moros and Cristianos represent?

Kurath: The Moros is the conquest of the Moors by the Christians. I wonder whether the Indians read into this the idea of the Conquest?

Beals: You get an obvious transformation, but you do have the Europeans burlesqued.

Kurath: They take off the bourgeoise.

De la Fuente: We have further secularization of these dances. The Indians come in, and there are bailes.

Kurath: Carnaval is a religious occasion and you have bailes too.

Tax: I wonder if there is an interpretation in terms of Indian ethos of why they keep dances in celebration of their own conquest?

Gillin: The dance symbolizes certain traits or elements in the culture.

Tax: But is there any interpretation? What is the function of the dance?

Paul: In San Pedro they have gorgeous costumes. The question of the theme of the context is nearly wholly irrelevant. The explanation has to do with the context of celebration. Also, just as they go to the cofradía, they put on the dance according to certain forms. It's the formalistic side of it, and not the text that's important, since it has all kinds of functions quite apart from its context.

Kurath: Possibly these dances replace ancient dances and they had sufficient similarity with the dances they replaced.

Paul: That doesn't answer Tax's question of why they use a theme that's definitely detrimental to the Indians. It is my impression that it isn't so much that the dances were introduced but the simplest thing to do was to say, "Go ahead and have your dances, but change the content."

Jimenez Moreno: I want to say that among the Aztec there already existed many dances of historical significance. With reference to the Moorish dances, the purpose of those dances was to enact the conquest of Granada in 1492 by the Spanish, but ever since that dance was enacted in Tlascala it was connected with the conquest of Mexico, in which the Tlascalans played an important role as allies. Thus the Indians were enacting both the conquest of Mexico and that of the Moors. Since the conquest of Mexico was so important, it's explainable why they kept that dance in so many places in Mexico.

chapter 13

THE SIXTEENTH CENTURY AND THE TWENTIETH: A Comparsion of Culture Types and of Culture Areas

Tax: I would like to report what the committee did. Our assignment was to put on a map degrees of acculturation of communities in Mesoamerica. We included only those communities we knew something about. We thought we could fill in this morning some we don't know as well.

We selected four criteria: (1) Monolingualism; (2) Technology; (3) Social Organization; (4) Religion. We took the Lacandon as a standard of 100 for each category; they total 400 by definition. (These are not percentages.) Then we considered the various places; the order was empirical. You see in the table that there are twenty groups that are used, of different size and importance. The order on the table is from most to least Indian.

If you look at Monolingualism, for example, Quintana Roo is also 100. Language seems to bring Guatemala up a little.

Technology goes down pretty regularly; Midwest Guatemala is brought up a little by having a primitive technology—no use of the plow.

Religion is where Midwest Guatemala goes down because the

cult of the saints is Spanish rather than a survival of aboriginal traits. We're not worrying about substitutions; we can't say that the saints are substitutes for gods. We simply took the actual trait retention rather roughly.

The number in the third column from the right on the Table is what's left when you subtract the trait retention total from 400—this represents loss. How much of this was lost early and how much was lost in recent acculturation? In most cases more was lost early than has been lost recently. Among the Lacandon, the loss is recent; in Northwest Guatemala 80 per cent early; in Quintana Roo, all early.

Note now that these conclusions have also been plotted on a map. There is a central area that's less acculturated; but the least acculturated area is peripheral. On the other hand, Beals says that if you take Mexico City and Guatemala City or Mérida, then you can say the areas marginal to the centers of acculturation are the least acculturated. One of the troubles with that is this: as you go twenty miles to the west of Guatemala City, you're in an unacculturated area, whereas if you go east of Guatemala City twenty miles, you're in an acculturated area.

Beals: The figures in this Table should not be taken very seriously by anyone, if taken seriously at all. They're just a set of hunches. This isn't exact at all, in any real sense. But with all this in exactitude, in doing this, when the committee got all through and added it up, everybody thought it looked right—it did conform to a common sense criterion.

INDEX OF ACCULTURATION

	Retention of pre-Columbian Traits					*Time of Loss*		
Area	*Mono-lingual-ism*	*Tech-nology*	*Social Organi-zation*	*Re-ligion*	*Total*	*Total*	*Early (16th Cent.)*	*Late (19th Cent.)*
1. Lacandon	100	100	100	100	400	. . .	. . .	(all)
2. NW Guatemala (Huehuete-nango & Ixil)	90	85	80	90	345	55	45	10
3. Tzeltal	70	90	90	80	330	70	60	10
4. Quintana Roo	100	90	40	40	270	130	130	. . .
5. Soteapan (Popoluca)	65	50	60	90	265	135	. . .	. . .
6. Chinantec	70	90	70	30	260	140	100	40
7. Mazatec	80	40	70	60	250	150	105	45
8. Mixe	75	55	50	50	230	170	150	20

Area	Retention of pre-Columbian Traits: Monolingualism	Technology	Social Organization	Religion	Total	Time of Loss: Total	Early (16th Cent.)	Late (19th Cent.)
9. Midwest Guatemalan Highlands	90	75	40	20	225	175	130	45
10. Sayula (Popoluca)	80	60	50	25	215	185	...	...
11. Totonaca	60	70	50	25	205	195	125	70
12. N. Guatemala (Kekchi)	80	75	30	15	200	200	130	70
13. E. Guatemala (Chorti, Pokoman)	20	70	80	30	200	200	100	100
14. Mixteca	60	40	40	50	190	210	145	65
15. Otomí	60	60	40	30	190	210	145	65
16. Huasteca	60	40	50	20	170	230	...	...
17. Zapotec	70	30	30	25	155	245	200	45
18. Maya of Yucatan	40	40	30	30	140	260	210	50
19. Tepoztlan	10	20	40	30	100	300	180	120
20. Tarascan	25	10	0	10	45	355	285	70

Tax: Let's see if everybody here will agree to that.

Kaplan: I wonder if it would be possible, instead of using the Lacandon as 100, to use the trait list which we have been preparing and to work in those terms.

Kelly: I think you're suggesting that when the trait list is made up, perhaps we'll have twenty elements in social organization. Then we'll have a more or less uniform guide.

Tax: But how can you weigh these things?

Beals: Also you have wide variation in the number of traits present. What we're trying to figure out is how much of the aboriginal traits have been lost.

Tax: You couldn't do that unless you got the universal traits and then weighed them statistically. Even then it would be subjective.

Wisdom: These figures may be all wrong but it's something to shoot at.

Beals: This does not express at all the degree to which Spanish elements were taken. There could be a complete loss, not necessarily a substitution—or a lot of new things from Spain.

Tax: This doesn't handle Kirchhoff's problem at all because the Lacandon didn't have much to lose.

Kirchhoff: Those who had least also lost least.

Paul: When Kirchhoff talks about 90 per cent loss, is he talking

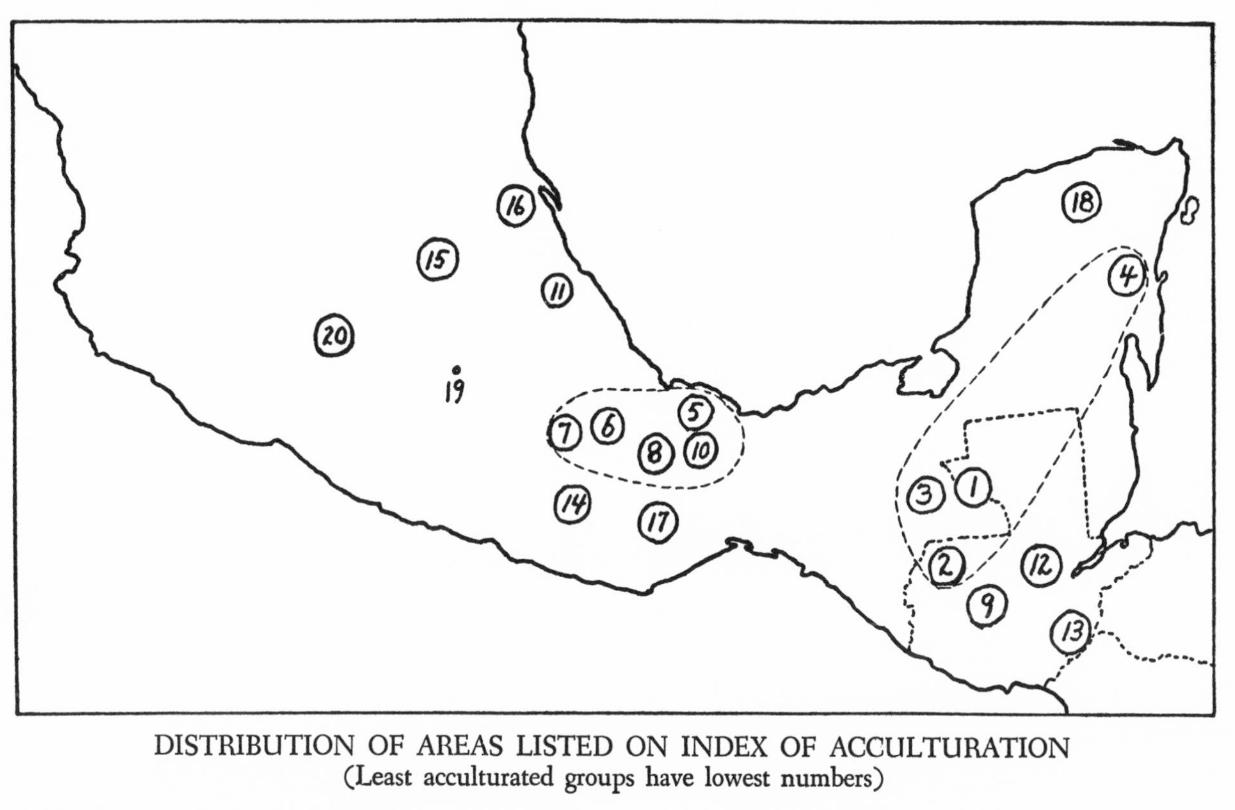

DISTRIBUTION OF AREAS LISTED ON INDEX OF ACCULTURATION
(Least acculturated groups have lowest numbers)

about art items in the hands of the upper group or total native culture? If he means the first, it's a good statement, but if it has to do with the total culture which the individual carries within him, a lot of these things have gone on.

Kirchhoff: I believe I started by saying that really it's not a question of given percentages. That was just a way of expressing myself in order to get an idea across. In a tremendously long trait list, it's entirely possible that I'm quite wrong. The statement that I made —and again I apologize for the absurd percentage—is that basic structural features and the key aspects of native life were lost. That, of course, we cannot settle here. That's a question of the interpretation of culture.

Paul: I want to point out the contrast between this and Mr. Kidder's feeling that basically the life of the people of the Guatemalan highlands isn't much different than it was before.

Kirchhoff: The subject we're talking about is only a small segment of the descendants of the aboriginal native population, located principally in backward mountain areas. Their relations to what at that time were the leading political centers may not have been very different from what the relations of the present Indian groups to Mérida and Mexico City are.

Beals: In dealing with the documents that still exist, we might study Aztec culture. We don't study Aztec culture now; we study the culture of an Aztec village.

Jimenez Moreno: I think that one of the most important things today in this study of acculturation would be to study the mechanisms of substitution. Some Chichimec, for example, who used to do hunting and gathering still carry on the same activities as in pre-Hispanic days, but now use rifles in their hunting. I think one has to study this problem of substitution in religion, technology, and social organization in order to have a clear judgment of the degree of acculturation.

Kirchhoff: While this discussion necessarily belongs in this kind of meeting, we could probably make more progress if we brought the modern and the old together. No one has brought out the picture of intergroup relations; we need to fill in this tremendous gap.

Tax: Could we get down what we know about the ethnography of the area at the time of the Conquest. Who's working on it at the moment?

Jimenez Moreno: Ralph Roys in Yucatan.

Kirchhoff: I have always been amazed that a single man, Ralph Roys, has been able to do for Yucatan what I think we need for the whole area—to show the contact ethnography. I am sure that there are not more than four or five people who have done anything like Roys' work in the rest of Middle America.

Tax: It's the impression of the social anthropologist that everything in Mexico has been along these lines.

Kirchhoff: Ralph Roys has confined himself to one single people, the Maya of Yucatan. Even there the differences are not as strong as they are in the rest of Middle America. His success is based on the fact that he took probably the easiest case. In the rest of Middle America the contact situation is very confusing; to this day we haven't been able to tell from a given source to what people the source refers. We have areas where it is a tremendous job merely to plot on a map the one-time existing groups which have long since disappeared. No one has ever dreamed of compiling the material, much less classifying it. We could never get more than ten people together, including those who are "just interested." That probably explains the hesitation of those who might be interested in the Colonial transformation. We should all understand that we should know about contact ethnography. If you culled Middle Americanists, you would find two large groups—archaeologists and this group—and the tiny group working on the contact situation.

There is very little specialized teaching in Middle America on the contact situation.

Jimenez Moreno: I think we have to stress the necessity of studying the Colonial background of Middle American history. It's a great fault of research to wait until all the information on the present-day situation has been collected before we begin informing ourselves on what happened prior to the present. I would prefer the opposite—to get as much information as possible on the historical background of the area and then to collect the material on the present.

Tax: We have to do both at the same time.

Kirchhoff: There are then, three areas of interest: (1) Contact ethnography; (2) the Colonial period; (3) present-day material.

Jimenez Moreno: Such developments as took place in the Colonial period should be studied more carefully. There have been many changes and the conditions of life of the Indians have changed during the three centuries of Colonial life. These things have to be studied for each area; we need more information about the Spanish background. Some people like George Foster are interested in this now. What region of Spain influenced certain sections of Mexico? I would like further to emphasize the necessity of studying the regions which are not so Indian but rather Mestizo.

Paul: On the question of who are the people working on contact ethnography, there are some at the Peabody Museum and the Department of Anthropology at Harvard.

Marshall: We have at least two people working on this problem: William Sanders, whose thesis was on Mexico City, and David Kelly. These people are trying to combine the archaeological and the chronological approach, from the original data, and they apparently are getting results.

Jimenez Moreno: At the Centro de Estudios Historicas, Morales is working on what happened in the sixteenth century, especially in art. Another student is working on religious acculturation in the Valley of Mexico. There are perhaps two or three others.

Gillin: Is there any good explanation as to why the Indians were cleaned out of Eastern Guatemala and not out of Western Guatemala, comparatively speaking?

Tax: We discussed that one day in terms of the retention of the Maya culture.

Gillin: But you have Maya groups left in the East.

Paul: Is the geography a differentiation?

Kurath: I would like to say that if you study culture contact you have to be aware of the corresponding European situation—not only in Spain but in other parts of Europe as well. Dr. Termer and I were agreed on the possible ceremonial influence from the Alps. It may not be Hispanic at all.

Termer: I would like to underline the things told us by Jimenez Moreno on the importance of studies of Colonial times. It seems very important to me.

Gillin: It's not only Spain but the whole Mediterranean culture that needs to be put together in functional form.

Tax: We ought to take a few minutes to touch on one of the basic problems of this whole field, the problem of whether it is possible even to tie the two time periods together, or whether you have to treat them in different terms. We have two fields which are different not only in time but in the interests of the people who are working on them. Many people are working in the high culture area of Mesoamerica itself. On the one hand you have people with historical interests, who come from archaeology and ethnology, who tie the two together in terms of historical problems. The kinds of problems you are interested in are considered antiquarian by the other people. The people who have been working in the modern tribes are interested in what one can learn about problems of culture and personality, about the relations of different kinds of institutions, etc. The result is that if some of us were writing the proposed Handbook, we would talk about various institutions and how they function, regardless of whether they are Spanish or Indian. For example we would talk about the institution of the *cofradía* as something of value in itself, ignoring its provenience. The problem of Middle American ethnology is to value both things and to value something in between to tie the two together. When we come to the people who are interested in the Handbook, as far as ethnology is concerned, there's going to be a pull in two directions.

Kirchhoff: I don't see why there should be. A man interested in Aztec political and social institutions values them regardless of where they came from. But as the next step, we have to know not only how at a given moment they function, but how they came to be that way. A man studying contact ethnography has to tie that up with the archaeological record. In each case we find gaps in between. I frankly can't see how a man who tells me he's not interested in historical perspective can refrain from fitting that into a general picture of human development.

Tax: The ideal is to know everything.

I think we ought to start drawing together our experiences about present-day acculturation. I take it we almost concluded before that the places which have retained Indian culture are those where there wasn't much to start with.

Beals: I have long had the suspicion from my Tarascan materials that the more complex the culture the more rapid the acculturation.

Tax: That is an area which was marginal to the great societies of the old days. I think we could probably think of correlations but I would rather that we return to our experiences of the present day on problems of modern acculturation. For one thing, talking about distribution, to what degree does the suggestion of a gradient as you go away from the city hold? My own experience in Guatemala is to the contrary. How is it that in many cases we have a spotty distribution of acculturation?

Termer: The Eastern part of Guatemala is a much more sparsely occupied area than in pre-Columbian times. The sparse population of Indians that existed here in the sixteenth century was taken as slaves to the mines of Honduras, so that in the 1650's and '60's most of this area was depopulated. Peasants from Spain came in greater multitudes to these parts of Guatemala.

Jimenez Moreno: We must consider the importance of roads in this situation. We have to take into consideration the roads the Aztec used. There was a road by Tuxtepec and through the isthmus to Guatemala; that explains how this nucleus was separated. Another road led from Oaxaca through the isthmus to Chiapas and Guatemala. This was the road followed by Alvarado. It is important to see what was the pattern of communications in pre-Columbian days, and later what was the system in Colonial days, because the latter more or less followed the former. Certainly those regions being more exposed to contact with Spanish Colonial culture retained less of their own culture than did those less exposed to the Spanish.

Gillin: I would say that the acculturation gradient in Yucatan is a special case.

Tax: That's my experience too. The point is that in Yucatan there was one large city and the rest was more or less homogeneous, so that the variation is due to distance from the city.

Wisdom: In Colonial times was Western Guatemala more conveniently reached than what we call Eastern Guatemala?

Gillin: The road ran along the coast.

Beals: I've had the suspicion, at least in terms of modern acculturation, that one of the important factors is the development of roads. In historic times the main salt road ran right through the Tarascan Sierra. That was an extremely busy thoroughfare from Mexico City to the West Coast; that may account for the advanced state of the Tarascans in Colonial times.

Jimenez Moreno: Another item which also shows the importance of tying up the historical data with modern ethnology is the fact that in pre-Columbian days the Tarascans were working silver. Later, when the Spaniards came, they took the Tarascans to the silver mines. So you see to what extent the new pattern follows the old one.

Tax: I wonder whether we can make the general statement that the woman's customs last longer. I'm talking about modern acculturation now, and suggest that technology connected with women in the household lasts longer.

Beals: In the parts of the Mexican area that I know, perhaps the two most universal items are the sewing machine and the corn grinding mill, which are primarily in the woman's sphere. Among the Mixe, everyone wanted to know how much a sewing machine cost. I think this is significant enough to give us pause.

Paul: In San Pedro the men's clothes are native but women's clothes are not. Yet the women are more Indian than are the men. The women learn Spanish in school but they forget it, whereas the men don't.

Kyte: I find a contradiction to that in Guerrero where women are much more willing to accept new things.

Paul: In San Pedro, I had the feeling that when it was being discussed whether they should bring in a modern *pila,* the women were for it.

Watkins: In general, in Western Guatemala the men are more un-Indian than the women.

Kaplan: Very often a woman would be anxious to try out new things but the man would see to it that the woman would stay in her place.

Tax: That might have been true all the time; that might be a part of the explanation.

Gillin: We made a statistical study in San Luis Jilotepeque of clothes. Almost all of the women have cotton dresses and wear them, but they can't get married if they don't also have a *vestido.* It seems to me that these matters of acculturation always involve very complicated theoretical considerations of the wants of the people involved.

Borbolla: A more complicated problem is that of whether women are less apt to acculturation than men. At the present time we have a revolution of dress in Mexico. Native industries are disappearing very rapidly; less expensive material is being used for dress. It seems that women have taken to new dresses faster than was expected. The question of whether women are less apt to acculturation depends on whether there are some social or economic phenomena tied in with this change. Economic factors and the thrill of wearing something new have contributed a lot. It seems to me that at the present time there is a greater amount of money in circulation in the small villages where formerly there was none. The economics of the village at the present time is more and more dependent on money than it used to be, which is another economic factor. There's the possibility of having access to less expensive materials—less expensive in time and money than the former materials in use. If money is accessible, then money is contributing to that change. I don't think it has to do with sex.

Wisdom: Even though the Chorti women are more conservative and have less Ladino culture, I found in getting texts in which I was trying to get attitudes that the woman seems uninterested in ladinoization, but the man will tell you what he thinks about the whole problem of ladinoization—he's an Indian and he's proud of being one. You never get that attitude among the women.

Tax: Do you think there are pressures on women? Why don't they think about it?

Wisdom: The men keep them from being ladinoized as much as they can.

Tax: They're not faced with an immediate choice as the man is.

Wisdom: Yes.

Goubaud: There are 193 distinctly Indian villages in Guatemala where women are wearing native costumes. Only in ninety-seven of those same villages are men wearing native costumes.

Tax: You still have Indian costumes which are distinctive but they are a kind of generalized Indian; originally the assumption is that each of these villages had a distinctive costume and that's still true in some places. But in some areas many villages use the same kind of skirt. In Huehuetenango, skirt material is still back-strap loom woven; they have begun to wear *huipiles* that are made on a foot loom. What appears to be happening is that when women begin to become acculturated they don't adopt Ladino clothes, they first adopt generalized Indian clothes—not distinctive of their own town but still distinctively Indian.

Paul: There are variations in which they buy their costume, but it's still made for their village.

Tax: It's still regional but some of the regional ones are expanding.

Kaplan: Is there a sex difference in who's using the loom? When the woman stops using the back-strap loom, she is, in a sense, again becoming more advanced than conservative. She's liberating herself from the work of making her own material.

Mason: In the mountains of northern Mexico, it's the men's costume that is distinctive. The woman's is identical with the Mexican peon's, but the men all wear white muslin *calzones* and blouses.

Kirchhoff: The question of different influences of missionaries in early change in dress of men and women show there was greater interest in having the women dress "decently."

Guiteras: Among the Popoluca in southern Veracruz, the women are starting to wear huipiles. Formerly they didn't wear anything over the shoulders and the breast.

Camara: Is this applicable to the women of Tehuantepec who wear sixteenth century dress but are acculturated?

Guiteras: Factory made material generally starts to be used by the men, and only afterwards by the women. In the Tzeltal region no woman will wear anything that isn't hand woven, but they will buy *manta* for the men's costumes.

Gillin: I think we're talking all around what is actually at the core of the acculturation problem. Is there any particular information on the self-assessment of the men with regard to the women and with regard to Ladinos?

Paul: Men are superior; men say so and women say so. This is in a formal social sense. There's a general recognition of men's superiority.

Tax: How is that related to the symbolization of costume?

Paul: Where men are socially superior they're more ladinoized and they have more control over women. Even in San Pedro la Laguna where men wear the old costumes, women do the weaving of the men's costumes. You can take status as a base line but status itself keeps changing all the time; the woman is the merchant and the man is not. This will change her status.

Borbolla: How does acculturation act on the status of the individual within the group?

Gillin: If you're going to get a new element taken into the culture you can consider: (1) The presentation. (Stimulus.) But presentation doesn't guarantee that it will be taken over. (2) Can the receiving group perform the new pattern? For example, in San Luis Jilotepeque no one knows how to operate a car. They don't have the muscular patterns. (3) More important is: Does the new pattern satisfy a want? This is within the pattern of acquired drives.

In San Luis women don't wear cotton dresses regularly because they don't get the approval of the group if they do. I don't see how we can make any generalizations about that. (4) To get the people to actually take over a new object. If it does satisfy the want better than the competing object in the old culture, then it will be accepted.

Borbolla: I would like to make some other generalizations. Roads or communications have been some of the factors mentioned as contributing to change. I am wondering if some of those factors could be outlined in some way that would give a clearer picture of how acculturation functions in spite of the reaction of the individual and the group to the forces that are playing upon their culture.

Tax: I think we could name the influence of schools and governmental efforts to educate people. It would be interesting to analyze the situation as you see it on the map in terms of such factors. Where are the places in which conscription into the army is more important? Where are the places in which the government has established schools? There is also the factor of time. In these more central areas that are more acculturated, you would assume that this has been going on for a long time. The obvious case of Tusik is due to special circumstances. The factors themselves would be obvious to all of us, but the complication of them would get us into trouble.

Gillin: Take communication, for example. I agree with you in general that the better the communications the more ladinoization or acculturation, but there are exceptions. There is a town right on the railroad and also on the main road from Guatemala to the coast, yet it's one of the four towns where Pokoman customs and costumes continue.

Tax: Certainly in Western Guatemala and Chiapas, there have been Indians living side by side with Ladinos for generations without becoming ladinoized. Furthermore, you have Indian communities which have many characteristics of our Western tradition which are very non-folklike. This makes them appear acculturated until you see that they're not learning Spanish and that their systems of values are quite un-Ladino. Basically they're not at all acculturated even though their outward characteristics are very Ladinolike. You wonder if you don't have to deal with the resistance rather than the opportunity.

Beals: Take the situation among the Mixe where you have progressive villages and conservative villages. The progressive village is looking outward; the conservative village is looking inward. There's a change in basic attitude that no one has put a finger on. It's a matter of shifting of interest as well. A shift in world outlook.

Gillin: The question of values is very fundamental. As long as the old values appear more rewarding they'll stick with them. We used to think that all you have to do is to expose people to education and they'll change their ways. In San Luis, Indian children go to school but they get out as quickly as they can because the Ladino teacher makes fun of them. It's punishing rather than rewarding.

Tax: Dr. Redfield has a new book in press concerning a revisit to Chan Kom; it will be called *A Village That Chose Progress*. I would like to ask Villa how different is Chan Kom from other villages that didn't choose progress?

Villa: That point has been taken into consideration by Redfield. Chan Kom is very similar to other villages of the region, but the historical process—the appearance of new leaders, the proximity to Chichen Itza where the Americans were working—all those accidental factors gave them an opportunity to change their point of view.

Beals: Another example of this: In Ecuador there's an Indian community that has developed an important hand-woven textile industry. They're better off than Mestizos, but they aren't becoming whites; they even take airplanes to Colombia to sell their goods. The whites are completely puzzled by all this, but the people are making progress.

Jimenez Moreno: I want to stress the importance of markets as one of the main factors in the process of acculturation. Things sold in the market have to do with the acceptance of certain materials.

Regarding Dr. Beals' statement that side by side with a completely urban civilization you find the Indians clinging to their own customs and costumes. I think this is an experience that all of us have had. I have seen a modern factory not far from Mexico City, in front of which are people living in caves.

I think that all this discussion leads at least to the impression that the main factor is a psychological factor. It's a question of attitudes; it's a question of why people are ready to accept new experiences and why people are not ready to accept those things. An illustration of the attitude of the people is shown in some materials I found in the Mexican archives. The people who had not accepted the Christian religion around 1544 didn't want to be dressed like the Spaniards. Whenever they found somebody wearing calzones, they would either cut them off or mock him as a coward. By 1570 the situation had reversed; most of the Indians had accepted many of the external elements of the Christian religion. Now they dress like the Spanish. A change takes place in their attitude. Why?

I want to stress the point that Dr. Beals has mentioned, that no matter how much the culture has changed in technology, a great deal of the Indian spirit has remained.

De la Fuente: These are questions which pertain to our studies of ethos and acculturation. Oscar Lewis is making a study of acculturation in Tepoztlan. There are more tourists, more ethnologists, more psychologists, but still Tepoztlan persists as a timeless place.

Guiteras: The Chamulas go to the fincas and dress like Ladinos. Then they come back and take on the costume of their own village again. The women are very sad about it but they know that in their milieu they will never be able to put on the Ladino type of dress again.

Gillin: This business of costume is always a matter of symbolization. The ethos of the Indian to merge with his group is illustrated by dressing like others.

Kirchhoff: What we're all groping for here is some general underlying principle of change: the contrast between the static situation and change. I want to pose this question to Dr. Tax: Shouldn't a group like this enter into a discussion of where this is going to lead? Shouldn't we make some predictions as to the rate of change and the probable outcome of this in 50 to 100 years?

Tax: We ought to compare notes on that now.

Kirchhoff: We should look at this from the point of view of what the world at large expects of us as students of this sort of problem. On the basis of that we should be able to show trends and the speed or slowness of these trends.

Tax: People who are interested in planning ought to have some notion from us as to what parts of the culture they can change without changing other things that they don't want to change.

Kirchhoff: May I express my strong difference to the point of view that Dr. Tax has presented? It is not the task of the student of such problems to actively participate in the framing of policies but only to present the basic analysis of the situation.

Tax: I wasn't suggesting that we become *indigenistas.*

Kirchhoff: I mean that we should make a general scientific prediction of where things are going.

Tax: One of the variables in the situation is that you have these indigenistas and others doing things.

Kirchhoff: Maybe my difference with you is based on the fact that I believe that the actual planned intervention of governmental agencies does much less in effecting change than some fundamental phenomenon such as industrialization, the extension of roads and communications, etc.

Gillin: As things are going now, Indian cultures are going to disappear into Ladino cultures in about 150 years. There is going to be a decreasing proportion of the population regarded as Indians. But the question of what the governmental policy is has to be taken into account. What is it that the indigenistas want? What's their goal? I've heard some of them say that the idea is to incorporate the Indian into the *cuerpo nacional.*

Beals: I want to agree in general with both what Kirchhoff and Gillin have said. I would say that you will get ladinoization of the Indian cultures. You will get regional variation of Ladino culture but it will still be Ladino. These broad forces are probably more effective than any planned governmental program, but the nature of the process may be very different depending upon the amount of intervention. Whether these people become a governed peasant class, an industrialized proletariat, or an educated labor class will depend upon government policy.

Gillin: Up to now you don't have a rigid prejudice system toward Indians. It's quite difficult to observe certain elements in the United States because of the culturally defined prejudices.

Jimenez Moreno: Looking at what is happening today, and to the future, I think the policy should be not to try to introduce cultural elements from industrial civilization that would be in sharp conflict with what already exists. We must be very careful now that many of these Indian groups are confronted with the industrial civilization not to take certain elements that would be in conflict with their own psychological traits and factors that have been operating in their whole history.

For example: Is Protestantism to be a good thing or is it going to cause a great deal of disturbance? Let's look at some other factors, for example, *camiones*. We must be careful of what the new changes will produce in certain towns because a crisis of values arises.

Beals: Isn't it a question of the security system? If the security system in which the individual finds his satisfactions changes too sharply then the individual himself is lost. He becomes a marginal man like those in the city of Oaxaca.

Villa: What are the things in which there is general agreement?

Mason: Here are a few preliminary observations.

The arid nomadic northeastern area was ladinoized or acculturated. The rural agricultural northwestern area has about the same economic pattern; the esoteric pattern largely ladinoized. The Mesoamerican plateau region less ladinoized than the northern mountains. It may be that the percentage of ladinoization is the same but they had more to begin with. The Gulf Coast and Yucatan considerably ladinoized. Guatemala and Chiapas least affected.

There is relatively little change in economy and no great change in technology. They have adopted iron tools, power corn-grinder and the sewing machine, but it's not universal. Also have wheat, sugar cane, bananas and coffee.

Paul: How about writing and communication?

Mason: One of the great changes is in the use of money.

In ethnic and intercommunal relations: There is the modern Ladino problem and the question of "passing." The aboriginal class structure. Disappearance of intertribal warfare.

Social organization: Is the aboriginal system in its entirety found anywhere?

Tax: Yes. There are places which are not European.

Villa: The Lacandon and Tzeltal, for example.

Mason: The most important change in social organization is the ritual relationship, the godparent system which is an entirely new system.

Gillin: There is some question as to whether the godparent relationship is entirely new.

Tax: We had a report from Spain that it's certainly not Spanish.

Kirchhoff: In many cases, one should not look just at Spain but to a larger area of European culture.

Mason: Major native deities are all gone.

Villa: Not entirely gone in Yucatan, and especially in Quintana

Roo, the names and functions of some of the main gods still remain. Also in Chiapas among the Tzeltal.

Tax: Also still among the Chorti.

Mason: Communal agriculture ceremonies have disappeared.

Tax: No. Eastern Guatemala has agricultural and rain ceremonies.

Kirchhoff: We spoke about looking at a large area in Europe. I wonder whether we could compare tribes which have preserved their aboriginal culture in America, north of Mexico.

Tax: I'm sure it would be useful, but we haven't time at the moment.

Kirchhoff: I feel very strongly that it would be. I think the cultural characteristics of ancient Mesoamerica were so remarkably different from groups north of Mexico.

Mason: Throughout the greater part of the area the native ceremonies have been replaced by Christian fiestas. The concepts and methods of curing remain the same. Minor supernaturals remain with both disembodied and unembodied spirits. There is little that is sacred in paraphernalia.

Villa: With reference to the Tzeltal Indians, the concept of the supernatural and the function of the supernatural is mainly Indian and exercises a great influence upon the social organization of the group. It exercises a very powerful role as a social control system.

Kirchhoff: In pre-Columbian days, religion was one of the strongest features making for group cohesion; it was always distinctive.

Jimenez Morena: I think that the disruption of the native religion meant disruption of the native cultures and it has to be studied more carefully.

Mason: Politico-religious organizations. There are now two types. The first is the Centripetal, in which the religious and secular functions are combined. This is more aboriginal, and for the benefit of the group, and is tending to disappear in favor of the Centrifugal or Ladino type, in which the religious and secular are separated and individualistic. Do we agree that in aboriginal days there was only the first system?

Tax: We would agree that there was probably only one system.

Kirchhoff: In the Christian religion, besides the institutional religion, there was always the possibility of mysticism, in which man could have a direct relationship with God without an intermediary.

Mason: The former aboriginal type prevails to a greater degree in the highlands of Guatemala and Chiapas; the Ladino type predominates in Mexico and Yucatan. There are no pure cases of either.

The life cycle is probably not greatly changed; baptism is becoming important, and ritual relationships. Less polygamy than in aboriginal days.

Watkins: Do you know what the life cycle was before?

Tax: We have some statements.

Mason: The naming pattern is generally entirely different. There are no puberty ceremonies anywhere at present.

Kirchhoff: Generally no ceremonies for the life cycle except by the church.

[There was general disagreement on this.]

Villa: The *hetzmek* is a ceremony in the life cycle.

Kelly: I know of areas where the birth ceremony is largely aboriginal.

Mason: Ethos and personality are probably changed least of all.

Tax: But we don't know very much about that in the old days.

Kirchhoff: We can only get that for the upper classes in the old days. No one has thought of making a study of the ethos of ancient Middle America.

Gillin: It's been strongly influenced by the caste relationship.

Beals: This seems to be one of our least illuminated areas.

Tax: It's not the one about which we should make the strongest statements.

Mason: There are tendencies toward the general psychology of a conquered people.

Gillin: I would like to compliment Dr. Mason for bringing this together. It's something we need very badly.

Tax: How shall we prepare our summary for the Congress?

Gillin: We could present what the Seminar agrees upon and then point out the areas of the field that we know nothing about, and suggestions for future research.

Tax: We might ask what are the major differences in the area? We agree on what is general and then we say what is different. There should be some discussion of why in both cases; relations between the old and the new. We ought to talk about the problems of method in the area. We've had a little discussion on what we know and don't know about various topics.

Kirchhoff: I would suggest that after a positive statement of what has been done, you would point out what auxiliary studies have to be made on the Colonial period, and on Spanish and Mediterranean culture. These are side branches that would have to be developed for a future meeting.

Beals: I have the impression that we're generally agreed that Mesoamerica is still a definable area, of interest in terms of the fact that Dr. Kirchhoff originally worked this out on the basis of contact ethnography.

Tax: In contact ethnology you see an area for which we who are working in the area at the present time discover that the generalizations we want to make also apply to this area. You have the persistence of an area, which is of interest.

Kirchhoff: Kidder has shown that for quite some time back this original unit persisted. We could seriously present one of several generalizations that would reach out quite far.

Kelly: The breakdown of the area into several subareas would be interesting.

Gillin: I'm not impressed by the fact that the area still persists. Is that much of a discovery? If you look at modern culture in Mesoamerica, I'm not convinced that it is very distinct from South America, for example.

Beals: Many of these things were also characteristic of the Andean region in South America but in terms of the discussion on Middle America, we could still find a differentiable boundary between the northern part of Middle America and the southern part of Middle America.

Kirchhoff: We have an interesting parallel with the past. I would suggest that at that meeting we should also try to speak to the specialists in Andean acculturation problems, who, in some future phase of our work, should be brought into close collaboration.

chapter 14

SUMMARY FOR THE TWENTY-NINTH INTERNATIONAL CONGRESS OF AMERICANISTS: The Major General Propositions as to the Culture That Distinguishes Mexico and Guatemala from Other Parts of the World, With Some Attention to the Problems of Method in Treating the Cultures of This Area Past and Present*

Tax: This is a symposium reporting the results of the Seminar. The first page of the Viking Fund program sets forth the idea of the Seminar. Many of us have been working in the field; we know our own areas but we don't know the areas of others as well. The object of the Seminar was to enable us to compare notes so that we could get a better picture of Middle America as a whole. Each of the nine sessions was devoted to one topic, for which an individual had prepared a paper covering that topic for all of Middle America, even though he might not know it all. We then spent three hours discussing the paper. We exchanged ideas and came out with some impressions which, on the whole, were better than those with which we went into the Seminar.

You will notice that there are some topics which could have been

* New York City, September 5, 1949.

included but which were left out. So far as areas are concerned, the major omissions were Nahua, the Otomí and some parts of Guatemala; we did have a good part of Mesoamerica represented however. Dr. Mason, Dr. Beals, and Mrs. Stone represented areas on the edge of Mesoamerica; others of us also have had some experience outside of the area. We did have a pretty fair, although not complete, representation.

We would like the comments of the people who were not at the Seminar. Those of you who did not attend any of the meetings can, I hope, make some points during the discussion at the end of this meeting.

In introducing the first part of our program, which concerns the traits characteristic of Mesoamerica, I want to explain in the first place that we did not intend to limit ourselves to anything short of what is commonly known as Middle America. Most of us had worked in a restricted area and were interested in seeing whether Mesoamerica as set up by Dr. Kirchhoff is a useful concept. What Dr. Kirchhoff found was in terms of the pre-Columbian distribution of cultures. Here was an area that was dominated by the great civilizations. Actually in Central America it is more or less limited to the Maya and Nahuatl intrusions and perhaps includes the Chorotega. Don't confuse Mesoamerica with Middle America; the latter includes everything from the Rio Grande down to Panama or thereabouts. One of our problems was to distinguish Mesoamerica from the land to the north and south of it.

Dr. Mason will present a summary which he has prepared entitled: The sixteenth century and the twentieth; a comparison of culture types and culture areas.

Mason: I am presenting this more or less in the guise of a reporter and an editor rather than an expert on Mesoamerica, which I am not, so if I have misstated any point I hope you will make a note of it and raise objections at the end of the presentation.

The area. Regarding the boundaries of the culture areas and subareas, they are probably essentially the same as in pre-Conquest days. However, they differ greatly in degree of acculturation.

The extra-Mesoamerican arid nomadic northeast of Mexico is entirely acculturated to the Mestizo pattern.

The extra-Mesoamerican rural agricultural mountain area of Northwest Mexico probably retains much or most of the economic pattern but otherwise is greatly changed.

Highland Mexico, from Oaxaca northward, is like the foregoing but, having a more complex culture to start with, retains a far greater number of aboriginal elements.

Yucatan (except Quintana Roo) and the Gulf Coast is considerably ladinoized.

Guatemala, Quintana Roo, Chiapas, and parts of Oaxaca are the least acculturated to the Mestizo pattern.

Economy and technology. The change in economy is relatively small. The introduction of the *burro* may be the greatest feature, plus the culturation of wheat, potatoes, coffee, sugar cane, and bananas. The use of money in place of barter is important, writing and communication less so. The introduction of iron tools, the plow, the cart, the sewing machine and the power corn-grinder, as well as factory-woven cloth, has had considerable influence.

Ethnic and intercommunal relations. Everywhere there is some blood mixture, varying from place to place. Intergroup warfare has, of course, disappeared. The aboriginal class structure has been replaced by ethnic class distinctions between Indian and Ladino.

Social organization. The most important new element is ritual relationship, the godparent pattern; this had some aboriginal prototype, but probably one of far less importance. Indians are generally bilingual, Ladinos monolingual. The systems of consanguinity vary greatly. The data on these are very deficient for pre-Conquest days. Probably among some groups the ancient system is found in its entirety, and complete replacement by the Spanish pattern is probably rare or even missing among Indian groups.

The supernatural world and curing. Present beliefs are a blend of: (1) A substratum of some fundamental pan-American or worldwide concepts; (2) Spanish, Mediterranean or European elements; (3) Mesoamerican elements; these are difficult to separate. In many places the major pre-Conquest deities have disappeared. Communal agricultural ceremonies have been replaced by Catholic Church fiestas in much of the region. The cult of the saints is the most important new feature, replacing local and family deities. Minor supernaturals remain, both unembodied and disembodied spirits. There is little sacred paraphernalia. The basic concepts of illness and methods of curing are probably slightly changed.

Religious organization. The aboriginal pattern was centripetal, in which religious and secular functions were combined. Its purpose was the welfare of the entire group, and service therein was practically obligatory. This remains in more or less full vigor in some communities while in others, the more ladinoized pueblos, it is being replaced by a centrifugal type of organization in which the religious and secular elements are separated. This operates more for the prestige of the individual, and service therein is voluntary. The former type is at present more common in Highland Guatemala and Chiapas, the latter in Mexico and Yucatan.

Life cycle. Though our information on this topic in pre-Conquest days is deficient, it is probable that it has not changed greatly. Details vary from place to place. The greatest change is probably in the importance of baptism, and of the godparent relationship. The system of naming is greatly changed; school education is entirely new. Most aboriginal ceremonies of the life cycle have been replaced by those of the Catholic Church, though the former are still observed in some less acculturated regions.

Ethos and cultural aspects of personality. On this phase we have almost no data for former days, but the presumption is that the change has been slight, though naturally the general psychology of a conquered people is evident. It is strongly influenced by class reactions. There are slight tendencies towards the modern or European pattern. All imperialistic tendencies, such as those of the latest Aztec theocracy, are gone.

* * *

Tax: Now I would like to call on members of the Seminar for any criticisms, additions or qualifications. Doris Stone, your impression is that these comments do not really apply south of the Mesoamerican border?

Stone: South of the area we have matrilineal clans; people don't accept baptism; don't accept marriage. There are puberty ceremonies; secret societies for men. Lack of church influence. Different economy: corn loses its importance; importance of tubers and yucca. The pig is important. And of course you have a great linguistic difference.

Goubaud: I would like to add to the list of Dr. Mason with regard to the early traits brought by the Spanish, wool—the material for the clothing of a large number of Indians. And perhaps steel tools.

Tax: We have a list of common denominators here. Dr. Beals has summarized the bases on which distinctions may be made within the area.

Beals: Dr. Mason has outlined in some detail certain aspects of this general area which, it is our impression, occurred over the whole area. There is also regional divergency. This is much less clearly defined. All I want to do is to indicate with an illustration or two what these regional differences may be like when we get the material pulled together. It is quite clear to most of us that although we didn't start out to test this hypothesis of Mesoamerica, it happened—the realization that modern Mesoamerica and ancient Mesoamerica more or less coincided in their areas. The kinds of differences that I want to point out are differences that may be defined particularly in areal or regional terms. Such differentiation will probably never be very easy because the area has had a very long and complex history. It presents highly varied and sharply contrasting conditions. You have a variety of forces at work in the differentiation of cultures that are pretty complicated. The impression is that this region is many times as complex as the Andean region.

One of the sets of differences which we suspect in this area is that which may be summarized as the difference between Highlands vs. Lowlands; differences which probably have their ultimate origin in contrasting environmental differences. When we say lowlands we mean the Gulf Coast. We don't know much about the Pacific coast lowland region.

The sorts of differences are in such things as certain aspects of technology, e.g., in the lowlands, the slash and burn type of agriculture. This seems to be generally a lowland trait. Perhaps the most marked difference that we could see in our discussion was the difference in the presence of a market economy throughout this highland region. Even where the market economy spills over into the lowlands, it is the highland people who are the traders. You have, in the highland region, a great emphasis on the market, trading, and on village and community specialization in occupations, handicraft manufactures and certain kinds of trade and social activities. The other type of differences that seemed fairly obvious is the differentiation today between the North of the area and the South of the area. There are suggestions that perhaps these differences might be related to the general Nahua tradition as opposed to Maya culture. However, we decided that it was better to call it "North" and "South" at the present.

In general, modern Indians are noted for lack of aggressive behavior—my impression is that it is more noticeable in the North than in the South. The Northern part shows greater acculturation and less retention of aboriginal traits, more movement toward the Mestizo pattern. In the Southern part of this area, you get the centripetal communities, whereas in the Northern part of the area, you get the centrifugal, approaching the Ladino type of community. There are probably other differentiations which could be made in this area but it seems to me that these were the two main ones we discussed and they more or less cut across each other.

There are other difficulties with this kind of classification: The boundaries are not clear, the classification doesn't adequately account for the fact that in a sort of central region between the North and the South you get a higher degree of retention of aboriginal traits. There are various possible explanations for some of these factors which may include such things as aboriginal and Spanish communications. The centers of colonization and the administration in Spain, on the other hand, may account for present-day differences.

Tax: Do the members of the Seminar more or less agree with this summary?

The problem that obviously comes out here, in Mr. Beals' presentation of some of the major differences in the area is the problem of acculturation, the differential degree to which these people have been subjected to Spanish or European influence. We had a lot of discussion on this and we want to spend the next half hour talking about acculturation and to try to bring out some of the material that we have been over in the last week. Mr. Villa will present an historical sequence of what happened in this area.

Villa: The sequence of cultures that I am going to present was originally presented by Dr. La Farge. After working in the Cuchumatanes in the northwestern section of Guatemala, he felt that the history of the region could be presented in five main periods. Later, when I was working among the Indians of Chiapas in southeastern Mexico, I discovered that the schema which he had prepared also applied to Chiapas, and now Dr. Beals feels that the schema is applicable to the highlands of Mexico. The importance of the schema is that it shows that the process of acculturation has not followed a single line. In general terms the dates that I am going to set forth are not exact but are approximate and differ according to the sections of the country. The sequences are as follows:

(1) 1524-1600: The period of the Conquest, when the Indian

culture declined very fast. That was a period of violent clashing of Indian and Spanish culture.

(2) Then from 1600 follows a long period of adjustment when the Indian groups were assimilating most of the Spanish elements—from 1620-1700, when the *encomiendas* were abolished. In this period the Indians get a new opportunity to reorganize their lives and they have a better chance of a more satisfactory living. Then they developed some of the Indian elements of the cultures. During this period, some of the Indian elements that were suppressed during the Conquest were revived and a new blending of Indian and Spanish elements took place.

(3) Then we have a period of another eighty years when this new type of culture was smoothly blended and integrated and a satisfactory adjustment took place.

(4) Then we come to the period when the communal lands were abolished and then by law you had a new system of land. Then the Ladinos and mixed people began to interfere with the property of the Indians and we have a very sharp decline of Indian tradition. This occurred from 1880, when President Barrios abolished the communal lands.

(5) From 1880 to the present time we have this period of conflict and acculturation. And now Dr. Beals adds a new period which, according to him, took place in Mexico with the revolution in 1910, when the Ladino recognized the kinship that he had with the Indian and abolished in high degree the caste system. Now we see, in Mexico at least, a very fast development of the culture, due to the new projects by the government, to better the way of life of the Indians, and so, within the next few years, the Indian cultures are going to decline very sharply.

Tax: Jimenez Moreno would want to suggest that there was a general retardation in Guatemala as compared with Mexico.

Wagley: 1880 in Mexico would correspond to 1891 in Guatemala.

Beals: There is one point to be added to what Villa said. Villa has dealt with the history primarily in terms of the retention of the Indian culture. You could consider this in terms of the rejection on the part of the Indian of parts of European culture. You get periods of rejection when they don't take any European culture. These are associated with a period of unpleasant relationships between Indian and white. When you get such a period, such as that about 1910, with more rapid acculturation coming in, it generally marks an improvement in relations. These are cases in which the government tries to do something constructive for the Indian rather than simple exploitation of him.

Tax: Do the members of the Seminar now agree?

The next point is the problem of which parts of this area seem to be more acculturated than others. Could we map differential acculturation in the area? Mr. de la Fuente will describe what we did in this connection.

De la Fuente: We worked in a purely impressionistic fashion to achieve an index of retention of pre-Columbian traits and loss of aboriginal elements.

[Here followed a description of the Table and Map.]

The most general conclusion that we have reached is that we have a relatively acculturated Northern area which includes such groups as the Chinantec, Mazatec, Mixe and Popoluca; a least acculturated area to the South which includes the Lacandon, Ixil, and Tzeltal; and farther away the Maya of Quintana Roo, who have been more isolated. In between we have the Isthmus of Tehuantepec, in which some groups can be linked up with the more acculturated groups toward the North and others with the less acculturated block to the South.

It is the attempt in the Table [see pp. 263-265] to differentiate the time of loss of aboriginal elements, probably the least accurate part of our work.

Tax: There are two principal periods of acculturation then: The original contact, in which there was great loss, and the modern contact which has been since 1880. For example, anything the Lacandon lost has been recent. On the other hand, some of the other groups—those in Quintana Roo, for example, lost everything early. It's interesting to consider when the loss occurred. There's another interesting thing that we stressed—when we make these assessments we're always convinced that something looks very primitive, but you can't say it's pre-Columbian. On the other hand, some of the other groups, even though they're not so strange, get a high score for the retention of traits.

Goubaud: It seems more logical to me to place the Kekchi closer to the circle—with groups one, two and three. I would say, with regard to language they would stand around 90, with regard to technology also about 90. In social organization they would be about the same as Midwestern Guatemala. In religion they would be about 80.

Tax: I don't agree with you. A score of 80 or 90 in religion in Huehuetenango or Chiapas includes the old calendar complex there. We disagree on that.

Gillin: Dr. Beals said there were no Indians along the Pacific Coast of Guatemala. I think this was just a generalization; there are about 3000 along there.

Beals: We still don't know anything about them.

Termer: All the Xinca Indians on the coast that I encountered were certainly acculturated. They had no single trait of pre-Columbian times left. I never found any survivals here. They are perfectly acculturated except for the language, but the Xinca in the highlands have not been acculturated.

Tax: I would like to mention one obvious fact: that some of these Indians are in places farther from city centers. Another obvious fact, brought up by Dr. Kirchhoff, that the people who had the least to lose lost least. The people who were most highly civilized were acculturated most rapidly. That is why these peoples in Northwest Guatemala and Chiapas, since they were on the margins of the ancient civilizations, had not so much to lose.

Beals: I would like to mention the fact which Jimenez Moreno indicated: that the Spanish expansion followed the Aztec pattern for the northern part of this area, but how far down this went is problematical. He pointed out that the two great roads of communication of the Aztec were the roads followed by the Spaniards in early times.

Termer: From what we know of Central America, in the altitudes above 600 meters the acculturation of the Indians is much more progressed than in altitudes below 600 meters. There has never been such intense acculturation as in the higher altitudes. The Spanish had here the best conditions for the development of the great encomiendas and the acculturation of Spanish elements.

Tax: I wonder if some of us would like to indicate some of the interesting points of content. For example, Mrs. Guiteras discussed with us the matter of social organization, clans, etc., and I think many of the people here would be interested in knowing where in this area some of these interesting features of social organization exist.

Guiteras: We find clans and lineages in these lowest acculturated regions. They extend, of course, beyond these regions. In a broken-down form we might still be able to call them clans but they are not crystallized as in this less acculturated region. Here we have patrilineal clans. Later on we have a change from the unilateral to the bilateral organization in several regions, first under the Nahua contact and later on, in contact with Western Civilization. We have a tendency in the whole region towards a bilateral organization with a unilateral tendency.

Tax: Are there any other features of the less acculturated areas that some of you think ought to be reported here? If not we would like to go on and indicate where we think we know the most and where we think we know the least, and the direction that future research should take. What are the places about which we know most?

Villa: In terms of the regions that are not known, I can say a few words, especially with reference to Mexico. We know least the most Indian regions, especially where ethnographic reports are lacking, e.g., the Isthmus of Tehuantepec. In this area we have Indians with the highest percentage of monolingualism. Out of 220,000 Zapotec, 111,000 are monolingual. We do not have any studies on the Mazatec. We have exploratory studies on the Chinantec, but very preliminary. In this region there are about twenty linguistic groups and every group is divided into dialects so that it is like a tower of Babel.

Then there is the region where the Lacandon are living now and we do not have a view of the whole culture. We are beginning to understand the nature of the cultures of the Indians living in the state of Chiapas. We know a little about the Popoluca. On the Maya, we have reports on Chan Kom and Quintana Roo, and several others that present a more or less complete picture of the culture of this region but we do not have reports for the Nahua because the knowledge of the position of this group is very inadequate. The only report we have is the one written by Redfield about twenty-two years ago. There are now some studies being made of the region by modern ethnologists. We know something about the Totonac and the Huastec and also something about Michoacán. I don't know if we have any other information on other regions.

Goubaud: Guatemala has been quite well studied in certain areas, but if we use linguistic terminology, Guatemalan subcultures are all community cultures. Studies have been made in the midwestern part of Guatemala mostly. I shall go over a list here that I have tentatively jotted down.

Studies are needed of the Quiché in the eastern part of the region and the northern part of the region—in places like Rabinal and others, and also around Quezaltenango. Studies have been made in Chichicastenango which is in the center of the Quiché area. In the Cakchiquel area we have studies mainly on the western part of the area; nothing on the eastern, northern, or southern part of the area. With regard to the Zutugil, this is pretty well covered, so far as communities around Lake Atitlán are concerned.

In the Mam area, a very good study by Dr. Wagley was made in the northern part of the area, and recently a study made in Todos Santos, but nothing in the central or southern part of the Mam area. Also there is a linguistic study of Aguacateca. The Kekchi area has been very little studied. We have Sapper's synthesis of the Kekchi cultures more or less on a linguistic basis, and no community studies. I have worked in one community—San Juan Chamelco. Also in between the Ixil and the Kekchi is the Uspanteca, which seems to be a kind of stepbrother of the Quiché culture. We are making surveys of all these communities simply to gather very elementary data for administrative purposes. It does seem that there's quite a bit to be done in Guatemala. Besides that, we are interested in a comparison of Indian and non-Indian cultures. Then we also have to consider the Ladino culture. Gillin and Tumin have made some very important studies in the eastern parts of Guatemala, and Redfield has made a study of Agua Escondida.

Tax: If I may make just one comment, when Mr. Villa talked about what had to be done, he said Chiapas was pretty well studied. Applying the same criteria, Guatemala has been pretty well studied, too. Apparently different standards are being applied here.

Mason: Modern ethnological studies are a great desideratum among all the tribes in the North. Many years ago, when they were investigated, an ethnologist never thought of ethos and personality. So from the modern point of view, we know hardly anything about Northern Mexico.

Stone: With the exception of the Lenca, none of the people to the South were townspeople. If you are speaking of ethnology from the point of view of Ladinos, nobody has touched the west coast. I am working on the Lenca now. The Jicaques certainly ought to be studied, not only in ethnology but also in linguistics. I don't know how many Rama are left, but certainly they ought to be studied. The Watuso in Costa Rica are disappearing completely. No one but Sapper has worked on them. It seems to me that somebody ought to take the linguistics of many of these people and work on it while there's still time.

Tax: Now let us see whether we have taken advantage of our methodological tools in these areas.

Paul: Despite all the gaps, in recent years we have accumulated a considerable amount of data in these areas. Gaps occur also in the field of methodology. I want to say something about what methods have been used. It's not too useful to talk about method when talking about the interests of the people involved. The interests applied in this area are the traditional range of interests you'd find in any area. Some people are primarily interested in the area for itself and others are interested in general principles, and in using areal data as it illustrates these principles. Perhaps another way of putting it is that interest have fallen into, roughly, four groups: (1) Reconstruction; (2) the acculturation period; (3) dynamic sociology; and (4) psycho-ethnology, which is the new growing interest. These are the kind of studies that have been made:

(1) Regional surveys. To find appropriate sites, like Mr. Goubaud's group in Guatemala.

(2) Topical studies. Interested in an institution rather than a community, things like costumes, on which three or four people have been working: Lily de Jong Osborne, Lila O'Neale and the Cordrays. Problem of markets, on which Malinowski, de la Fuente, McBryde, Tax, and Goubaud have done work.

(3) Community studies. The most common kind of study and that which employs the traditional method is the community study made without reference to a particular problem. These have been made in various numbers.

There is also the beginning of some studies on communities which we might call cities—Oaxaca, Mexico City, etc.

Of particular interest here are "before and after" studies. Good community studies made long enough ago to make revisitation possible. I think particularly of Chan Kom revisited by Redfield. Tepoztlan: original study by Redfield and now Oscar Lewis. This gives us an excellent opportunity to study change. Obviously there are other places that are becoming available for this kind of approach. Perhaps the Chorti, and San Juan Teotihuacan.

Regarding techniques which are used in the field—the standard kind of technique used in anthropology, but in addition to the standard use of informants, participant-observer method, genealogical method, use of census data, native texts, etc., there's been a slow invasion of techniques from sister disciplines, as from the field of psychology, for example, so there now have to be systematic life histories from the point of view of the ongoing individual, and the beginning of work in projective techniques. TAT's have been given in two or three communities, and Rorschachs in two or three; studies of doll play in two or three communities and so on. Also different kinds of interviews. Also from rural sociology have come attitude studies. Also there has been an increase in use of statistical techniques.

Two things of particular interest here are that in dealing with Middle America, we are dealing with communities that are large and complex. Two problems arise out of this: (1) Sampling and statistical problems. When you get into the larger communities the traditional techniques are good but perhaps not good enough. (2) The problem of how to work with teams of experts. This has been tried but has not always been successful.

This area has also been used as a testing ground, for example, in Redfield's study at Chan Kom and nearby towns, in which he took the opportunity to test certain general hypotheses in his *Folk Culture of Yucatan*, and made certain propositions about the nature of social change.

Another type of approach in which the area has been used as a testing ground is a matter of testing the reliability of the ethnographers. In at least three instances there have been independent studies of the same community by two different people. Chamula: two investigators; Chichicastenango: Bunzel, Schultze-Jena and Tax; San Pedro: two investigators.

In connection with action research, both Guatemala and Mexico are directing activities toward bettering the lot of their people. The Papaloapan project is one of these.

Characteristics of action research: (1) Areal; (2) Standard of living; health, housing, etc.; (3) implies need for teams of experts; (4) consideration of Indian and Mestizo communities; (5) in studies of the kind that are taking place now in Mesoamerica, we have an excellent opportunity to establish a base line against which rapid changes are going to be projected. This is an ideal laboratory for people to observe differential reactions to change, and the unforeseen consequences of social change.

Types of comparison with respect to Mesoamerica as a whole: (1) Inductive comparisons—trying to build up from local communities a total picture of Mesoamerica as a whole. (2) Comparisons in space. Comparisons of this area with other areas. It is being compared with people of typically Mediterranean culture, by Foster, Lewis and others. Termer tells us we will also have a chance to get data from the European archives. (3) Comparisons in time, these are comparisons which we can make with reference to the historical base line.

I want to close with the problem of method involved in doing what we have been doing this last week. (1) Does a trait which is to be considered diagnostic have to be universal to the area; (2) must it be unique to the area; (3) the whole problem of the magnitude of traits—minute traits or larger institutions? (4) Are we ultimately to characterize the area in terms of an inventory of features, or in terms of some kind of configuration—an organization of traits, rather than the traits themselves?

Tax: Dr. Kirchhoff mentioned the problem of getting a baseline—in fact, he mentioned two baselines: (1) the present stage of culture as a basis of study for the future, and (2) the ancient baseline.

Kirchhoff: The two outstanding features that came out in the Seminar were that in the groups studied, their cultures are of known mixed origin. We are very definitely aware of several historical moments when new ingredients came in. At the moment we are studying now, changes are going on. These two aspects—mixture and change—are important in our approach to this material. They lead us into the feeling that we have to try to project into the past a series of changes which we have observed recently, not only, as it were, to have an earlier date line but also to have the possibility of seeing a continuous flow of historical movements and transformations. I would say our great interest in studying present-day cultures in present Middle America is that we want to be able to compare them. We want to be able to say what is of native provenience. Secondly, we want to be able to compare historical processes of change as we observe them now with earlier processes of change.

I would like to repeat the point of view that I presented in the Seminar. In that respect, following the contrast established by Redfield between folk cultures, or tribal cultures, on the one hand, and urban or city cultures on the other hand, it seems to me that we get much more out of the study of the present if we confine ourselves not only to present change but to earlier changes as well. We have three great periods of clash between the urban and the folk cultures. One took place in pre-Columbian days. Definitely situations in which, on the one side, you had city-states, with a firmly established ruling class with its own system of values, and on the other hand, we have in the rural area surrounding these cities a totally different type of culture.

The next period is, of course, the coming of the European culture in the Spanish Conquest.

Then we have no longer such a dramatically sharp division, but a number of consecutive changes, resulting from changes which have taken place in Mexico from city culture and eventually from the inroads of modern industrial civilization—Anglo-Saxon rather than Mediterranean. We need at least as full a coverage of earlier periods in history in Mesoamerica as has been pulled together in a very satisfactory manner in this last week's Seminar. It seems to me that on the two extremes of this historical sequence we have a reasonable coverage. We are not all satisfied with what we know of modern Mesoamerica, but we know much more about it than we know about the time of the coming of the Spaniards. We need to know more about contact ethnography. We have perhaps four centuries of descriptive material, chronologically dated, of this contrast between city-states and still simpler cultures. We have people who have studied the archaeological material and people studying the present-day Indian. We have a strong need for the period in between, for what I would call "pre-contact ethnography," as well as for contact ethnography. I think this is highly important, for a better understanding of the present is based on a better understanding of the past. Then we will be able to bring together, on one front, people who are interested in all of these areas of study. We have plenty of material.

Gillin: If we take this area and compare it with other areas, I think we can say that the general character of ethnological work during the last twenty years has been unusually high. There are very few other parts of the world where the native cultures of modern times have been so well studied from so many different points of view. This is not something that North Americans or Europeans can take exclusive credit for, because the quality of work of the Mexican and Guatemalan ethnographers has been very high.

This Seminar has been primarily concerned with modern Indian cultures, but this is only one kind of culture. The Indians are well in the minority. We have at least half the population in Guatemala and probably two-thirds at least in Mexico who are modern Latin Americans, or whatever we want to call them. This culture has to be understood too, and it will probably be soon because of international policy. The people at the United Nations are interested in this, so that if anthropologists do not take the responsibility of trying to define the basis of modern Latin American cultures, someone else will have to do it. I don't think anthropology can do the job alone. So far as the future goes, we can think of some new approaches which are known as interdisciplinary cooperation; such are: sociology, psychology, and medicine—the latter to tie up local beliefs in illness with modern medical theory. We will also have to look toward the humanities also being brought into the picture. We have literature in Mexico by experts in the humanities, discussing what the Mexican soul or ethos is—how the Hispanic is combined with the native. There is the matter of translation of concepts from one discipline to another. I think anthropologists and the other experts should get together. On the question of art, of course, anthropologists have done a good job on the native arts, but we also need to know what's going on in modern art. As Dr. Kirchhoff has pointed out, this is the time for historical investigation. My plea is for several approaches to be used so that we can understand what this whole culture situation is now and in what direction it is moving. Studies of modern area are now under way in Japan; several of the modern contemporary cultures of Europe are under study by a group right here in this city—the study of Russia, for example—and in all of these, not only traditional ethnological material but everything that can be gathered from the social sciences and the humanities is centered or concentrated on the focal problem.

Tax: We have seen some of the problems with which we are involved. The problem of time differences. The sixteenth century and the twentieth. We've just said that we've been talking about the

Indian cultures and not about the non-Indians. Of course, there's the difficulty of telling who is an Indian and who is a non-Indian. We decided not to try to define the manner in which they are to be distinguished. But there is a kind of a two-class system with the Indians subordinate in the whole area. And there is also the difficulty which we've come across of defining the community that you are studying: the larger, political community, or the small local community.

BIBLIOGRAPHY

THE following bibliography is not intended to cover all the literature on Mesoamerica, but rather to give some sources which may be used as a guide to further study. The first section is a highly selective list of monographs reporting the results of field observations; the works in this list deal with most of the places and peoples mentioned in the papers and Seminar discussions.

A. *Monographs*

Beals, Ralph L. *Cherán: A Sierra Tarascan Village.* Smithsonian Institution: Institute of Social Anthropology Publication No. 4. Washington, 1946.

———. *Ethnology of the Western Mixe.* ("University of California Publications in American Archaeology and Ethnology" Vol. XLII, No. 1.) Berkeley, 1945.

Bevan, Bernard. *The Chinantec and Their Habitat.* ("The Chinantec: Report on the Central and Southeastern Chinantec Region" Vol. I.) Instituto Panamericano de Geografía e Historia Publication No. 24. Mexico, 1938.

Brand, Donald F. *Quiroga: A Mexican Municipio.* Smithsonian Institution: Institute of Social Anthropology Publication No. 11. Washington, 1951.

Bunzel, Ruth. MS. on Chichicastenango, Guatemala, to be published in 1951 as a Monograph of the American Ethnological Society.

Cámara, B., Fernando. *Monografía sobre los Tzeltales de Tenejapa.* ("Microfilm Collection of Manuscripts on Middle American Cultural Anthropology" No. 5.) Chicago: University of Chicago Libraries, 1946.

De la Fuente, Julio. *Yalalag: Una Villa Zapoteca Serrana.* Museo Nacional de Antropologia; Serie Cientifica No. 1. Mexico, 1949.

Foster, George M. *Empire's Children: The People of Tzintzuntzan.* Smithsonian Institution: Institute of Social Anthropology Publication No. 6, Washington, 1948.

———. *A Primitive Mexican Economy.* ("American Ethnological Society Monographs" No. 5.) New York: J. J. Augustin, 1942.

Gann, Thomas F. *The Maya Indians of Southern Yucatan and Northern British Honduras.* Bureau of American Ethnology Bulletin 64. Washington, 1918.

Guiteras Holmes, Calixta. *Informe de Cancuc.* ("Microfilm Collection of Manuscripts on Middle American Cultural Anthropology" No. 8.) Chicago: University of Chicago Libraries, 1946.

———. *Informe de San Pedro Chenalho. Ibid.*, No. 14, 1946.

Kelly, Isabel. *Tajin Totonac: Part I.* Smithsonian Institution: Institute of Social Anthropology Publication No. 13. Washington. To be published sometime in 1952.

La Farge, Oliver. *Santa Eulalia: The Religion of a Cuchumatan Town.* Chicago: University of Chicago Press, 1947.

——— and Byers, Douglas. *The Year-Bearer's People.* ("Middle American Research Series" Publication No. 3.) New Orleans: Tulane University of Louisiana Department of Middle American Research, 1931.

Lewis, Oscar. *Life in a Mexican Village: Tepoztlan Restudied.* Champaign: University of Illinois Press. 1951.

Lincoln, Jackson Steward. *An Ethnological Study of the Ixil Indians of the Guatemala Highlands.* ("Microfilm Collection of Manuscripts on Middle American Cultural Anthropology" No. 1.) Chicago: University of Chicago Libraries, 1946.

Oakes, Maude. *The Two Crosses of Todos Santos.* ("Bollingen Series" XXVII.) New York: Pantheon Books, 1951.

Parsons, Elsie C. *Mitla: Town of the Souls.* Chicago: University of Chicago Press, 1936.

Pozas A., Ricardo. *Monografía de Chamula.* ("Microfilm Collection of Manuscripts on Middle American Cultural Anthropology" No. 15.) Chicago: University of Chicago Libraries, 1947.

Redfield, Robert. *Ethnographic Materials on Agua Escondida.* ("Microfilm Collection of Manuscripts on Middle American Cultural Anthropology" No. 3.) Chicago: University of Chicago Libraries, 1946.

———. *The Folk Culture of Yucatan.* Chicago: University of Chicago Press, 1941.

———. *Notes on San Antonio Palopó.* ("Microfilm Collection of Manuscripts on Middle American Cultural Anthropology" No. 4.) Chicago: University of Chicago Libraries, 1946.

———. *Tepoztlan: A Mexican Village.* Chicago: University of Chicago Press, 1930.

———. *A Village That Chose Progress: Chan Kom Revisited.* Chicago: University of Chicago Press, 1950.

——— and Villa R., Alfonso. *Chan Kom: A Maya Village.* Carnegie Institute of Washington Publication No. 448. Washington, 1934.

Rosales, Juan de Dios. *Notes on San Pedro la Laguna.* ("Microfilm Collection of Manuscripts on Middle American Cultural Anthropology" No. 25.) Chicago: University of Chicago Libraries, 1949.

Schultze Jena, Leonhard. *Leben, Glaube und Sprache der Quiche von Guatemala.* ("Indiana" Vol. I.) Jena: Gustav Fischer, 1933. Non-text portions translated by Antonio Goubaud C. and Herbert D. Sapper as *La Vida y las Creencias de los Indigenas Quiches de Guatemala.* ("Anales de la Sociedad de Geografía e Historia de Guatemala" Vol. XX, Nos. 1, 2, 3, and 4.) Guatemala, 1945.

Taylor, Paul S. *A Spanish-Mexican Peasant Community: Arandas in Jalisco, Mexico.* ("Ibero-Americana" No. 4.) Berkeley: University of California Press, 1933.

Tax, Sol. *Notes on Santo Tomas Chichicastenango.* ("Microfilm Collection of Manuscripts on Middle American Cultural Anthropology" No. 16.) Chicago: University of Chicago Libraries, 1947.

———. *Panajachel: Field Notes. Ibid.*, No. 29. 1950.

———. *Penny Capitalism: A Guatemalan Indian Economy.* Smithsonian Institution: Institute of Social Anthropology, Washington. To be published in 1952.

———. *The Towns of Lake Atitlan.* ("Microfilm Collection of Manuscripts on Middle American Cultural Anthropology" No. 13.) Chicago: University of Chicago Libraries, 1946.

———. (ed.) *Notas Sobre Zinacantan, Chiapas. Ibid.*, No. 20. 1947.

Thompson, J. Eric. *Ethnology of the Mayas of Southern and Central British Honduras.* ("Field Museum of Natural History Anthropology Series" Vol. XVII, No. 2.) Chicago, 1930.

Tozzer, Alfred M. *A Comparative Study of Mayas and Lacandones.* New York: The Macmillan Co., for the Archaeological Institute of America, 1907.

Tumin, Melvin. *San Luis Jilotepeque: A Guatemalan Pueblo.* ("Microfilm Collection of Manuscripts on Middle American Cultural Anthropology" No. 2.) Chicago: University of Chicago Libraries, 1946.

Villa R., Alfonso. *The Maya of East Central Quintana Roo.* Carnegie Institution of Washington Publication No. 559. Washington, 1945.

———. *Notas Sobre la Etnografía de los Indios Tzeltales de Oxchuc.* ("Microfilm Collection of Manuscripts on Middle American Cultural Anthropology" No. 7.) Chicago: University of Chicago Libraries, 1946.

Wagley, Charles. *Economics of a Guatemalan Village.* ("Memoirs of the American Anthropological Association" No. 58.) Menasha, Wis., 1941.

———. *The Social and Religious Life of a Guatemalan Village. Ibid.,* No. 71. 1949.

Whetten, Nathan L. *Rural Mexico.* Chicago: University of Chicago Press, 1948.

Wisdom, Charles. *The Chorti Indians of Guatemala.* Chicago: University of Chicago Press, 1940.

To the North of Mesoamerica lies the area of the Greater Southwest, concerning which there is a wealth of literature. A few works are listed, all of which contain bibliographies of the area:

Beals, Ralph L. *The Comparative Ethnology of Northern Mexico Before 1750.* ("Ibero-Americana" No. 2.) Berkeley: University of California Press, 1932.

———. *The Contemporary Culture of the Cahitá Indians.* Bureau of American Ethnology Bulletin 142. Washington, 1945.

Bennett, Wendell C. and Zingg, Robert M. *The Tarahumara: An Indian Tribe of Northern Mexico.* Chicago: University of Chicago Press, 1935.

Mason, J. Alden. "The Tepehuan Indians of Azqueltan," *Proceedings of the Eighteenth International Congress of Americanists.* London, 1913.

Concerning the area to the South of Mesoamerica, the literature is well summarized in:

Steward, Julian. (ed.) *Handbook of South American Indians,* Vol. 4. "The Circum-Caribbean Tribes," Bureau of American Ethnology Bulletin 143. Washington, 1948.

For the historical background of Mesoamerica, one may refer to:

The Maya and Their Neighbors. New York: D. Appleton Century Co., 1940.

Roys, Ralph L. *The Indian Background of Colonial Yucatan.* Carnegie Institution of Washington Publication No. 548. Washington, 1943.

Sahagun, Bernardino de. *Historia General de las Cosas de Nueva España.* 5 volumes. Mexico, 1938. (Various other editions.)

Tozzer, Alfred M. *Landa's Relación de las Cosas de Yucatan.* Translation with notes by the editor. ("Papers of the Peabody Museum of American Archaeology and Ethnology" Vol. XVII.) Cambridge, 1941. (Various other editions.)

B. *Bibliographic Sources*

For more detailed bibliographies on Mesoamerica, see:

Boletín Bibliográfico de Antropología Americana. Mexico: Instituto Panamericano de Geografía e Historia. (Annual.)

Handbook of Latin American Studies. Cambridge: Harvard University Press. (Annual.)

C. *Periodicals and Scientific Series*

The following journals and scientific series contain many references, articles and special studies concerning Mesoamerica and adjacent regions:

Acta Americana. Washington: Inter-American Society of Anthropology and Geography.

Acta Anthropologica. Mexico: Fondo de Cultura Economica.

America Indígena. Mexico: Instituto Indigenista Interamericano.

Anales del Instituto Nacional de Antropología e Historia. Mexico: Secretaría de Educación Pública.

Anales del Museo Nacional de Arqueología, Historia y Etnografía. Mexico: Museo Nacional.

Antropología e Historia de Guatemala. Guatemala: Instituto de Antropología e Historia de Guatemala.

Boletín Indigenista. Mexico: Instituto Indigenista Interamericano.

Contributions to American Anthropology and History. Carnegie Institution of Washington.

Ibero-Americana. Berkeley: University of California Press.

Microfilm Collection of Manuscripts on Middle American Cultural Anthropology. Chicago: University of Chicago Libraries.

Middle American Research Records. New Orleans: Middle American Research Institute, Tulane University of Louisiana.

Middle American Research Series. New Orleans: Middle American Research Institute, Tulane University of Louisiana.

Notes on Middle American Archaeology and Ethnology. Washington: Carnegie Institution of Washington.

Papers of the Peabody Museum of American Archaeology and Ethnology. Cambridge: Harvard University Press.

Publicaciones Especiales del Instituto Indigenista Nacional. Guatemala: Ministerio de Educación Pública.

Revista Mexicana de Estudios Antropológicos. Mexico: Sociedad Mexicana de Estudios Antropológicos.

Revista Mexicana de Sociología. Mexico: Instituto de Investigaciones Sociales de la Universidad Nacional Autónoma.

CHIAPAS ~ GUATEMALA AREA

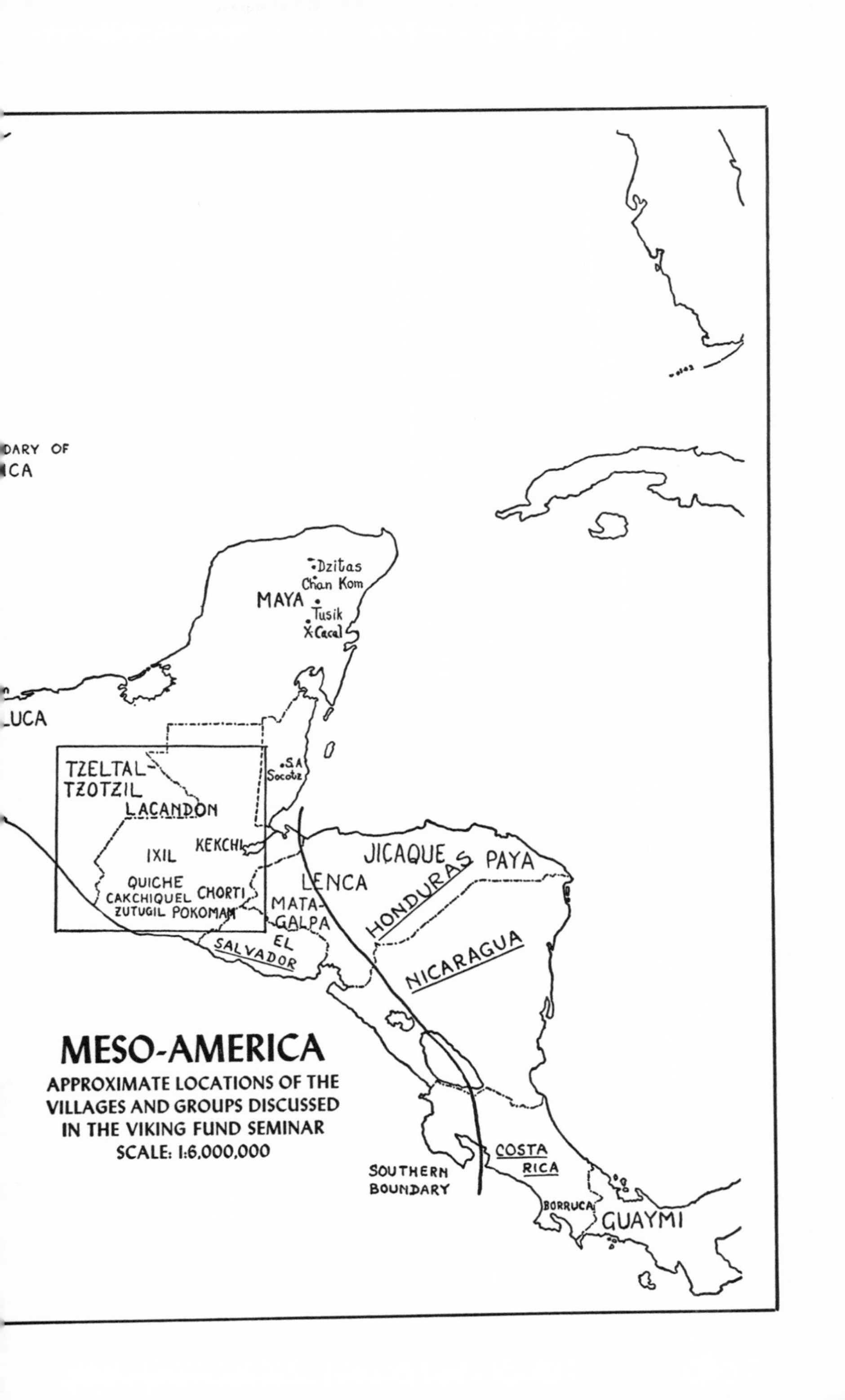

MESO-AMERICA

APPROXIMATE LOCATIONS OF THE VILLAGES AND GROUPS DISCUSSED IN THE VIKING FUND SEMINAR

SCALE: 1:6,000,000

INDEX

D

E